THE
★ PROPHETS ★
OF

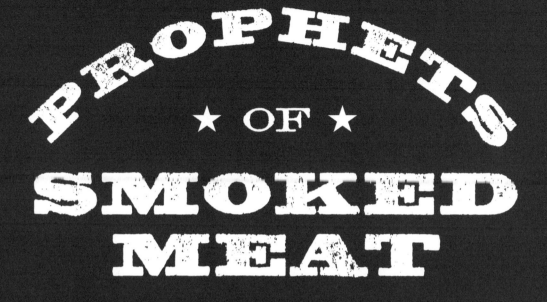

SMOKED
MEAT

· ·

A JOURNEY THROUGH TEXAS BARBECUE

· ·

DANIEL VAUGHN

WITH PHOTOGRAPHS BY

NICHOLAS McWHIRTER

An Imprint of HarperCollinsPublishers

HarperCollins books may be purchased for educational, business, or sales promotional use. For information please write: Special Markets Department, HarperCollins Publishers, 10 East 53rd Street, New York, NY 10022.

Interior design by Suet Yee Chong
Map design by M. Brady Clark, mbradyclark.com

Library of Congress Cataloging-in-Publication Data has been applied for.

ISBN 978-0-06-220292-5

13 14 15 16 17   OV/QGT   10 9 8 7 6 5 4 3 2

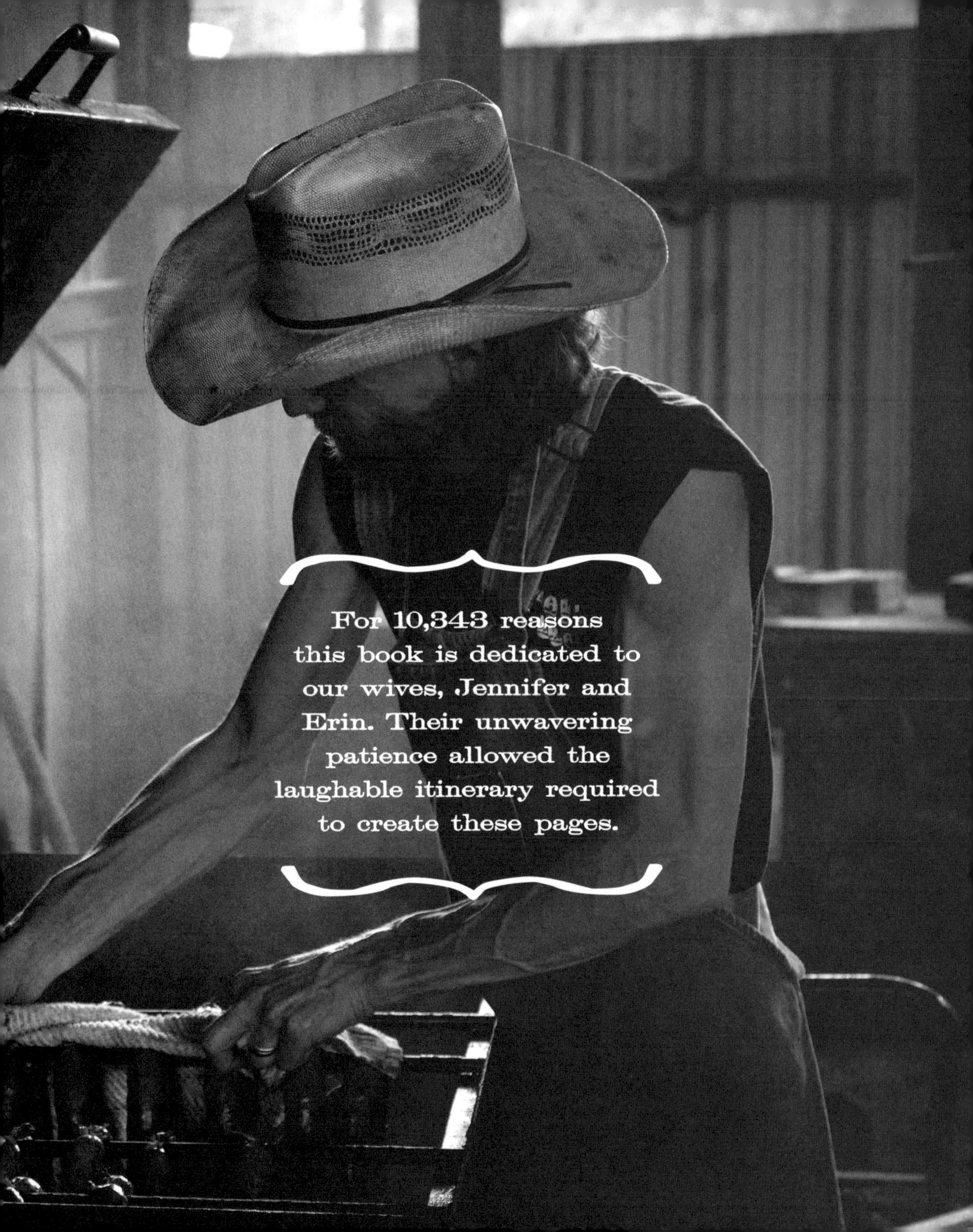

For 10,343 reasons
this book is dedicated to
our wives, Jennifer and
Erin. Their unwavering
patience allowed the
laughable itinerary required
to create these pages.

"In the end, it was made deliciously clear that, whether your taste be for barbacoa, brisket, or ribs, you'll find no better quality and variety than that in Texas."
—LOLIS ERIC ELIE

"Smoke is mysterious, fire is uncertain, and pitmen are expensive. So the mystery, uncertainty, and expense of taking the chance to make great barbecue is being replaced by the quantifiable methods of always making pretty good 'cue."
—JIM SHAHIN

CONTENTS

★

TEXAS BBQ
BY THE CORD

#	Name	Location	#	Name	Location	#	Name	Location
001	Betty Rose's Little Brisket	Abilene	069	Doc's Hot Links	Gilmer	137	Rattler's Pit BBQ	Navasota
002	Sharon's Barbeque	Abilene	070	McMillan's World Famous Bar-B-Q	Goliad	138	Butcher's Korner	Nederland
003	Joe Allen's	Abilene	071	Gonzales Food Market	Gonzales	139	Van's Bar-B-Q	Oakville
004	The Original Willie's Bar-B-Q	Alamo	072	Mr. B's BBQ	Grand Saline	140	Fermin's Smoked Bar-B-Que	Odem
005	Dyer's Bar-B-Que	Amarillo	073	Capistran's Tortillas & BBQ	Harlingen	141	Rockin' Q Smokehouse	Odessa
006	Big Texan Steak Ranch	Amarillo	074	Rucker's BBQ	Hearne	142	Sam's Bar-B-Que	Odessa
007	Texas Style BBQ	Asherton	075	Hemphill BBQ	Hemphill	143	Jack Jordan's Bar-B-Q	Odessa
008	Stiles Switch BBQ and Brew	Austin	076	Bob's Bar-B-Que	Henderson	144	The Rose Bar-B-Que	Odessa
009	Franklin Barbecue	Austin	077	Heavy's BBQ	Hondo	145	Rear of the Steer	Omaha
010	JMueller BBQ	Austin	078	Billy Bob's Hamburgers	Hondo	146	JB's BBQ	Orange
011	Lamberts Downtown Barbecue	Austin	079	Gatlin's BBQ	Houston	147	Dyer's Bar-B-Que	Pampa
012	Broussard's Links + Ribs	Beaumont	080	Gerardo's Drive-In	Houston	148	Hashknife on the Chisholm	Peadenville
013	Patillo's Bar-B-Q	Beaumont	081	Burns Original BBQ	Houston	149	Pody's BBQ	Pecos
014	Sonny's BBQ II	Beaumont	082	Burns BBQ	Houston	150	Uncle Roy's BBQ	Pharr
015	Willy Ray's Bar-B-Que Co	Beaumont	083	Burns Old Fashioned Pit Bar-B-Q	Houston	151	Pittsburg Hot Link Restaurant	Pittsburg
016	Miller's Smokehouse	Belton	084	Pizzitola's Bar-B-Cue	Houston	152	Rusty Jeep Hickory Pit BBQ	Port Aransas
017	Big John's Feedlot B-B-Que	Big Spring	085	Virgie's Bar-B-Que	Houston	153	Comeaux's Bar-B-Que	Port Arthur
018	Hog Heaven B-B-Q	Big Spring	086	Hunt Store	Hunt	154	M&M Café	Quemado
019	Fritze's BBQ	Boerne	087	Dairyland Bar-B-Que	Jacksboro	155	Hobbs Que	Robinson
020	Old Sutphen's BBQ	Borger	088	Larkin's Bar-B-Que & Catering	Jasper	156	Sam's Bar-B-Q, Lidia's Road-Kill	Robstown
021	Mac's Bar-B-Q	Brady	089	Cooper's Bar-B-Q & Grill	Junction	157	Hiway 77 Café	Rosebud
022	Vera's Backyard Bar-B-Que	Brownsville	090	Lum's Bar-B-Que	Junction	158	Lil' Joe's Bar-B-Que	Rosebud
023	Fargo's Pit BBQ	Bryan	091	Polak's Sawsage House	Karnes City	159	Jake 'n Boo's Backdoor Bar & Grill	Rosebud
024	Martin's Place	Bryan	092	Bill's Bar-B-Que	Kerrville	160	Highland Grocery	San Angelo
025	Wilhite's Barbeque	Buda	093	Buzzie's Bar-B-Que	Kerrville	161	Smokehouse Bar-B-Q	San Angelo
026	Perini Ranch Steakhouse	Buffalo Gap	094	Country Tavern	Kilgore	162	Bubba's Smokehouse	San Angelo
027	Dziuk's Meat Market	Castroville	095	CB's Bar-B-Que	Kingsville	163	Packsaddle Bar-B-Q	San Angelo
028	Bad Dog BBQ	Columbus	096	Belli Deli BBQ	Kirbyville	164	Two Bros. BBQ Market	San Antonio
029	Lou's Landmark Saloon	Corpus Christi	097	Milt's Pit BBQ	Kyle	165	Congers Smoke Shack	San Antonio
030	The Bar-B-Q Man Restaurant	Corpus Christi	098	Prause Meat Market	La Grange	166	Barbecue Station	San Antonio
031	Mr. G's BBQ	Corpus Christi	099	Felix Meat Market	La Joya	167	The Big Bib	San Antonio
032	Old Coupland Inn	Coupland	100	Briskets & Beer Smokehouse	Laredo	168	Cowboy Chuckwagon BBQ	San Augustine
033	Striedel's Fine Meats	Cuero	101	The Hog Pen	Leakey	169	Watts and Watts Bar-B-Que	San Augustine
034	Outlaw's BBQ	Daingerfield	102	Snow's BBQ	Lexington	170	Bo-Bo's B-B-Q	San Augustine
035	Hodie's BBQ	Dalhart	103	Cooper's Old Time Pit Bar-B-Q	Llano	171	Laredo Taco Company	San Benito
036	Peggy Sue BBQ	Dallas	104	Laird's BBQ	Llano	172	Longhorn Cattle Co. BBQ	San Benito
037	Pecan Lodge	Dallas	105	Inman's Kitchen Pit Bar-B-Q	Llano	173	Hays County Bar-B-Que	San Marcos
038	Mac's BBQ	Dallas	106	Black's Barbecue	Lockhart	174	CBQ Eatery	Schertz
039	Lockhart Smokehouse	Dallas	107	Smitty's Market	Lockhart	175	Doc's BBQ	Schulenberg
040	Smoke	Dallas	108	Chisholm Trail Bar-B-Q	Lockhart	176	Johnny's Bar-B-Que	Seguin
041	Deanville Sons of Hermann Hall	Deanville	109	Kreuz Market	Lockhart	177	Davila's Bar-B-Q	Seguin
042	King's BBQ	Deer Park	110	Carter's Bar-B-Que	Longview	178	Shiner Restaurant and Bar	Shiner
043	Border Stop One	Del Rio	111	Wild Blue BBQ	Los Fresnos	179	Curly's BBQ	Sierra Blanca
044	The Salt Lick	Driftwood	112	JB Smokehouse	Los Fresnos	180	West Texas Style Bar-B-Que	Silsbee
045	Paula's Bar-B-Q	Dumas	113	Mustang Creek BBQ	Louise	181	Maywald's Sisterdale Smokehouse	Sisterdale
046	Austin's BBQ	Eagle Lake	114	City Market	Luling	182	Zimmerhanzel's Bar-B-Que	Smithville
047	Wagon Wheel BBQ	Eagle Pass	115	Luling Bar-B-Q	Luling	183	R.O.'s Outpost	Spicewood
048	Charlie's BBQ	Eagle Pass	116	Cele Store	Manor	184	Opie's BBQ	Spicewood
049	Piedras Negras Tortilla Factory	Eagle Pass	117	Texas Traditional Bar-B-Q	Manor	185	Big Boy's Bar-B-Que	Sweetwater
050	Vincek's Smokehouse	East Bernard	118	Inman's Ranch House Bar-B-Q	Marble Falls	186	Louie Mueller Barbecue	Taylor
051	Chuy's BBQ	Eden	119	Peete Mesquite BBQ	Marble Falls	187	Taylor Café	Taylor
052	Smitty's Pit Bar-B-Q	El Paso	120	Food Shark	Marfa	188	Davis Grocery & Bar-B-Q	Taylor
053	Smokey's Pit Stop	El Paso	121	The Que Shack	Marlin	189	Stanley's Famous Pit BBQ	Tyler
054	Rib Hut	El Paso	122	Whup's Boomerang Bar-B-Q	Marlin	190	Rhea's Hot Links	Tyler
055	Southside Market	Elgin	123	Pic 'n Pay	Marshall	191	Smokey's BBQ	Tyler
056	Meyer's Elgin Smokehouse	Elgin	124	BBQ Express	Marshall	192	Caddo Grocery	Uncertain
057	Cattleman's Steakhouse	Fabens	125	Porky's Smokehouse and Grill	Marshall	193	Evett's BBQ	Uvalde
058	Pollok's Grocery & Market	Falls City	126	Neely's Sandwich Shop	Marshall	194	Merle's Bar-B-Q	Victoria
059	Bar H Country Store	Fannett	127	Cooper's Pit Bar-B-Q	Mason	195	Mumphord's Place	Victoria
060	Cistern Country Store	Flatonia	128	Lone Star BBQ	McAllen	196	Rusty Star BBQ	woodway
061	Off the Bone BBQ	Forest Hill	129	Keese's Café & Bar-B-Q	Medina	197	Balderas Grocery & Bar-B-Que	Waelder
062	Cooper's Old Time Pit BBQ	Fort Worth	130	Mesquite Bean Bar-B-Q	Merkel	198	R Place	Washington
063	Smokey's BBQ	Fort Worth	131	Sam's Bar-B-Que	Midland	199	Hog's Heaven BBQ	Weatherford
064	Sugar & Smoke	Fredericksburg	132	Johnny's Bar-B-Que	Midland	200	Fat Daddy's BBQ & Burgers	Weslaco
065	Dozier's Bar-B-Que	Fulshear	133	KD's Bar-B-Q	Midland	201	Nors Sausage House	West
066	Leon's World Finest Bar-B-Que	Galveston	134	Pappy's Bar-B-Q	Monahans	202	Hinze's Bar-B-Q	Wharton
067	Meshack's Bar-B-Que Shack	Garland	135	The Garven Store	Mountain Home			
068	City Meat Market	Giddings	136	Mr. Will's Restaurant	Nacogdoches			

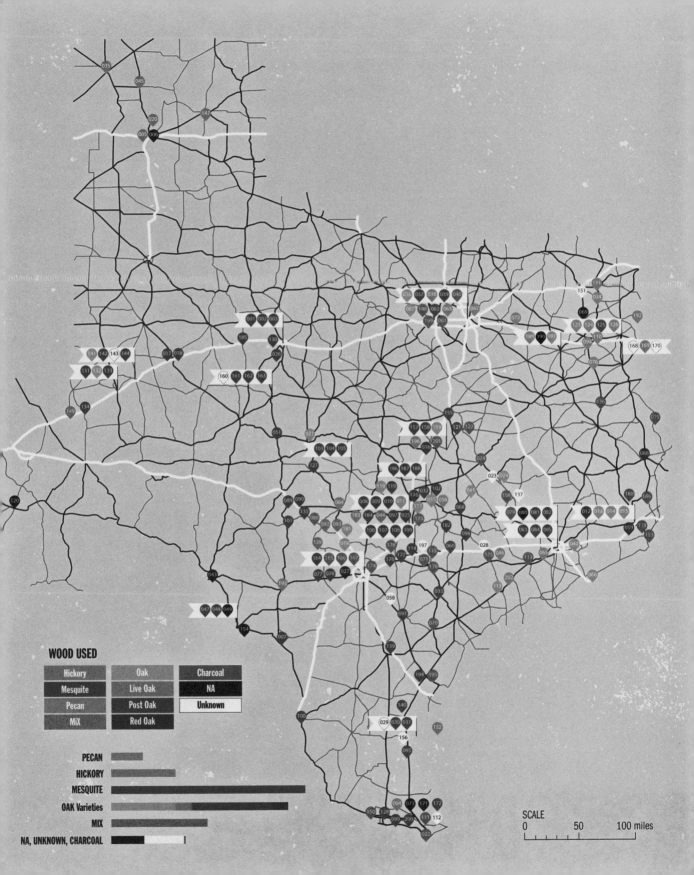

WOOD USED

Hickory	Oak	Charcoal
Mesquite	Live Oak	NA
Pecan	Post Oak	Unknown
MiX	Red Oak	

PECAN

HICKORY

MESQUITE

OAK Varieties

MIX

NA, UNKNOWN, CHARCOAL

SCALE
0   50   100 miles

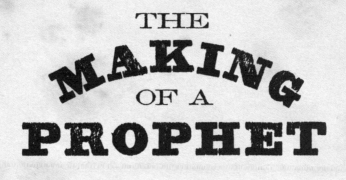

THE MAKING OF A PROPHET

I make no pretense—I am not a native Texan. I first set foot in Texas in 1998. My Oklahoma-born girlfriend and I were in Dallas for the annual football game held at the State Fair of Texas between the University of Texas and their archrival the University of Oklahoma. Her father—who would become my father-in-law six years later—had bought us both our plane tickets and game tickets, and I was giddy with excitement to take in my first live big-time college football game. The Sooners were playing the Longhorns, and my girlfriend's father was a Sooner fan, so I was obliged to wear crimson. Come halftime, the outlook for the Sooners with just three points was grim, and our group's spirits were low. My enthusiasm dampened, I darted out to the concessions to get some food—in this case, a rib sandwich from the Smokey John's tent. I had always loved ribs. I paid quickly and ran back to our seats with my bundle of foil-wrapped smokiness. The band was leaving the field as I hurriedly unwrapped and bit ferociously into my sandwich. "Those idiots left the bones in!" I exclaimed to no one in particular. I was just an infant when it came to Texas barbecue and didn't realize. . . .

Three years later I returned to Dallas for good. I didn't know it, but I was about to experience a personal awakening similar to the one I'd had five years earlier, when I arrived at Tulane University in New Orleans, just a naive kid from small-town Ohio. Everything about life in the Big Easy was radically different from the hay fields and dairy farms of my youth, and I found my place in New Orleans through food. Before my first semester was complete I was exploring new parts of the city for that perfect po'boy, navigating what seemed like a whole new language just to get the right steaming bowl of seafood, and relishing the social lubricant of a crawfish boil, where hands stained red from spice could barely grip that third bottle of Abita. Lessons in food are lessons in culture, so the more food discoveries I made, the more at home I felt. After graduation, spurred by love, I drove straight to Texas. Once I arrived, it was again food that I sought to guide me as well as ground me in this strange new place.

My first week in town, Jessica, a good friend and Dallas native, suggested we dine at Peggy Sue BBQ for a taste of authentic Texas barbecue. Peggy Sue BBQ is a sit-down joint with table service and a decidedly fifties' vibe in the upscale University Park neighborhood. But all I remember about that meal was the bold smokiness of the brisket, which I doused in the house's signature spicy sauce that comes warm in a miniature metal pitcher. In Ohio, brisket is corned and boiled and served with a side of limp cabbage. My first taste of Texas brisket was a revelation. It awakened a desire for more of it.

A few years later my smoked-meat palate would be revolutionized all over again. My good friend Sam and I took a weekend road trip to Central Texas, the promised land of Texas barbecue. We planned a pilgrimage to all the hallowed barbeque joints there. In these sacred spots, butcher paper soaked to transparency is the only thing that resembles a plate, and forks are considered superfluous—instead, you use your hands, lubricated with animal fat, to convey the meat to your eager mouth. Even hours after you leave one of these barbecue joints, the smell of your clothes gives away your journey. But before Sam and I hit Central Texas, I knew none of this. I was a sheltered Dallasite who was used to a knife and fork and plenty of sweet sauce. But after repeating the primal experience a total of sixteen times over that weekend, I was never again able to enjoy mediocre barbecue the way I once had, and my quest to taste the best of real Texas barbecue began.

It's taken me years to understand, but Texas barbecue is defined more by what it isn't than what it is. A basic (and correct) definition might be "simply seasoned meat cooked to tenderness over hardwood smoke," but Texas barbeque encompasses so much more than that. Tell someone outside of Texas that barbecue sauce is actually peripheral to smoked meat in the Lone Star State and you'll get the same blank stare you're sure to receive when attempting to explain to a Yankee that beans don't belong in chili. Ask a pitmaster for his or her rub recipe and surprisingly, they'll usually give it to you—along with a grin that lets you know the secret to the transcendent barbecue isn't in the ingredients but in the technique, a process they've repeated a few thousand times. Sadly for you, that pinch of onion powder isn't getting you on that mountaintop. Texans cherish the simplicity that the best barbecue joints in

this great state deliver, and any outsiders lucky enough to get a taste of it will return home with a hole in their charred soul.

After visiting more than five hundred barbecue joints across the state, I still yearn for new horizons. In my search for great Texas barbecue I've sampled some of the best of what this state has to offer, but the potential rush of discovery continues to lead me down back roads and through questionable neighborhoods. There's always so much to keep learning—and tasting. The city of Memphis alone requires two barbecue styles (wet and dry) of its own, so why shouldn't the Lone Star State— largest in the lower forty-eight—contain more than one style? Still, my experience has taught me that many people are surprised to learn that there are four distinct styles that characterize Texas barbecue, and that we eat more than just brisket. Each individual style has a loose geographical origin, but none have strict boundaries.

THE FOUR MAJOR STYLES OF TEXAS BARBECUE

★ HILL COUNTRY STYLE

The pitmasters west of I-35 in the Hill Country don't have the patience for low-and-slow smoking. They use direct heat from mesquite coals to sear heavily salted briskets in half the time it takes in Central Texas. In the Hill Country, it's common to order your barbecue by pointing at the hunks of meat sitting in a warming pit, ready for carving. All you need is an active index finger to compose a hearty meal. Though you can often order a side of a thin, vinegar-based sauce, thick, sweet sauces are few and far between in Hill Country–style barbecue. The cuts of meat typically on offer can vary from the standard brisket, beef ribs, turkey, and chicken to more unusual cuts like lamb ribs or goat meat, called cabrito. The Hill Country style of barbecue is more commonly referred to as West Texas–style or even cowboy-style barbecue, but in my travels it is rarely found outside of the Hill Country. It *is* straightforward, with little pretense—just like a good cowboy. Of course, the appellation more likely originates in the style's speed and its use of direct heat, a method that cowboys, camping out on long cattle drives, would have used. Most pitmasters who cook this way would be pleased if you complained that their meat lacked a smoky flavor. It's just not the point. Ironically, the further west we got from the Hill Country, the less of this style we encountered.

★ EAST TEXAS STYLE

The most common form of barbecue found in Texas's urban centers and suburbs is East Texas Barbecue. The style originates in the culinary traditions of the slaves who emigrated from the Deep South, especially Arkansas and Louisiana, into East Texas. Incredibly tender beef, ribs with the meat falling off the bone, beef hot links, and pork sausage—all of it drenched in thick, sweet sauce—defines this style. In East Texas–style barbecue, meat is more often chopped than sliced. East Texas hot links are particularly different than the hot links you'll find in other parts of the state. Pittsburg Hot Links, made in the small, East Texas town of Pittsburg, Texas, are the most famous of this specific type of link, and their century-old recipe is still used for the links sold in stores and barbecue joints today, but you'll rarely find these outside of the northeast part of the state. These links embody the roots of sausage making—as a way to use up leftover scraps of meat and offal. The strong, livery flavor predominant in these tiny links may have something to do with the proliferation of barbecue sauce in East Texas.

★ SOUTH TEXAS STYLE

Finally, at our southern border barbacoa reigns supreme. In barbacoa, whole cow heads are cooked overnight until the meat is falling from the skull. In the past, traditional barbacoa style would have dictated that the heads be wrapped in leaves and cooked slowly in the ground, but these days steamers and ovens do most of the work. This silky meat is nothing like brisket, and its richness is best cut with salsa rather than traditional barbeque sauce. Forget about cheap white bread or a sleeve of saltines— fresh tortillas are the best vehicle for sopping up all that barbecue deliciousness. South Texas also has its ribs, brisket, and sausage, but it's barbacoa that's worth seeking out. If you're lucky you might even get an eye to munch on. Be brave and seize the moment.

★ CENTRAL TEXAS BARBECUE

Many Central Texas barbecue joints frown on sauce, and a few flat-out forbid it. Low-and-slow smoking is the essence of the Central Texas barbecue technique. Pitmasters here typically rub meat, most famously

...BRISKET...

Brisket is king in Texas. This cantankerous muscle couplet is the hardest to tame with a fatty half and a lean half that do not agree much when it comes to choosing a cooking method. The true pitmaster cannot be called such until they tame the brisket. It hasn't always been this way. Before the brisket was popularized in the middle of last century, the beef shoulder clod was more popular, and it still makes a few appearances.

beef brisket, with a simple combination of salt and pepper and leave it to smoke by indirect heat for hours at a time—resulting in an intense, smoky flavor.

Despite the popular belief outside the state that Texans eat only beef, pork—especially pork ribs—is commonplace in almost any barbecue joint around Texas, and Central Texas is no different. Instead of dainty baby backs though, you'll usually find behemoth spareribs. Even larger beef ribs are not uncommon here. One item that really distinguishes central Texas barbecue is its sausage-making tradition. Heavy on beef, Central Texas sausages are usually made in-house from secret family recipes rather than being delivered from a food-service truck. The meat is coarsely ground and then packed loosely in its casing. Bite into one of these sausages with caution: thanks to their high fat content, they often release a spray of hot juice. If those links have jalapeño or chipotle in the name, take heed—you better believe they're going to be *spicy*. The Texas state legislature proclaimed the Central Texas town of Lockhart the Barbecue Capital of Texas, and it boasts four of the best joints in all of Texas.

Noted barbecue historian John Shelton Reed wrote, "Barbecue is the closest thing we have in the United States to Europe's wines or cheeses; drive a hundred miles and the barbecue changes." So just what might change in the eight hundred miles between Orange and El Paso or the nine-hundred-mile stretch between Dalhart and Brownsville? The fantastic possibilities embedded in the answers to those questions were just what I set out to discover, along with my friend and photographer, Nick McWhirter, over several months of unabashed gluttony.

Over those months, we not only discovered barbecue, but Texas itself—a state slightly larger than the country of France. We had to cover more than a few thousand miles of asphalt to give it its due. Our destinations were both known and unknown. We lit out with a set itinerary, determined to document the best of each barbecue style, while at the same time keeping our minds open to new protein-based experiences.

No active smokestack was ignored. Checking off a list of conquests might be rewarding, but nothing equals the thrill of discovering a great unknown joint, communing with smoked-meat sages, and discovering the nuances of a regional style, which can only be found on the road. Unlike what you might read in other barbecue guides, I don't believe there are easy markers with which you can identify good barbecue. Antlers on the wall, a stack of wood outside, a good mix of cars in the parking lot, or any of those other "signs" we're told to look for are, simply put, bullshit. If it were that easy, all the great barbecue joints would have been discovered by now.

Embarking on the journey with an ambition the size of Texas was the only way we could accomplish the search. A Texas-sized appetite helped, too: we ate at up to ten joints in a day to cultivate our appreciation for the variations from pit to pit, town to town, and region to region. These ridiculously lengthy journeys tested our intestinal stamina, tolerance for automobile confinement, and the patience of our families back home.

Come on and join us for the ride. You won't have to drive ten thousand miles, defy the surgeon general, or abandon your family, but you will discover the heart and soul of Texas barbecue.

Who's hungry?

7 Days
Without Beef
Makes One Weak

CHECKS
MUST HAVE
PHONE-ADDRESS
AND
LICENSE

CASEY

CHAPTER ONE

FEW AND FAR BETWEEN IN THE TEXAS PANHANDLE

Walking across one of Texas's largest rivers is an unsettling feeling, especially when you don't even get your feet wet in the process. No, I'm not blessed with messiah-like water-walking skill. It's just too damned hot and dry in Texas. And this particular afternoon, the day I walked across the Red River, fell smack in the middle of the hottest three-month stretch ever for any state in the history of the United States. The land was so parched that the

Red River, one of the largest in Texas, had been reduced to a bed of crunchy, sparkling, crystallized salt that concealed the rust-red dirt of the riverbed itself. Nick McWhirter—my friend, cohort, and photographer—and I were headed for the World's Largest Free BBQ at the XIT Rodeo and Reunion in Dalhart, a Panhandle town in a far corner of rural Texas. We were 250 miles into our 500-mile trip when the sight of the Red River, sparkling but waterless, stopped us in our tracks.

The wake-up call that morning had been painful. I had picked up Nick at the unholy hour of 5:00 A.M.—there were five hundred miles between us and Dalhart, and we had just one day to get there, to make it in time for the barbecue and rodeo that night. Nick was waiting dutifully under his front porch light when I arrived with two cups of steaming convenience-store coffee. We hit the road in silence, enjoying the quiet predawn road. We made a quick pit stop nearly two hundred miles into the trip to fuel our bellies with some roadside burritos packed full with chorizo and eggs, and made our way toward the Panhandle, hands stained red with chorizo drippings. We continued on past several heavily perfumed feedlots packed with beef cattle at which point Nick noted, "Well, that's where the barbecue comes from." Our first planned stop was supposed to be for some barbecue in the town of Pampa, about 350 miles from Dallas, but the apparition of the dry, salt-covered Red River was too intriguing to just drive past. We pulled off US Highway 287 and explored the riverbank. As we kicked around spent shotgun shells and bottle caps, the sound of a lonely rooster's crowing echoed beneath the concrete overpass. The sound of a domesticated animal was

... TABLE SERVICE ....

It's a powerless feeling when your barbecue is prepared and plated out of sight back in the kitchen. What arrives can be a surprise since there is no way to gauge the quality of any cut or to specify how you'd like it sliced before it lands at the table. The variation from cut to cut of meat and even within cuts of meat is what makes barbecue special. No rack of spareribs is the same from rib one to rib thirteen and a whole brisket is made up of two distinct cuts. The flat, or lean side (the *pectoralus profund*) is thin, with little intramuscular fat, tight muscle strands, and a nice layer of fat lining one side (the fat cap), while the point (the *pectoralus superficialis*), also called the fatty or moist side, is a thick, well-marbled cut with large visible strands of muscle meat loosely banded by generous sheaths of collagen, which—if properly cooked—will melt, resulting in lots of delicious gelatin. Once you've tried both cuts of brisket, you'll find your preference between lean and fatty brisket. You might also learn to appreciate the crusty edges of fatty brisket, known as burnt ends. The problem is, if all of this carving and portioning is going on back in the kitchen, it's much harder to control what you end up with. And even if you are well informed and very specific with your server about what you want, chances are the server might not even understand your request, meaning your order might get lost in translation by the time it reaches the kitchen, let alone come out to your table as you might have imagined it.

Ordering smoked meat from a cafeteria line prevents more than just a potential error in translation. At that closer vantage point, you can see if there's a pile of dried-out cuts that have been sitting heaped under a warming lamp for too long—which should prompt you to ask for a fresh brisket or rack of ribs. As the carver slices the meat, you can be sure to chastise the carver if he attempts to trim away good fat or throws away a side of good, crusty meat that should end up on your plate. This small bit of communication alone may clue in the carver that you recognize the good stuff—and he will treat the rest of your order accordingly. Not only can you ask him to cut you some fatty or lean brisket, you can also ask for it to be sliced thicker depending on your tastes. If ordering by the pound, you can gauge (sometimes dangerously) with your eyes how much meat looks like enough. For example, when ribs are cut from the short end of a rack, you might need three to fill you up, but two cut from the center of the rack might be enough. Finally, when the carver reaches for the sauce ladle, you can stop him before it's too late. Sauce on the side, please. These small, informed decisions can turn what could be an otherwise mediocre barbecue experience into a great one. If you're just sitting there with your napkin on your lap, then you lose that power and the best judgment of the line cook might not yield the best barbecue.

startling given our desolate locale, but it served as a quick reminder that we still hadn't had any barbecue that day.

It was August and we hadn't spotted so much as a raindrop since before summer, so the line of clouds ahead was worth noting. A sign alongside the road read Satan called and he wants his weather back. As the clouds drew nearer, we left the elevation changes, however mild, of North Texas behind us as we climbed onto the Llano Estacado, which is the ultraflat land formation that gives the Panhandle its wide-open identity. After many miles of nothingness we spotted the grain silos on the outskirts of Pampa through the heat-distorted horizon.

It's rare that I wait seven hours into a road trip to grab some smoked meat, but it was still only about noon when we rolled into Pampa. Our destination was the original **DYER'S BAR-B-QUE** (there's a second outpost in Amarillo). It wasn't hard to spot their big red sign along the main drag through town. It was fashioned like the side of a barn with weathered singles on top and rusty poles supporting it from below. It screamed "We've been around here a while." Once we arrived, we saw that the interior decor sent a similar message—the place didn't look like it had been redecorated since 1967, their first year in business. Unlike many barbecue joints, where cafeteria-style or counter service is the norm, this place had a hostess and full wait staff. The dining room was sparsely populated, and more than a few diners looked on curiously as Nick snapped some shots of the heaping combo plate that arrived at our table.

Alongside the piles of smoked meat on the plate, there was a ramekin of mysterious orange goo. After consulting the staff, we discovered the goo was actually apricot preserves but our waiter gave us no further clue as to what it was for. We ate it straight with a spoon, and its sweetness was somewhere between applesauce and jelly. It would have been great on pancakes. Along with preserves, there were sides of stale, chewy Texas toast, bland potato salad, and a forgettable slaw. Thankfully the plate also held what would be the meal's shining star: fresh, crisp onion rings. A tempura-like batter enveloped thick-cut onions, which held up well to the hot oil. I wanted more.

For the most part, the meat was also unremarkable. The meat on the long, thin spareribs had dried out a bit, but the ribs were well smoked and sweetened with both a sugary rub and a light glaze finish. The tender meat came off the bone with just a tug. But the underdone brisket, thickly sliced, would have been better served by thin slices. Just like in Dallas and the rest of North Texas, hickory was the wood of choice, and the meat could have used more of its flavor. The inch-thick slabs of pork loin looked promising, but the meat was as dry as the rib bones stacked on the plate. Just before leaving we asked the hostess about the apricot puree, which neither Nick nor I had encountered before. Was it a ubiquitous side for barbecue in these parts? Nope, as far as she knew, Dyer's was the only place around that served the stuff.

Less than an hour later, a bowl of nearly the exact same apricot puree arrived at our table at **OLD SUTPHEN'S BBQ** in downtown Borger. Joey Sutphen started the joint in 1950 (in a spot just up the road in the town of Phillips, before moving to Borger in 1963) and continued to run it through the late nineties, when *Texas Monthly* named it one of the top fifty barbecue joints in Texas. Joey Sutphen sold the business in 2000, and the owners swore to stick to tradition when it came to the recipes. But one of the recipes they should consider rethinking is

the brisket. Rather than the expected slices of brisket, what arrived on the table were chunks of meat completely enveloped in a sauce. It was like pot roast stewed in a thin cooking sauce, and it definitely didn't meet my definition of barbecue—meat that has been slowly transformed by dry wood heat.

To my great relief, everything else was excellent. The combos were so large it took three plates and a bowl just to contain all the food. There was ultrafresh and crisp slaw, well-seasoned potato salad with chunks of dill pickle, perfectly crunchy, golden onion rings, and subtly seasoned pinto beans. We got a quick lesson in the correct use of the apricot sauce from our server—"Dip your toast in it." The Texas toast was already fantastic—grilled and buttery—but a dip into that apricot puree took it to a whole other level. Chunks of ultratender pork had a hint of smoke and plenty of sweet rub and sauce. While not my preferred presentation for smoked meat, this was markedly better than the brisket. Meaty St. Louis–cut ribs (pork spareribs with the rib end removed) turned out to be the best we would have in the Panhandle. Their good smoke wasn't overpowered by the sweet glaze, and the kick from the black-pepper seasoning was the perfect counterpoint to the sweetness. The ribs' tenderness could have won some competitions, and by the end of the meal, there wasn't a shred of meat left on any of the bones on the plate. Nick, who was a newbie to the idea of barbecue road trips, was now seeing the point of seeking out multitudes of meat.

From Borger we made our way to Dumas. The road to Dumas descended through a desolate landscape of exposed rock populated by as many oil pump jacks as shrubs. We crossed a bridge over the Canadian River—our second dry riverbed of the day. Climbing back up the river valley we twisted and turned until reaching the flat plains of the Panhandle once again. Technically, we were now crossing the southernmost edge of the United States' Great Plains. The highway was flat and straight as a needle. A few miles before we reached Dumas,

we saw a highway sign that read—in all caps—Texas Beef Road. The road led to a feedlot five miles north, but to us the sign felt more like a portent than a directional aid. Those three simple words symbolized our journey. There was now only one stop left between us there at the intersection of State Highway 152 and the Texas Beef Road and the ninety-five hundred pounds of free meat awaiting us at the World's Largest Free Barbecue.

We almost missed that last stop, though, as **PAULA'S BAR-B-Q** was set back from the street edge formed by motels and fast food establishments, its classic symmetrical facade with a wood clad overhang painted red and matching red letters on a yellow background just spoke barbecue. Real cowboys, dressed in hats, boots, and buckles that weren't for show, occupied the tables in this bright dining room, and looked on with curiosity at the guy snapping photos with his fancy camera. The owners worked the front counter, and they didn't seem to mind Nick taking pictures as they filled our order, though.

We ordered our food to go—we were in a hurry to get to Dalhart—and ate the meal in the front seat of my car. The food felt increasingly familiar: more great coleslaw and crunchy onion rings along with superb fried okra, which we hadn't come across thus far. The brisket was only average. Not surprisingly, the gray meat was a bit dry and needed more smoke after losing both fat and bark from a zealous trimming knife. The ribs had a bit more smoke, but tasted like they'd been stored in a warmer for a while. But the meat *was* tender and moist, and a dip into the sauce bumped up its flavor. Given the quality of the sides, I was hoping for more with the meat, but we settled for finishing every last onion ring to fortify ourselves for the last forty miles to Dalhart.

A couple of months later I learned of the demise of Paula's Bar-B-Q. In an ever-changing world, barbecue joints seem to switch hands or close down at a more rapid pace than other restaurants do, and this wouldn't be the last of our many stops to close before this book was completed. Paula's owners were elderly, so the restaurant's closure didn't come as a huge surprise to me. It seems that few people care enough about family tradition to keep these restaurants going in the face of the long hours required to run them, especially given their relatively low profits. Paula's became a Mexican restaurant. Due to the convenience of having a smoker on site the restaurant still serves smoked meats, but it's not their focus. We were lucky to have had the chance to try Paula's.

Actually, Nick and I *had* planned on one other stop before hitting the XIT rodeo and reunion—but that stop was also in Dalhart: **HODIE'S BBQ.** The Hodie's sign and its brightly lit enormous arrow pointing the way to "hickory-smoked BBQ" looms high above nearly everything else in town save the water tower and the grain elevator. Sadly, when we got to the restaurant's front doors, a Closed sign greeted us. Who could blame them, though? It was XIT Reunion weekend and they would be competing with the World's Largest Free Barbecue just down the road. The sting

...SAUCE...

The thing is, even though Texas (for example) has a reputation for eschewing barbecue sauce, only a few of the most well-known and revered joints in Central Texas refuse to serve it altogether. Nearly every joint you walk into in the Lone Star State will have sauce, and too many of them will try to ladle it onto your meat without asking first. If the meat has a chance of being good, then you need to ask for it on the side at the outset because they're sneakier with those sauce ladles than you'd think. But, by all means, if your nitwit brother-in-law dragged you there and you suspect the meat is subpar, then worship that sauce. You're gonna need it.

of Hodie's locked doors wasn't as sharp as it might have been, though—honestly, Nick and I were still full from Paula's, and the Feed—the locals' affectionate and, to us, curious, nickname for the barbecue—started in less than an hour.

Nick and I received a fast education in the Feed. As we queued up just outside the rodeo grounds in one of ten distinct lines, each one at least fifty people deep, in order to receive mammoth piles of food produced in massive quantities, we couldn't help but feel a little bit like cattle—even if we were there by choice.

Each line terminated at a booth where teams of food servers clamored for the crowd's "business" with cowbells, loud hollering, and even louder outfits. Nick and I quickly chose Booth One because, well, mostly because the barbecue slingers were wearing silver bikinis—and then we stood in a relatively informal line. The crowd's anticipation grew as we waited for the meat to arrive. While Nick saved my spot, I walked around the backs of the booths to witness the meat delivery. A local told me to keep my eyes peeled for a commercial-sized dump truck that would be carrying the meat. As I stood in wonder blinking at what were definitely industrial metal trash cans full of beans being delivered to each booth, the steady beeping from a reversing vehicle led my gaze to the far end of the park. There was the dump truck. Its bed was lined with industrial-strength black plastic and was heaped full of burlap-covered sacks of meat. A few men slung these steaming bundles to meat couriers waiting at the tailgate, and those runners brought the "feed" to each of the booths to be cut and portioned.

While most people generally associate strong smoky odors with barbecue, this meat was most definitely not smoked. Back in line my hunger grew exponentially as the smell of black pepper permeated the air. At the XIT barbeque, they season the beef heavily with salt and black pepper, then double wrap it in butcher paper and burlap. The packages are tied with wire and placed in a coal-lined pit. The pits are covered with

corrugated metal panels and then topped with dirt to seal in the heat. The pits sit undisturbed for more than twenty-four hours before the dirt is scraped back and the meat removed. The meat isn't smoked, and it's not intended to be. Some people from the older generations argue that true barbecue should not taste of smoke. But no matter your definition of barbecue, I don't see them changing the way they cook it in Dalhart. The XIT Rodeo and Reunion has been going strong since 1936, after all. Back in the 1880s, the XIT Ranch was the largest fenced ranch in the world. At one time, the ranch ran more than 150,000 cattle. But in the 1920s, the ranch was broken up, sold, and divided into smaller ranches. Beginning in 1936, the old cowboys and ranch hands who had worked on the XIT began gathering once a year with their families to reminisce and remember the old days—and every year for the last seventy-five years, they've continued to do so, along with the whole town of Dalhart and anyone else who feels like dropping by, for the rodeo or the Feed.

When we finally made it to the front of our feed line, we each received a plate quickly filled with a mountain of beef slices and chunks, a scoop of beans, and some applesauce. The meat was incredibly moist and tender from the day's worth of cooking. The meat's outer surface was heavily flecked with black pepper, which complemented the bold, beefy flavors of the cut very well. This single plate had been the primary goal of our road trip, and both of ours were gone—devoured—within ten minutes. Lingering cross-legged in the grass we watched as the lines dwindled to nothing at the booths.

By then, a crowd had massed around the dump truck turned meat conveyor. A weathered-looking truck driver told us that the crowd was gathering to buy the leftover beef. The XIT reunion cooks ninety-five hundred pounds of beef for the feed, but there's always a lot left over. A twelve-pound hunk of beef would cost you thirty bucks cash. Not a bad deal from any food truck. The sale was fast and furious. Three men toasted from both sun and plenty of beer collected tens and twenties. "One for thirty or two for sixty!" they cried. Neither of us had an appetite or a cooler, so we watched the show from the sidelines.

The drone of a helicopter intermittently overcame the roar of the crowd, and we soon learned that it was for hire. After forking over seventy-five dollars each, we received two tickets for a five-minute helicopter ride. Our excitement built as we waited our turn. When the helicopter landed and discharged its passengers, Nick and I scurried forward under the whirring blades. I kept my hat on just so I could hold on to it with one hand while squinting as I ran, like every television and film actor does. Once in the helicopter, we ascended quickly and were soon overlooking the park and the rodeo grounds. A few stragglers and those looking for seconds were still in line at the Feed and a tractor hauling a large rake was readying the adjacent rodeo grounds. We then swung wide and the pilot flew us parallel with US Highway 87 as it passed through the middle of town. There was a whole lot of nothing beyond the tall grain elevators on the north side of Dalhart. As we moved away from the highway, fields of green circles stretched beneath us, despite the drought, fed by the Ogallala Aquifer. While not exactly bucolic, the fields—the product of the center pivot irrigation method that transformed the Panhandle from a Dust Bowl scarred landscape to a lush horizon of corn, cotton, and wheat—were no less mesmerizing. I couldn't help but think about all the feedlots in this part of the state, too, full of cattle that subsist on that corn, cattle that may well have ended up as the beef at the World's Largest Free BBQ.

Back on solid earth, we moseyed over to the rodeo grounds. Despite the rain clouds threatening on the horizon, the rodeo stands were searingly hot. Sunlight bathed the west-facing seats, which sat completely empty until the shaded seats had been filled to capacity. Nick and I found a shade tree to stand under and watch the festivities. We talked with a couple of Oklahoma cowboys who'd spent a total of only three nights of the previous month at home. They were here to rope steer and win some prize money doing so. Over the course of the event many cowboys were thrown and many more steers wrestled and roped. From the rodeo program we learned that there would be no bull-riding climax, so we walked slowly back to the car while admiring the sunset that painted the entire sky. We were exhausted and had booked reservations at the Big Texan Motel in Amarillo an hour and a half away. The World's Largest Free BBQ was officially behind us.

The tallest thunderstorm clouds I'd ever seen loomed ahead of us for the entire drive back to Amarillo. The thunderheads emitted razor-thin lightning strikes with such frequency that the night sky never seemed to go completely dark. The towering steel windmills perforating the horizon were eerily backlit and the blinking lights atop every irrigation post in the surrounding fields acted as giant mechanized fireflies. But the lights of Amarillo blotted out the night within fifteen miles of the city.

Before long, the Hollywood-Western kitsch of the Big Texan Motel greeted us. The facade of the motel is composed of a series of fake Old West–style buildings pieced together to resemble the main street of a platonic Deadwood. But with no energy left for a gunfight, Nick and I decamped to our room, took a few turns pulling from a bourbon bottle that I'd packed, and then hit the hay. In the morning, an enormous statue of a Hereford bull welcomed us as we emerged from our room. It was draped in an advertisement for the seventy-two-ounce steak eating challenge the motel's restaurant, The Big Texan Steak Ranch, is famous for. Feeling ambitious? Well, if you can consume an entire seventy-two-ounce steak in an hour, it's yours for free. This being Texas, the restaurant also serves barbecue, but we had some time to kill before we could try it. Nick and I decided to take a little barbecue break and walk off some of the food we'd spent most of the previous day eating, but despite our best intentions we couldn't resist a slight detour after spotting a billboard for another **DYER'S BAR-B-QUE** location. Just like the Pampa location, we found some great onion rings and nothing much else of note.

The next stop was a hardware store, where we picked up a few cans of spray paint and headed out of town. A few miles west of Amarillo, the city quickly disappears, and in a cow pasture just off Interstate 40 a row of ten Cadillacs lay half-buried. This is Cadillac Ranch, a public art installation created in 1974 by Chip Lord, Hudson Marquez, and Doug Michels—members of the art collective Ant Farm—and eccentric local art patron Stanley Marsh 3. It's considered an interactive exhibit where spray-painting the cars is welcomed and even encouraged. Without trash cans nearby, many of those spent cans and caps, strewn across the surrounding field, become a part of the art installation as specks of color on the dry, brown earth. Nick and I had our fun with the paint and posing for photos, but after a while the call of the Big Texan became hard to resist.

Moving from one Texan landmark to the next, we took our seats under the numerous animal busts that line the walls of the **BIG TEXAN** dining room. A lit display booth at the front entry presented a life-sized model of the seventy-two-ounce steak meal. We were after less ambitious portions of barbecue, so we split a three-meat combo plate between us. When the plate arrived it struck me that tourists would assume this was real Texas barbecue. I felt dismayed. None of the meat had even been licked by smoke, and I had serious doubts that there was even a smoker on the premises. The ribs were tender with plenty of sauce flavor,

but they had definitely been baked. The brisket, also baked, wasn't even a good take on roast beef. From the salty flavor to the soggy texture, all the signals were there that it may have been presliced and stored in broth. The sausage was large and mushy, oddly flavored with unidentifiable but overly aromatic spices. Again, all smoke flavor was missing. The fried okra and mashed potatoes were also forgettable, but were at least more representative of real Texas cuisine than the barbecue. For the sake of this state's barbecue reputation, I hope the tourists stick with the steaks at the Big Texan Steak Ranch.

The Big Texan was the last official stop on our barbecue trip, and because of that, we left even more disappointed than we might have been otherwise. Yes, we had discovered a distinctive Panhandle twist to Texas barbecue in the form of apricot puree and otherworldly onion rings, but we were leaving a bit defeated, not having found much in the way of incredible meat. We decided to try to find just one more spot on the way home, to end the trip on a happier, smokier note. Almost every small town on the way back to Dallas from Dalhart boasts its own barbecue joint. Unfortunately, it was Sunday, the day on which nearly every small town pitmaster chooses to take his or her day off. Each Closed sign we encountered only added to my ever-growing barbecue to-do list—not to mention my craving—and after a few hundred miles, I was beginning to think we'd have to settle for a burger. About an hour and a half northwest of Dallas–Fort Worth, a wall of gray smoke painted the horizon as we approached the town of Jacksboro. We decided to try our chances in Jacksboro and give the smoke from the wildfire some time to clear.

After a sharp bend in US Highway 281, which also serves as Jacksboro's Main Street, I spotted a low-slung, homey, bright red building. The bold yellow sign out front read Dining Room **DAIRY LAND**, but my eyes were focused on the wonderful promise written on the front awning: Brisket, Ribs, Ham, Sausage. Pulling toward the back of the parking lot, we saw a home-made brick smoker lurking beneath a suburban 1970s-style carport. Jackpot.

Nick and I both thought we'd had our fill of onion rings by then, however delicious they might be, but we were wrong. More delicious golden orbs made their appearance here. These babies were thick, wide, and crisp, with a thin flour batter. The onions beneath were not yet translucent and offered some bite. Nick decided then and there to start an onion ring blog. Next we ordered a combo plate. The third meat in a three-meat combo is always a toss-up for me. I'll always try brisket and ribs, but I usually save the third meat for home-made sausage, a regional specialty, or a staff recommendation. I decided to ask our waitress what to order and she recommended the sausage, which ended up being a very boring, mass-produced, commercial-quality

kielbasa. Luckily, the ribs and brisket were both commendable. The St. Louis–cut ribs were perfectly moist and tender and had a decent bark (that crunchy crust that forms on the meat's surface as it smokes) even with a heavy, powdery rub. A roasted-pork flavor was up front, but a good hint of smoke was evident on the finish. The tightly trimmed brisket slices were a little dry, but tender enough, and had a great smokiness in the black crust. This was some good brisket made better by a dip in the subtle home-made sauce that used mainly ketchup and beef broth. As we dined at a picnic table out back, we realized we had been led to the Dairy Land Drive Inn by the barbecue gods so we could end this epic trip on a high note before making our way back into the concrete tangles of Dallas–Fort Worth, where good onion rings are hard to come by.

Ninety miles later I dropped Nick back at his front door, now lit by the blazing sun rather than the lone porch light of just one day ago. The journey had been long—thirty-six hours and almost a thousand miles—yet rewarding in its wealth of new experiences. As the days passed after our asphalt adventure, we were both left with an enduring impression of both the Panhandle's stark landscape and its smoked-meat traditions. Nowhere else will I expect to find pureed apricots next to my brisket and I'll never forget those perfectly seasoned ribs at Old Sutphens Bar-B-Q or the vision of a dump truck filled with meat.

Mostly, I will miss the onion rings.

2 Days, 998 Miles, 6 BBQ Joints

CHAPTER TWO

WEEKEND BARBECUE IN SOUTHEAST TEXAS

The cumbersome task of removing car seats
from the back of my Audi is even less pleasant
when I leave it until the morning of a big trip.
It's not that it's difficult to unclip a few straps,
but the task is a reminder that I'm not going to
see my wife and children for at least a couple of
days. Who wants to be reminded of such a thing
just before heading out to meet his mistress? The
siren song of smoked meat was luring me back to

the road and I couldn't resist. Clark Key, my friend and a stalwart barbecue eater, would be joining Nick and me. By the end of that day, three grown men would have traveled hundreds of miles to eat more than twice as much as any reasonable person should. We would need every extra inch of room in that car.

We were headed for the center of the Texas Triangle, the swath of the state bounded by the interstates (45, 10, and 35) that connect Dallas–Fort Worth, Austin, San Antonio, and Houston—and within which more than 70 percent of Texans live. Along southbound I-35 just north of West, Texas (very different than West Texas), we passed the weathered concrete pad that once served as the foundation of the bar where Willie Nelson first got drunk at the age of nine (it's since been dug up). It was too early for a beer, but not for the kind of treat that would get the trip started off on the right foot.

We took the next exit for downtown West to pick up a few treats for the road. This little Czech-founded town, more commonly known as "West comma Texas" is *the* place to go for excellent kolache. A kolach is a Czech pastry (*kolach* is the proper singular and *kolache* the proper plural), a square of sweet dough with a fruit-filled depression in the middle. They bake up fluffy, unlike their flatter cousin, the Danish, and are sprinkled with a streusel-like topping called popsika. West has three kolache bakeries to choose from, all excellent, making it hard to choose. But the oldest in town is the **VILLAGE BAKERY**, where they warm the kolache to order. The fruit-filled kolache at Village Bakery are sweet enough to be dessert, but people usually eat them for breakfast. If you need more fortification, then the sausage-filled klobasniki is the ticket. The klobasniki is a Village Bakery invention: a sausage link wrapped in sweet kolach then baked like a pig-in-a-blanket. The Village Bakery fills their klobasniki with Slovacek sausage from Snook, Texas—they are dangerously good. I almost bit into my third one of the morning before reminding myself that we had eight barbecue joints to hit that day. The local Nors Sausage House was a few hours from being open, so it would have to wait until our Central Texas trip.

South of Waco we turned east along State Highway 6. Though the majority of the state's population lies within the Texas Triangle, most of those people live along the corridors of the interstates. The inside of the triangle is sparsely populated by comparison, dotted with a number of forgotten small towns we hoped to mine for good barbecue. The town of Marlin was our first destination. The little Internet research we had been able to dig up on Marlin turned out to be out-of-date. We drove around town, from one closed or out-of-business barbecue joint to another until, seemingly out of nowhere, we could see and smell heavy, meaty smoke. Under the awning of a used-car dealership (which also appeared to function as a check-cashing business and bail bond service), three large smokers were going strong. A gaggle of men decked out in various forms of camouflage surrounded the smokers. They pointed us in the direction of the building across the street, a restaurant called **THE QUE SHACK**. The Closed sign was still hanging on the front door, but we pushed through anyway with the encouragement of the group across the street. We startled a woman smoking a cigarette behind the counter, who wondered aloud why we were so anxious for barbecue at ten in the morning.

It didn't take long for the kitchen to stock up from the smokers across the way. We soon had a plate of ribs, sausage, and beef, but the beef wasn't brisket.

They served tri-tip at the Que Shack. The tri-tip, sadly, had been covered in sauce back in the kitchen. I tried to rescue an untainted slice from the bottom of the pile, but it was futile. Another helping—no sauce—was in order, and it was worth it. The meat from the corner of the tri-tip had a heavy rub and just a kiss of flavor from the fire. Tri-tip doesn't take near the time to cook as a brisket, and with such a short time over the coals there wasn't much of a chance for any crust to develop, but the meat had flavor that comes only from cooking over charcoal. I can't say how tri-tip is usually prepared in Texas barbecue joints because you just don't find it on barbecue menus outside of California, where it is a feature of the Santa Maria style of barbecue. In more than ten thousand miles of travel across the state, that was the only barbecue joint we stopped at that served this cut of beef.

Midway through our meal, Jim Mitchell, the owner of the Que Shack, came by and introduced himself. Turned out Jim owned the triumvirate of businesses across the street, too. He'd been a cattle man, then owned a convenience store, then sold that business and came to Marlin. Jim had sold tri-tip back at his store, too—it provided a lot better yield than brisket since there was no trimming required and much less fat to render. Jim learned his barbecue from local legend Ben Jefferson, who barbecued just about anything, including armadillos and coons, but always only used direct heat. When I asked Jim what kind of wood he was smoking with, his retort was "We don't smoke meat, we cook it." He also didn't use wood, or much of it anyway. Kingsford charcoal provided all the heat for the barrel pit, though Jim told us he added in a log of mesquite at the end for a little color and twang. Jim's opinion is that those who smoke meat just haven't figured out how to adequately nurse a direct fire. Those would be some fightin' words just a couple hours away in Lockhart.

Jim invited us to stop by and check out the pits when we were through, then he brought out a few slices of the previous day's pork loin.

At a day old, the meat wasn't at its best, but it was still damn good. The cumin in the rub—which was otherwise a pretty straightforward combination of salt, pepper, garlic powder, and cayenne—gave it a unique flavor. I took a bite of a limp-looking sausage and wished it had sat in the pit a bit longer. The ribs were coated in the same sauce that had obscured the quality of the tri-tip. Fortunately, it had pooled on the back side of the ribs and was easy enough to wipe off, revealing some excellent baby backs with that same simple rub and plenty of flavor from the coals. The meat was moist and perfectly tender—so much so that I ate more than I should have so early in the morning. It's a good thing that I got my fill since a few months later when I called Jim for a recipe he informed me that he had had to close the Que Shack. But he'll be happy to cook some up for you if you ask nice next time you need a bail bond.

We drove through Marlin on our way out of town. In the early twentieth century, Marlin was a popular tourist destination, due to the reputed healing powers of its mineral water. In 1929 Conrad Hilton even built a beautiful hotel there. The town had clearly fallen on hard times in the intervening years. An old motel way past its prime, still advertising "refrigerated air," looked like the only place in town to get a room and a sign on an old bar with the words Enter If You Dare painted on the door still advertised the last year's New Year's Eve party. A crumbling house had broken windows through which we could see an open closet, eerily still full of clothes.

We had high hopes of **WHUP'S BOOMERANG BAR-B-Q** on the south side of Marlin. While the local sausage and well-smoked hot links were enjoyable, the overcooked ribs and chewy brisket had us back on the road quickly. Another stop an hour south in Hearne at **RUCKER'S BBQ** did little to ease our wanting for good brisket, although the ribs weren't bad at all.

Next stop, Bryan, and **FARGO'S PIT BBQ**. As we closed in on Bryan, my nerves began to creep. Three years earlier I had had some of the best ribs and brisket at Fargo's that I've ever had anywhere. I drove all the way home—about 172 miles—with a rib in one hand, the steering wheel in the other. The thing is, most professional food critics make at least three visits to a restaurant before completing a review or issuing a star rating. Given the mileage I've got to cover in my search for smoked meats, I don't have this luxury. I routinely provide a rating based on a single visit, knowing the restaurant might have been having an off day or an unusually great

one. I was nervous that my previous meal at Fargo's would turn out to have been a fluke. Luckily for me, I needn't have worried a bit: Fargo's turned out to be just as great as I remembered, one of the finest purveyors of smoked meat in the state.

Fargo's owner and pitmaster, Alan Caldwell, is a man full of secrets. Ask him to see the smokers? Nope. What's in that rub? Not a chance. What wood are you using? Nada. But what he lacks in a forthcoming attitude, he and his wife, Belinda, make up for in warmth and hospitality—and a heart-stopping meat case filled with beautiful, black-crusted briskets, rust-hued racks of spareribs, links of brick-red sausages, and perfectly bronzed half chickens begging to be chopped and bagged. I had to have them all even though I rarely order chicken.

Fargo's is a take-away joint, so we opted for a picnic spread on the trunk of my car. Smoke and saltiness was perfectly balanced in the large spareribs, and their touch of sweetness combined with black pepper kept me coming back for bite after bite. Each bite through the yielding crust and the layers of rendered fat came easily off the bone. Pork ribs of this size can have issues with consistent texture throughout since the tips can dry out easily, but these ribs were perfectly moist and tender

from end to end. Clark thought they might be the best ribs he'd eaten anywhere. The texture of the chicken was also commendable. Neither chewy skin nor dry meat afflicted this bird. The skin was crisp, salty, and luscious. The meat beneath was smoky and ridiculously moist. This was a good bird.

After a few bites of a snappy and peppery sausage link, I went right for the brisket, most of it cut from the lean end. The long, pencil-thick slices broke in half under their own weight as we lifted them from their Styrofoam box. This can be a sign of dry brisket, but it wasn't in this case. Smoked just beyond tender, each slice had a thick border of rich, velvety fat bursting with smoky flavor. A thick, red smoke ring sat beneath a thick, black crust that brought even more smokiness to the table. I had eaten several meals already that day, but I couldn't keep my hands off the brisket. Near the bottom of the box sat some fatty slices. I didn't think the brisket could get any more satisfying until I sank my teeth into the buttery meat of a fatty slice. An intense rush of salt and smoke came with the juices that immediately covered my tongue as I began to chew. I was in barbecue bliss, one unrivaled by almost all my previous experiences.

Our next stop was also in Bryan. While Fargo's is less than a decade old, **MARTIN'S PLACE** has been owned and operated by the same family since 1925, and might be the only barbecue joint in Texas with a marker from the Texas Historical Commission. Steve Kapchinskie, the third-generation pitmaster and owner, took over the business from his father, Albin Kapchinskie, who took it over from his father, Martin Kapchinskie. Very little has changed about the smoking methods at Martin's over the last eighty-eight years. Mismatched stools surround a Formica-topped U-shaped bar at the center of the restaurant. If a white surface ever existed inside the building, years of smoke have hidden it completely. Even the ceiling tiles are tan. In the pit room, stalactites of hardened creosote hang from the rafters.

In keeping with this timeless sensibility, Steve eschews adding anything more than a light dusting of salt and pepper to his oak-smoked briskets and thick slabs of pork ribs. When our plate of barbecue arrived, the brisket slices were circled by a thick black crust, so I expected a big punch of the oak smoke. Sadly, the smokiness was fleeting, as was the moisture in the dry slices. They lacked a whole lot of any flavor. The ribs were even drier, though they were a bit smokier than the brisket, but just as lacking in overall flavor—a bigger hit of salt or pepper would have helped. The bright spot in the meal came from the unexpected menu item of sliced pork shoulder. Ribbons of nicely

rendered fat made for a moist cut, with plenty of smoke and loads of clean, pork flavor. The pork alone, along with a side of the ultracrispy onion rings, would be more likely to bring me back than the ribs or brisket, but regardless of the meat, just sitting in this space with the knowledge that they've kept a viable barbecue business going in the same family since 1925 and still use the same smoking methods is incredible to reflect upon.

With a long while to go before our overnight stop in Houston, there was little time for reflection. A much anticipated stop in Navasota to visit the storied Ruthie's Pit Bar-B-Q was in vain as we found **RATTLER'S PIT BBQ** had recently taken over the space.

··· SMOKE RING AND CRUST/BARK ···

I've never found a better explanation for the science of the smoke ring than the write-up on the blog Steel Town BBQ by Ed Maurer of Youngstown, Ohio. "Nitrous oxide (NO), a gas, is being produced by the combustion of the wood. Nitrous oxide is a relatively unstable molecule and in the presence of heat and oxygen is oxidized to nitrous dioxide (NO_2). As the NO_2 passes over the moist meat, it comes in contact with water forming nitric acid ($HNO3$). The acid dissolves on the moist meat surface and forms a nitrate ion ($NO3^+$). This nitrate then combines with the myoglobin forming a pink compound. This myoglobin—nitrate pigment is responsible for the "smoke ring" found in barbecued meats. The smoke ring is generally only 1/4 to 3/8 of an inch thick. The depth of the smoke ring is limited by the ability of the nitrate ion to penetrate the meat and by the temperature of the meat. Myoglobin proteins begin to denature (break apart) at about 120°F. Denatured myoglobin is no longer able to combine with the nitrate to form the pink pigment. It is important to remember that the formation of the smoke ring occurs early in the barbeque process and its maximum development requires plenty of oxygen at the fire, moisture on the meat, and relatively cool meat surface temperatures."

The bark (or crust) is the darkened exterior on a cut of smoked meat. The longer the meat is exposed directly to the smoke, the better defined the bark becomes. One should not be alarmed to see an uncut brisket that is completely black. It is not burnt or charred; it just has a great bark.

A plate of fried gizzards were more memorable than the barbecue, which may be why it closed soon after. Just a few miles away in Washington on Brazos we found the site where the Texas Declaration of Independence was signed; right next door, we enjoyed some excellent peach cobbler at **R PLACE** along with some merely promising brisket and pork ribs.

Our stomachs adequately fortified, we hit the road for the last stretch to Houston, where we were meeting friends for dinner at **GATLIN'S BBQ** on the northwest side of the city. Gatlin's owner, Greg Gatlin, had his heyday on the gridiron as a defensive back for the Rice Owls, but barbecue is his game now. He's still a young man whose brow is not yet creased by years of smoke from the pits, but his skill is no less than some pitmen twice his age. With all of the smoking completed for the day, he was manning the counter with his mother when we arrived. We had met a group of friends there. One, who was equally eager to be a good host and show off his status as a regular, made a sweeping motion with his arm,

moving our group back from the counter as he slurred, "I got this." Neither Clark, Nick, nor myself were the least bit hungry. All we needed was a taste, but our friend had just returned from an all-day craft beer festival and needed large amounts of meat to soak up some of the beer. He ordered inside as the rest of the group waited at picnic tables on the attached covered porch, not sure what would arrive at the table. Soon, a team of employees carried over large foil trays brimming with all types of smoked meat and myriad bowls of side items, sauce, and cobbler. I was thankful to take part in the feast, but was only able to muster a few bites from the bounty. My joy turned to dismay at the end of the meal when my

inebriated friend asked for an equal share of cash from all parties at the table to cover the large bill as he stuffed the leftovers into heaping takeout containers that would be worthless to the three of us. Not wanting to spoil the fun I paid up with a clenched jaw and we moved on to beers at a bar a few doors down. In the end, my memories of the meat outweigh the cash that I had to part with.

The grayish hot links, made without red dyes or nitrates, may not have looked like typical grocery-store hot links, but they packed some heat. The casings were a bit chewy, but the meat was smoky and delicious. The regular sausage had a great snap and good black-pepper flavor, but the hot links had superior flavor from both the smoke and an extra layer of heat. The rosy pulled pork, both toothsome and silky, was flecked with black bits of highly seasoned crust. The perfectly tender ribs were sweet, smoky, and magnificent, with a sugary rub that didn't overwhelm the well-formed crust.

All of the meat at Gatlin's was excellent, but it was the brisket that had me considering a fortnightly Dallas-to-Houston road trip. Many barbecue connoisseurs will go for the fatty brisket over lean brisket (I prefer a bit of both). At Gatlin's the thick slices of the fatty brisket were just on the edge of disintegration—strands of well-cooked fat barely held the slices together. They had good smoke and great flavor from the subtle seasoning, but much to my surprise, it was the lean brisket that stole

the show for me. When done properly, a lean cut of brisket with a quarter-inch-thick layer of fat remaining can be a thing of smoked wonder. The fat locks in the smokiness more so than the meat itself, so a bit of each makes for a perfect bite of brisket. The fat layer on this lean brisket was the epitome of what I like. It was nearly clear and barely clinging to the meat. A pinch of my fingers went clean through without a hint of resistance.

A thick, black crust enveloped the whole smoky slice and provided a slight crispness to the very edge. My brain overruled my bulging stomach as I went for another bite.

After a good sampling of meat, I turned my attention to the large bowls of family-style side items. The dirty rice was the best I've had anywhere. It was rich, with just a touch of gaminess from being fortified with offal. The mix of rice, meat, and veggies had been cooked together to form a bond that could be eaten in heaping forkfuls rather than having to round up the scattered elements of the dish with a spoon. With almost as much meat as rice, it could have easily made a meal in itself. Prompted by my dining companions, I mixed a bit of barbecue sauce into my rice, taking an already great side to an even higher level. I'll take this Gulf Coast flavor with my Texas-style barbecue any day. Before we arrived at Gatlin's, I couldn't imagine ingesting more than a few bites of anything, let alone eating dessert. But that was before the kitchen sent out some peach cobbler—the bowl was clean before I left the table. There always seems to be room for sweets no matter how much protein I've eaten in a day. Even so, if my job description didn't require gluttony I'd have been ashamed of myself, but I slept easy that night.

Before we left Houston the next morning, my friend Michael Fulmer, who knows where to find good food in general, took us out for what he considers the best barbacoa in Houston. At **GERARDO'S** they wrap cow heads—cabeza de vaca—in foil and steam them, the method Gerardo's

owner, Jose Luis Lopez, learned in the Mexican state of Michoacán. Though barbacoa isn't usually seasoned, Gerardo's uses a mixture of salt, pepper, and oregano on the meat, and the results are incredible. The silky, salt-soaked fat combines with the chunks of beef for a deep, rich flavor. Scoop it up with a fresh-grilled tortilla and top it with Gerardo's famous salsa verde, and you'll have one of the finest breakfasts that can be had.

In addition to cabeza de vaca, Gerardo's also serves chicharrones, pork carnitas, and mutton barbacoa. The mutton was free of the gaminess I had braced myself for and was just as good as the beef. It was more tangy and a bit dryer—but not too dry. The meat also had a nice, reddish hue, different from the dark brown flesh of the beef. Having both on the table was a dangerous way to begin a day with six barbecue stops ahead. I had eaten barbacoa before, but never had it been so rewarding. A couple of months later, in South Texas, I reached a personal barbacoa apex, but at this point Gerardo's was the best I'd eaten.

For the rest of the trip we focused on the traditional Texas barbecue to be had in the small towns south and west of Houston. It seems like all small-town barbecue joints usually follow a few rules: They're named after the owner, they only take cash, and they're closed on Sundays. I'm not sure if there's a particular moral depravity in this part of the state, but I noticed a while back that a large number of the notable joints here had Sunday hours. As

a weekend barbecue hunter, I usually reserve Saturdays for the hunt and Sundays for either seeking out the chains that might be worthwhile or, more likely, just finding my way home—so this region held a unique opportunity.

First up was **DOZIER'S GROCERY & MARKET**, in Fulshear, about a half hour outside of Houston, barely beyond the reach of the suburban housing developments. I had heard that Dozier's was one of the best barbecue joints in Texas back when Ed Dozier was manning the pits. We ordered at the meat counter, where bacon and sausage were on display in a glass case. We chose the three-meat plate of ribs, brisket, and sausage. The sausage had good seasoning and a pretty good snap to the casing. The meat had been ground a little more fine than I like, but it was a solid link. The brisket had good smoke from the pecan wood, but all of its fat had been scraped off the meat, leaving it dry. A good smoke ring and nice black crust made for pretty slices, but the meat just wasn't as good as it looked. The ribs had a thick rub that hindered a good crust from forming, or they may have just been stored a little too long. Either way, the meat was still tender, moist, and enjoyable. While their reputation has receded since Ed Dozier's passing, on this day they still put out some respectable, if not incredible, barbecue.

After crossing the Brazos, the longest river in Texas, the housing developments disappeared for good. Corn and cotton fields, fed by the Brazos and the Colorado rivers, lined the road. We were just a few minutes away from East Bernard and our destination in the middle of town: **VINCEK'S SMOKEHOUSE**. When we pulled into Vincek's parking lot, the first thing we saw were several pickup trucks, their beds filled with deer carcasses. It turns out that deer processing and venison sausage production is a big part of Vincek's business.

Sausage is the house specialty here, and it shows. The meats are ground rather than chopped, resulting in a coarse consistency. This differs from the monolithic texture of most commercially made sausages, and that coarser texture is one telltale sign of a house-made sausage.

Spiced with black pepper and garlic, the links are smoked until the casings are nice and crisp—they were some of the finest sausages I'd had anywhere. Other folks must feel the same way—Vincek's sells two to three thousand pounds of sausage per week. The St. Louis–style ribs had taken on the flavor of the oak-lump charcoal they had been cooked over. They tasted similar to ribs I had had all over Memphis, where direct-heat charcoal cooking is popular. The high heat hadn't rendered out the fat, so the ribs were still tough, but their flavor was great. The brisket, which is first smoked for twelve or more hours over pecan wood before being finished over oak charcoal in a concrete cooker, was a bit dry, but the slices had great smoke and a crisp crust. Even with the dryness, this was some fine brisket that any joint would be proud of.

After we ate, Gary Vincek showed us around the entire operation. He's owned Vincek's for more than twenty-five years, but before that he worked for Ed Dozier back in Fulshear. The huge concrete smokers out back of Vincek's were there when he bought the place. Gary raised the large, metal lids on the smokers to reveal grates full of chicken and ribs, charcoal—but no wood—glowing beneath the meat. Over in the bricked smokehouse, the sausages and briskets are indirectly smoked with pecan. Vincek is a busy man and a great host—and between the deer processing, the shelves of goods inside, and the meat case that runs the length of his joint, you might think that barbecue is an afterthought here, but that couldn't be further from the truth.

Twenty minutes down the road, we hit **AUSTIN'S BBQ** in Eagle Lake. Austin's had been on my personal list for some time—it's one of only two barbecue joints in Texas to make it onto *Texas Monthly*'s top fifty barbecue

list three times without cracking the top five. The haphazard pile of pecan logs taking up several spaces in the parking lot was a promising sign. Pecan is the only wood Austin's uses in their very large indirect smokers, the location of which—right next to the entrance—made for an appetizing odor and a solid advertisement for their smoking methods.

At Austin's you order from a window in a small indoor hallway that leads to the register. The options were limited, so I went straight for the Texas trinity of brisket, ribs, and sausage, sauce on the side. A home-made sausage made from a mixture of beef and pork was heavily seasoned with black pepper. The links were good, but could have had more smoke and a better snap. The grind made for an almost cohesive sausage but without reaching commercial sausage consistency—I have to admit I might have been a little too picky here, having just chowed on the transcendent sausage at Vincek's. The ribs, on the other hand, were incredible. A heavy black-pepper rub helped create a beautiful crust. The smoke penetrated deeply into the meat, and the rendered fat within made these ribs perfectly juicy. The brisket had the same heavy rub and well-rendered fat. The smoke was bold on the tender slices, and the fat that remained had excellent flavor. All the standard sides were available, but I went with the duo of potato salads. Both types were mashed pretty heavily (I've only encountered this style of potato salad in Texas, but it may exist elsewhere), which makes for an odd texture if you're used to the more common chunky potato salad, but the flavor is still great if you can get over the texture of what amounts to cold mashed potatoes. The mayo-based salad had a vinegar kick and a little hint of sweetness, while the mustard-based salad was pale yellow and had a milder flavor. Both potato salads were some of the better potato salads I'd had. With all of these quality meats and sides, it's no wonder Austin's has received such steady and frequent accolades.

It didn't seem possible to eat more barbecue than we had that day, but there were still two stops to check off our itinerary—you've got to sacrifice some intestinal comfort to find the best barbecue, after all. **HINZE'S BAR-B-Q**, in Wharton, has come a long way from the tiny metal shack that housed the joint in 1970. The current restaurant is as expansive as its menu: there's a banquet room for private parties and the large covered front porch is built around a couple of very tall trees.

Just inside the doors you'll normally find a sizable line. We placed our order at the register and took our number placard to our table. The plate of meat that arrived at the table looked great. The pecan-smoked brisket had a good bark and beautiful smoke ring. The meat was a bit tough and trimmed extra lean, but remained moist. It had decent smoke but really needed some seasoning. The lean, thin ribs were even better. The meat had good smoke and excellent flavor from a sweet rub and subtle glaze. The texture was on the dry side, but in a pleasing way. The meat didn't crumble nor was it juicy. It came away from the bone easily and had great flavor. The three sides—green beans, potato salad, and onion rings—were all good, if not great, versions of these basic accompaniments. We weren't disappointed with the pie selection, either. The mile-high meringue that topped a lemon pie looked impressive, but
the custard beneath and the buttery

crust that supported it were the stars of the show. A warning sign behind the register announced "Our lemon pies are made with real lemon juice. They are very tart." It *was* tart, and that was just fine with me.

We now had to hurry to the next joint. I wasn't quite sure when it closed—independent barbecue joints in gas stations aren't known for keeping long hours. Fortunately, the Open sign was still turned outward in the window of **MUSTANG CREEK BAR-B-Q** when we pulled up. Located along US Highway 59 between El Campo and Louise, this joint has garnered recent fame for a sandwich called the Bohemian Special, which *Texas Monthly* featured in 2006. In 2009 Texas barbecue expert Robb Walsh called it the best barbecue sandwich in Texas, and in 2011 *Garden & Gun* magazine named it one of the top twenty-one barbecue sandwiches in the United States. Let's just say the place has been discovered, and I was going in with high expectations.

We watched with anticipation as pitmaster Cecil carefully assembled the sandwich from peppery slices of brisket, smoked sausage, dill pickles, sliced white onions, and plenty of spicy and sweet barbecue sauce. When it all came together, it made for a behemoth of a sandwich. I have a friend named Scott Slagle, who has a habit of never setting down his sandwich during a meal. In our group the practice is known as "Slagling" a sandwich. For some it's a practice reserved for an incredible sandwich, for others a structurally unstable sandwich. The Bohemian Special was both, and even after having consumed several meals that day, I still Slagled that sucker.

We were too late for the ribs, but added a plate of sliced brisket to our order. The smoked meat on its own was a disappointment. The slices came from the lean end and were underdone and rubbery, though well-seasoned and smoky. I could see their potential, but the sandwich was definitely the better vehicle for them.

We all kept our eyes peeled for some roadside barbecue as I pointed the car back north toward Dallas. Roadside barbecue can be a great source for quality, small-batch smoked meats. It can also be a low-overhead outlet for someone experimenting with a new smoker. **BAD DOG BBQ**, in Columbus, seemed to still be in the experimentation phase. Now we had really had enough.

Sated, stuffed even, our day was coming to an end. Sunday had been good to us. Before the trip, my mind had said that fifteen joints in two days was a great idea. At this point my stomach was saying otherwise. Nick was definitely done—he had barely eaten all day. Even Clark's iron stomach was feeling fatigued. The rest of the drive up US Highway 77 served as a preview for future trips. It was dark as we passed City Meat Market in Giddings, then Snow's in Lexington, and a few oddball joints in Rosebud. All three of us had to return to reality at our day jobs the next morning. We ended the trip knowing that fine smoked meats could be had in Southeast Texas, especially on a Sunday, and that weekend road trippers all over our state would be glad to know it.

Clark Key was my friend and dedicated barbecue companion. I started writing this chapter on the day he was taken away from us by a vile disease. I'll miss you, Clark, and I certainly hope that heaven got some of the good pitmasters.

2 Days, 781 Miles, 15 BBQ Joints

CHAPTER THREE

COWBOY-STYLE BARBECUE IN THE HILL COUNTRY

Nick and I were rolling as a duo on this leg of
our tour of Texas. Southbound on I-35, a flatbed
carrying a soon-to-be-hoisted highway exit sign
for Luling, Texas—a Texas barbecue mecca that
houses the famous City Market—was our cue that
we were on the right track. With day jobs behind
us, the pedal was to the proverbial metal so as not
to miss a barbecue dinner in Austin.

STILES SWITCH BBQ AND BREW is an upstart in an emerging neighborhood in Austin. It opened just a month before our visit, but it didn't come quietly onto the barbecue scene. Lance Kirkpatrick, who mans the pits, honed his skills in Taylor, Texas, under the watchful eye of barbecue legend Bobby Mueller, of Louie Mueller Barbecue. When Kirkpatrick was brought into the Stiles Switch fold, word on the street spread that the Muellers might be involved in Austin's newest barbecue spot. Wayne Mueller, Bobby's son and the current owner of Louie Mueller, didn't take kindly to the possibility that the Stiles Switch crew might be playing up its connection to his place, so he filed a cease-and-desist on the use of the Louie Mueller name in connection with the Stiles Switch opening. Cue every local food-related media outlet.

While the menu at Stiles Switch bears a strong resemblance to that of Louie Mueller, on our visit the vibe was totally Austin. A row of local beer taps lined the long wooden bar, and a huge neon sign with a fedora-clad pig announced the place to the street. Inside, an optimistically large waiting area was cordoned off from the main space. Instead of a decades-old brick pit, the pit room contained a new steel Klose pit, from Houston, which has been dubbed Megatron by Mr. Kirkpatrick. The steel pit—with massive lids and counterweights to match—is fed only by post oak.

It was late on a Thursday night when we got there, so I didn't expect all eight meat options to still be available—it's common practice for barbecue joints to smoke only as much meat as they think they will sell on any given day. We grabbed some of everything except the chicken. (No matter the cooking method, I have a hard time granting chicken the elevated status of barbecue. A brisket is a tough cut of meat that is thoroughly transformed after bathing for hours in a smoky chamber. Chicken can only stand little more than an hour in the smoke lest it dry out completely, and the smoke barely penetrates the meat.) But it's brisket and sausage that define the Central Texas barbecue tradition that Lance comes out of, so that's what we focused on. The brisket and beef ribs were rubbed with an aggressive amount of black pepper. The lean brisket slices were pathetically dry and overtrimmed, I guess to satisfy the Weight Watcher's crowd coming over from the nearby UT campus. If you're looking for lean, then I'd suggest a few slices of the excellent smoked turkey breast, but I had fatty brisket on my agenda, and Stiles Switch did not disappoint. Well-rendered fat ran through each moist and deeply smoky slice. The beef ribs had a similar smokiness, but the meat was scant on what I had hoped would be a hefty short rib. Because of their large size, beef ribs are sometimes called "dinosaur ribs," but this one must have come from a velociraptor rather than a brontosaurus.

Sausage making is a time-consuming and therefore dying art in barbecue houses across the state. Bobby Mueller taught Lance most of what he knows about beef links (while he was still working at Louie Mueller Barbecue, Lance provided an on-camera beginner's course on sausage making when they were featured on the Food Network), so I was a bit miffed to discover that Stiles Switch has their sausage made for them by a (still respectable) meat market about an hour north of Austin, in Thorndale. The meat market's namesake sausage—a peppery, all-beef link—was the least exciting, while an all-pork, jalapeño-cheddar sausage, while spicy, was child's play compared to the signature Switch Original sausage, a plump link that seemed ready to burst from the juice coursing through it. My first bite released a hot and satisfying explosion of grease as the spices and smoke from the pork and beef sausage enraptured my taste buds. I was in sausage nirvana—and no longer miffed.

The next morning found Nick and me enrobed in swirling smoke as we sat at a grease-stained picnic table hidden from view by the blazing pits surrounding it. A few scraps of butcher paper and empty espresso cups littered the table, which is mainly for staff use, but if you know when, who, and how to ask, it can be cleared off for an early, preopening meal of smoked meat. With a front-row seat to all that fire, smoke, and meat, some might call it the chef's table, but I prefer to call it the Pitmaster's Table. Aaron and Stacy Franklin could make some ridiculous cash if they auctioned off no-wait seats at the table, but that's not their style. They're the owners of what has become the most popular restaurant in all of Texas in just over three years of operation—**FRANKLIN BARBECUE**. Lines of people waiting two hours for a seat are a common sight at Franklin, so I called in a favor. I consider both Aaron and Stacy Franklin friends, so I asked if Nick and I could come in before opening to get some photos of the calm before the storm. There were already people lined up outside, and they peered through the windows at us as we chatted barbecue, beer, and the pressures of perfection. A lot of folks ask me if the meat at Franklin's is worth the wait, and I can say with authority that it is. I've stood in that line many times before, and I have never been disappointed. The promise of achieving smoked-meat perfection is what keeps this couple in the restaurant for sixteen hours a day and keeps Aaron tinkering with his welder on his only day off, attempting to perfect the pits. They do not want to let anyone down. Of course their meteoric popularity brings detractors, but I have never dined on anything short of perfect here.

Pork ribs, sausage, and pulled pork all shine at Franklin Barbecue, but it's the fatty brisket that steals the scene. As we took the full tour with Aaron, our enthusiastic host unwrapped a fresh brisket for photographic documentation purposes. He then started slicing it—and I didn't tell him to stop. Pressing my luck, I asked if all of the ingredients for the Tipsy Texan sandwich were ready. Affirmative. I felt a sort of unexpected and involuntary cringe as Aaron quickly chopped some brisket.

I had just asked one of the state's best pitmasters to essentially

...SUPPLY AND DEMAND.........

Supply and demand doesn't work the same way in barbecue that it might in other businesses. Barbecue joints often run out of meat early in the day, and sometimes disappointed customers can't help but wonder if the joint has purposely kept supply low to increase demand. But a smoker can only produce so much meat. Take Snow's BBQ, in Lexington. They went from cooking three hundred pounds of meat on a Saturday morning to more than twelve hundred pounds after they received considerable state and national attention in 2008. But even with a new smoker and increased capacity, their meat is often still gone as early as an hour and a half after opening. Larger outfits like Kreuz Market are designed to smoke a ridiculous amount of meat and serve hoards of people. Their busiest day of the week is Saturday, when they cook about two thousand pounds of meat, which lasts them most of the day. A smaller joint of similar quality like Pecan Lodge can have a line of ninety minutes or more, but can still only smoke 530 pounds of meat in their smoker. If they rapidly increased their capacity, they might be able to stay open later than 2:00, but the quality of their meat would likely suffer. Franklin Barbecue has the same risk/reward conundrum for their current meat output. In the three huge smokers that Aaron has built, he can fit about twelve hundred pounds of meat for a normal Saturday service. But the lines stretch a hundred or more people deep, and the food is usually gone in just two to three hours after they open at 11:00 A.M. That seems like a quick sellout, but they're still cooking an incredibly large amount of meat. Providing more just to keep the doors open longer might affect the quality, and would most certainly make a line that is already unbearable for most even longer. In short, there's no barbecue joint I know of that would actually benefit from shortening their supply to increase their demand. If there is the capacity to smoke and sell more meat in this business of low-profit margins, then any pitmaster I know would be smokin' it.

...CHOPPED BEEF...

A chopped beef sandwich is what keeps many minor league BBQ joints in business, even the downright bad ones. Chopping the meat hides any of the tough texture you might find in under-cooked slices, and adding in plenty of melted fat and other collected juices invigorates other-wise dry meat. A warm buttered bun topped with saucy, tender meat is hard to screw up. With a modicum of effort, most places can make a decent chopped beef sandwich, but it's hardly an accurate measuring stick for a good barbecue joint. It is, however, a safe-haven menu item for a barbecue connoisseur who is dragged to a questionable joint against his will.

desecrate some beautifully smoked slices of beef to assuage my curiosity about one of his bestselling items. Having only partaken of naked smoked meat here over multiple visits, I wanted to branch out. But I hadn't foreseen the unsettling feeling I had. This reaction might make little sense to a barbecue newbie, but chopped brisket is usually made up of not-so-handsome scraps of meat and fat unsuitable for serving as sliced brisket; these are collected unceremoniously in various iterations of barrels, tubs, and buckets. Instead, Aaron had just chopped the beef from a half-pound of beautiful, center-cut brisket slices, which amounts to making hamburger out of a rib eye, but what a beautiful sandwich it made: Aaron piled the chopped brisket on the bottom half of a simple white bun that he had already prepped with raw white onion and dill pickle slices. He capped the chopped beef with a mound of beef sausage slices, house-made espresso barbecue sauce, and a crisp red-cabbage slaw. Breakfast was served with a side of fatty brisket slices.

There is no polite way to eat the Tipsy Texan, and I was conscious of Nick and his camera. But it took only one bite for my focus to shift to the sandwich and only the sandwich. The cool cabbage, the salt-and-pepper-flecked beef, the smoky sausage links, and the arresting rush of white onion and pickle. . . . Damn. When it all got too overwhelming, a snack of Texas's finest brisket was waiting. What separates the Franklin brisket from the pack is its tenderness, which they take right to the brink of being overdone. A black crust provides a smoky punch, and the fatty chunks of brisket cut from the brisket's ends are smoked to an almost crunchy consistency, which concentrates the flavor of the fat, bringing out a sweetness to which the salty rub provides a pleasurable counterpoint. I call the flavor sensation a sugar cookie because of how well it resembles the humble baked good that gets its flavor from fat and sugar. My breakfast required a halftime, but with Nick's help, we finished strong.

Still half-dazed from breakfast, we pointed the Audi west, away from the city. The Hill Country would be our host for the next four days. Folks outside of Texas seem to be confused as to just where to find the Hill Country. A recent *USA Today* article erroneously placed Lockhart and Luling in the Hill Country, while Zagat commandeered Taylor into the region as well. Even in Texas, real estate types exploit the allure of the Hill Country when "Central Texas" is deemed lacking in panache. But unlike geographical areas with ambiguous boundaries—like West Texas, say—the Hill Country's boundaries are formed by geology rather than perspective. From just north of Waco to just south of San Antonio, a limestone formation called the Balcones Escarpment rises from the Texas coastal plain. The escarpment forms the eastern and southern borders of the Hill Country. If you're driving south on I-35, just look to your right. The escarpment runs alongside the highway for two hundred miles, rising and dipping. The Hill Country only exists west of I-35, while Lockhart, Luling, Taylor, and Elgin are in the fertile plains of Central Texas that lie to the east of I-35. Unless you climb the limestone edifice of the Balcones Escarpment, you have not entered the Hill Country.

Our first stop in the Hill Country was at **R. O.'S OUTPOST** on the east side of Spicewood. It has since closed and reopened in another spot down the road, so our source for an incredible jalapeño-apple pie, which squarely outdid their barbecue, is still safe. Moving on.

As we descended into the Pedernales River valley, we surveyed the effects of the prolonged drought of 2011. We parked on the shoulder of the highway and walked down to the nearly dry riverbed. The Pedernales, typically known as a white-water rafting destination, had slowed to a trickle whose movement could barely be detected. Rain was not in the forecast. Before the end of January the town of Spicewood would make national news by becoming the first town in Texas to have to haul in drinking water due to their drought-starved wells.

After a hike back up the steep slope to the highway, we were hungry again. **OPIE'S BBQ** was just a few miles away on the far west side of Spicewood. At Opie's, you order directly from a pit just inside the door. All of the meats you'd expect to see at a Texas barbecue joint were on display, along with their specialty—sweet and spicy baby back ribs. You can get them by the whole or half rack—just don't come here without ordering them. Smoked to a perfect texture, the meat on these ribs wasn't falling off the bone, nor did it need to be gnawed off, and it still retained plenty of moisture. Cayenne further fortified a heavy, black-pepper rub, giving the ribs a not-so-subtle kick and the brick-red glaze beautifully set off the paler pink of the meat and the white of the bone.

Unfortunately, the brisket was overcooked; the texture of both the lean and fatty brisket was waterlogged and offered no resistance to being pulled apart. The simple salt-and-pepper rub was tasty, however, and the brisket did have a good smokiness from the all-wood-burning smokers out back.

Todd Ashmore, Opie's owner, gave us a tour of the whole operation. He and a few buddies had set up some chairs outside by the pits to watch a live Anthrax concert that was blaring from a big-screen television hung from the rafters of the pit-room roof. A painted wooden sign saying Welcome to the Shithole hung above it, reminding us that the chairs were set up just over the restaurant's septic tank, which shared some real estate with the pits. These guys definitely have a sense of humor, but they're serious about their meat. Todd's staff might be just as serious about desserts, given the myriad options on offer. The banana pudding

. . . FALLING OFF THE BONE . . . .

Let's use this opportunity to address a cliché oft used to describe ribs—"falling off the bone." Somehow this phrase has entered the lexicon as a way to describe the ultimate in pork rib texture, but all it really signifies is overcooked meat. It takes little skill to achieve denture-friendly ribs. They can either be boiled or baked before smoking or they can be left in a smoker to steam for hours wrapped tightly in foil. Apple juice, beer, water, or other liquids can be added to this foil package if braised meat fit for a teething toddler is the goal. On the competition circuit the highest marks for texture are given to ribs that, when bitten into, the single bite of meat should come cleanly from the bone while leaving the rest of the rib meat attached. A rib that displays a clean bite mark with visible white bone should be the postbite result. If you're just left clutching an empty bone when you attempt to lift a rib off your plate, then what was the point of cooking ribs in the first place? Along with well-smoked ribs comes one of nature's perfect meat handles, so let that bone do its thing.

highlighted in an episode of the television show *The Day Tripper* was gone for the day, but an homage to Dallas's own Neiman Marcus was there for the taking—a blondie brownie named after the tony Dallas department store was bigger than my hand. It was just what we needed to perk up for the drive to Marble Falls.

I had tried to visit **INMAN'S RANCH HOUSE BAR-B-Q** in Marble Falls twice before, but each attempt had been thwarted by Inman's short Saturday hours. My anticipation grew keener as we walked through the screen door. It took several minutes for my eyes to adjust to the dark pit room, lit only by a single fluorescent fixture. An exposed ceiling covered in black soot was a good sign that the brick-enclosed pit had been smoking for many years. Their menu was more tightly focused than anywhere else

we had been; all Inman's served was brisket and home-made turkey sausage, which they cooked over the direct heat of burning oak. We placed our order at a counter adjacent to a cutting table with an attached scale. No frills were offered, and none were needed.

I kept track of owner Billy Inman's whereabouts as we ate, because I wanted to praise him personally for the bounty of beautiful meat that sat in front of me. The brisket had a deep and dark bark. The meat glistened with moisture, and the fat was tantalizingly translucent. The sausage links had wrinkled skin, indicating they had spent some serious time in the smoker. I was salivating, but where the hell was Nick? I had given him first dibs on the plates for documentation purposes, but he'd gotten distracted by the bloody pans and random

piles of knives and ill-used forks back in the kitchen area. Brimming with impatience, I politely summoned him to photograph the container full of meat. Finally, I could dig in. That's when the confusion set in. That dark crust on the brisket was so dry that it cracked in my teeth. The fat didn't hold the concentrated flavors from the smoke, time, and salt it should have. Instead it was washed-out and flavorless. The wrinkled skin of the sausage was really just a sign of lost moisture. Since it's made from 100 percent lean turkey, I wasn't expecting it to be dripping, but I had had a better version of the sausage a few years back at an event where Inman's provided samples of their sausage. My brain wrestled with what I was seeing versus what my taste buds were telling me. Finally, my taste buds overruled. The food just wasn't that great. Any joint can have a bad day, and that brisket might have been the single bad one of that day. The sausage might just have been dry because we showed up after the lunch rush. There are a lot of reasons why my experience at Inman's did not match up with other opinions that I sincerely respect, but it'll take another visit before I can call Inman's a great destination for barbecue.

Just up the street in Marble Falls sits **PEETE MESQUITE BBQ**. The small red building is adorned with a very large sign that reads "Voted best BBQ in Burnet County 12 yrs. in a row." Consensus about barbecue tends to be worthless at determining quality, but I had had decent meat there a year earlier. I was back for a second round because I had missed out on the pork ribs on my last trip. And damn if they weren't out again this time. The owner and pitmaster, Wayne Henderson, told us that they're the most popular item. We settled for a few slices of fatty brisket and a few more of lean brisket, pork steak, and some excellent sides. I don't normally go on about sides, but the attention Peete paid to their coleslaw and macaroni salad was commendable. Just about every barbecue joint in Texas offers potato salad, coleslaw, and beans. At their worst, they come straight from a can and/or tub, but at their best they can be like the sides here: the macaroni salad was mixed with fresh-cut green peppers, chunks of celery, and a creamy dressing seasoned with black pepper and celery seed. For the slaw, the cabbage was roughly chopped and mixed with shredded carrots. A light, sweet, mayo-based dressing bound it all together without being overwhelming. If only it were always that easy to get roughage out on the barbecue trail.

Wayne is essentially self-taught in the barbecue arts. He bought the joint in 1999 after having plenty of experience in hotel dining. The previous owner who sold him the place agreed to stick around for about a month to get him acclimated, then called it quits two days into the training sessions. For Wayne it was either sink or swim, so he did all he could to keep his head above water. Now he sells out of ribs every day. He also has good taste in brisket, preferring the fatty stuff to the lean, but then it's hard to disagree, given how dry the lean slices were. He said his customers prefer the lean that way, but I couldn't finish it. A thin pork steak (which is just a slice from the shoulder) still had plenty of moisture. Both the pork and fat had been cooked to tender, and the well-seasoned meat had a unique smokiness. As we were finishing up the meal on the trunk of the car, Wayne invited us back to the pits. I immediately asked if the pork steak had been cooked over coals and if the brisket had been smoked indirectly. He confirmed but noted that he uses mesquite for both, just the way his predecessor did it. I'd identified two different cooking methods by taste alone, and I was feeling pretty proud.

Nick had heard that there was a bald eagle's nest somewhere along State Highway 29 between Marble Falls and Llano. As the sun was setting we waited alongside the highway with a few other photographers for the eagles to leave their nest. All I could ponder was how the breast of a carnivorous eagle would taste compared to a grain-fed turkey. As night fell we decided it was a better idea to drive the half hour back to Marble Falls for the Blue Bonnet Cafe. We were a few hours late for Pie Happy Hour (it really exists here, from 3:00 to 5:00 P.M. on weekdays), but the signature peanut butter cream and the coconut meringue were just as sweet at regular price. They were also the perfect complement to a crisp, hand-battered, chicken-fried steak. Don't worry, I got the small steak. We drove in the dark hoping to avoid any wildlife on the curvy roads that led to nearby Horseshoe Bay to stay for the night in my boss's house. She was nice enough to let us use it, and we were happy for a big-screen television and the good bourbon that was kept in the cabinet. We slept well.

A thick fog partially obscured a dozen or so white-tailed deer crossing the road as we left Horseshoe Bay and Lake LBJ behind us. We were going to earn our breakfast with an early-morning ascent up Enchanted Rock. This enormous granite mound rises over the landscape as if the earth had taken a gentle inhalation, forcing the igneous rock up above the soil and shrubs. The formation is the most visible component of the granite Llano Uplift. Once at the top of Enchanted Rock, the vicious wind did its best to tear our hats and water bottles from us. We had only a few minutes to comfortably take it all in. We could almost see Llano from there, where we would be hitting **COOPER'S OLD TIME PIT BAR-B-Q**, considered the holy grail of Texas barbecue by many barbecue pilgrims.

The people who pack Cooper's crave the unique flavor of the meat offered there, but many don't realize that the flavor is the result of a barbecue method that is completely different than the one used in the smoked-meat temples in more famous barbecue towns like Lockhart, Luling, and Taylor, Texas. But then, that is Central Texas, and this is the Hill Country. In Central Texas, barbecue is usually done in the low-and-slow manner that is replicated in Texas-style barbecue joints outside of Texas. Oak wood is burned in a firebox adjacent to the cooking chamber, and the smoke and heat from the burning wood is pulled through the smoker, over the meat, and out the chimney or exhaust. The meat within the chamber is most decidedly smoked and the flavor of the meat announces this at once. The crust of the meat is smoky, and usually the flavor penetrates into

the meat. Any untrimmed fat left on the meat is transformed from a hard white substance into a translucent, sticky treat with a buttery texture. At Cooper's and other joints like it all over the Hill Country, they cook over direct heat. The wood of choice is mesquite (oak, hickory, and pecan don't take kindly to the Hill Country's soil conditions), which is burned down in large steel chambers. Burning is usually done on a rack held above the base of the chamber so that as the wood breaks down, the coals will fall into a pile at the base of the chamber. A man with a very long-handled shovel then transports the coals to a rectangular steel pit, where he deposits them at the bottom of the smoker, a few feet below the meat rack. These burning-hot coals are spread out to evenly heat the entire cooking rack. The meat is then placed on the racks to cook, and the pits are covered with huge metal lids. Most proponents of this method will snap at you if you call this smoked meat since they don't consider this process smoking. Nor do I. In the words

of owner Terry Wootan, "We don't smoke our meat, we cook our meat just like you're cooking a steak." But this grilling is done over hardwood coals instead of gas or charcoal. As the meat cooks, its juice and melting fat drip onto the fire, which sizzles and creates steam and smoke. This does just as much to provide flavor as the coals themselves, but perhaps nothing (aside from the meat) provides as much flavor as the massive amount of salt in the rubs used at most barbecue joints that use this direct-heat cooking method. Due to the high heat, the cooking times can be as short as five hours for a whole brisket. When it's complete it's like a whole other animal from one that's done low-and-slow. The texture, the flavor, and even the color are different.

At Cooper's, just as at Opie's back in Spicewood, you order directly from the warming pit. The beauty of this method is that you can quickly assess the quality of each cut and leave those behind that look past their prime. A warning is also in order. All of those options in front of you will make it tempting to overorder, and the staff here will be happy to help you overfill your tray. A request for a slice of brisket can get you a two-inch-thick cut if you don't specify how much you want. I started with a pork chop. While Texas barbecue is known for its beef, Cooper's dubs itself Home of the Big Chop. They season pork chops an inch and a half or two inches thick with salt and black pepper on every surface, then cook them quickly over the coals. The meat's color is not bronze, reddish, or black like a smoked cut of pork would be. Instead the surface is pale flesh speckled with cracked black pepper. The interior meat is white with the faintest pink outline. Because it's already a nice cut of pork with high-quality fat, this direct-heat method is perfect since the transformative powers of a long cooking time are not required to tenderize the meat or break down any hard fat. On this visit the juices ran out of the pork as I sliced through the behemoth chop. The salty meat was surrounded by crispy fat that held on to the salty rub better than the muscle. This was an excellent cut of meat and one of the finest pork chops I'd eaten anywhere, but a little more smokiness would have made it even better. On a couple of other visits to Cooper's my chops had been dried-out, and it was on this trip that I realized why. On most barbecue trips, I don't get to Llano until late in the afternoon. At Cooper's they hold their meat in an uncovered warming pit. Think of it like a Chinese buffet. If you get the first meat of the day (as we had) or if you hit Cooper's during the massive weekend lunch rush, then you'll get fresh, moist meat just due to the high turnover. If not, your meat is bound to be a bit dry.

The beef rib I ate next was just as impressive as the chop. The thick short rib had shrunk up on itself, revealing enough bone to show me it was done. The fat had rendered throughout the short rib, and because of the cut's low surface-area-to-meat ratio, the heavy seasoning on the rib didn't overpower it. The brisket had the same supple moisture, but the crusty end bits were sodium bombs that were just plain hard to enjoy—an unfortunate consequence of the direct-heat method. Due to the gobs of salt on the meat and the lack of smoke, the flavors in the ends of fatty brisket can become unbelievably concentrated. This isn't anything that a bowl of gooey and crunchy pecan cobbler can't fix, but it is a casualty worth noting.

In a converted two-story house just across the Llano River, Kenneth Laird, the owner and pitmaster of **LAIRD'S BBQ**, turns out some fine, fine brisket. Even better than what we had just had at Cooper's, this brisket had a deeper mesquite flavor from the coals, and its seasoning was thankfully a little more subtle than at Cooper's. The fatty line that ran through the meat was perfectly rendered, and the texture of the brisket was flawless. Along with the brisket, we ordered ribs and a pork steak, which arrived on a Styrofoam plate with a full slice of white onion, flavorless beans, and a sweetened-up potato salad. The long, thin spareribs were curiously dried-out beneath their coating of sauce. They tasted like yesterday's smoked meat. The pork steak also suffered from a lack of

···PRICEY BARBECUE··········

The skilled labor required to thoughtfully tend a pit isn't cheap. An interview with Cooper's owner Terry Wootan in *Republic of Barbecue* revealed that he runs eight pits on a busy day and requires two men on each pit. This can't be two newbies, but must be folks who are well trained in cooking quality meat. That's sixteen well-trained employees required for a busy day at Cooper's. When you compare that to the hourly wage of any high schooler who can hit the On button for the overnight cooking session in a modern gasser pit, and it's no wonder the barbecue at Cooper's is more expensive. Whoever said barbecue was cheap must have been eating in a joint that didn't require well-paid talent. The high waste (about forty percent of a brisket's precooking weight is saleable), long hours tending to the pit, the high cost of wood (unless you're using gas), along with the high cost of the well-trained labor we just discussed all add up to an expensive business to run.

moisture, but that was due to its thin profile, which couldn't really hold up to the high heat of the coals. Still, the brisket alone was worth the price of admission. I knew Kenneth to be cantankerous from previous visits—that is, when I could actually get a few words out of him. On this visit he asked about my shirt—it was from a barbecue competition that I had judged. "You tell those boys they don't know what competition is until they try to run a barbecue business in Llano, Texas. Now that's competition."

Before getting out of Llano, we made one last stop at **INMAN'S KITCHEN PIT BAR-B-Q**. Yep, this joint has the same name as the Marble Falls spot, but they aren't affiliated—at least they aren't anymore. Lester Inman once owned them both, but when he passed in 1988, his business partners in the Llano location, the Oestreiches, bought out his half, and Lester's brother and nephew took over the Marble Falls location. Though the two Inman's are separate businesses, the Llano Inman's is also known for its turkey sausage. The original recipe turkey link here had a more aggressive seasoning than the Marble Falls location, and may have had some pork fat in it, given the juiciness. It was a pleasing link of sausage that was downright healthy compared to the rest of our usual menu of fatty hunks of beef and thick pork ribs. A patty-sized link of jalapeño-Swiss sausage had a synthetic casing and lots of black pepper. I enjoyed the flavor just fine, but something about it felt too homogenous and overprocessed. I didn't have to linger on it since there were a couple of promising pork ribs on the plate. I hadn't gone into this Inman's hoping for much, but the ribs were exceptional despite—not because of—my low expectations. Juicy meat seasoned with lots of black pepper and the right amount of salt had just enough bite, but the tender meat was still easy enough to get off the bone. On a long barbecue day like that one, I would normally stop after a few bites, but I cleaned those ribs to the bone. I needed a few bites of slaw to cleanse my palate, and it was great: tender cabbage tossed with celery seed and dressed with a sweet, tangy dressing that hinted of sour cream. It had a nice crunch and a great, unique flavor.

When I reached for the brisket, alas, I could immediately feel its rubbery texture. I have a multistep method for judging the quality of brisket: first, I perform a visual inspection as it's being cut. I end by tasting. In the middle, I handle the meat. This is where I check to see if it feels moist or tough or if it's going to fall apart too easily. If the slice stays together then I get a feel for its tenderness by pulling it apart. It should take little effort, but sometimes the pesky collagen will hold the protein strands together so that it pulls apart in a prolonged manner like an accordion. In the case of Inman's, the brisket simply wouldn't pull apart. It was so underdone that I struggled mightily with the slippery slice before having to resort to a knife.

As Nick stood on a chair taking a few shots of the food, the management somehow took notice. Owner Horace Oestreich came over and sat with us for a chat. He was genuinely curious about our experience. I had to level with him about the brisket, and he was visibly embarrassed. As he took us on a postmeal tour of the pit room, another serving of brisket found its way to us. Not too surprisingly, it was far superior to the first in both texture and flavor. My guess is that if Horace were still taking the knife to every brisket, then the slices we were served originally would never have made it to the dining room.

Thirty-four miles west of Llano lies Mason, a charming town with a less-than-charming past. Its historic downtown, with its quaint town square, limestone buildings, and still-operating, art deco–era Odeon Theatre belies the fact that more than a dozen people were killed here between 1875 and 1877 in the Mason County War. Also known as the Hoo Doo War, the killings were the result of clashes between ranchers and newer German settlers over cattle rustling. The famous outlaw Johnny Ringo took part in a few of the killings. Just a couple of years later he would find himself a suspect in the killing of Wyatt Earp's brother Virgil in Tombstone, Arizona. The war came to a fiery conclusion when the courthouse was burned along with all records of the troubles. Only one person was ever jailed for the violence, and none of those involved would ever talk about it.

We tried to start a Mason County War of our own with a stop at Texas Deadwood BBQ so we could pit it against the well-known **COOPER'S BAR-B-Q** in Mason, but Texas Deadwood was closed until the weekend. Mason is home to the original Cooper's, which George Cooper opened in 1953. In 1962 George sent his son, Tommy Cooper, to Llano to expand the business. Sadly, Tommy died in an accident in 1979, and the family sold both locations. Terry Wootan bought the Llano location in 1986 while Duard Dockal purchased the Mason location, which he still operates. As at the Llano joint, in Mason they cook the meat directly over mesquite coals in steel pits, and you still order straight from the pit. This visit would be my third. My first visit had led me to conclude that the Mason Cooper's had some of the best barbecue in the state, while my second visit—oddly— had been almost entirely forgettable. This was to be the tiebreaker, but as soon as we arrived I had a sinking feeling it wasn't going to go well. The offerings looked a bit sad for so early in the afternoon, though they did have some cabrito (young goat) available along with a new house-made goat sausage. We ordered both, along with a beef rib and some brisket, and took a seat at an outside picnic table.

The beef rib had great flavor, and although the crust was dried-out, the interior meat was still moist and pleasant. The brisket tended toward waterlogged; it had been stored in a foil wrapper, and its flavor couldn't overcome the poor texture. The cabrito was mostly bone. At seventeen dollars per pound, it was even more demoralizing that the salvageable meat was dried-out and flavorless. The only savior on this day was the goat sausage. A mix of pork and goat, the link had a kick of heat, excellent smokiness, and great snap. The meat was moist, with just enough fat. It was some of the best sausage of the trip. Even with the other missteps, I would return to the Mason location of Cooper's just for that sausage.

From Mason, we opted for a slightly longer drive to Junction along the farm-to-market roads, the paved two-lane roads the state developed to connect rural and agricultural towns to market areas. This route took us over a few picturesque low-water crossings that spanned the Llano River, one of which was used by the old cattle drives along the Great Western Trail, and was thus named the Old Beef Trail Crossing.

In Junction we sampled the meats from the third independent joint in the Cooper family at **COOPER'S BAR-B-Q & GRILL**, which was opened by a grandson of George Cooper. While their jalapeño sausage had plenty going for it, the ribs and brisket were poor. They had all the saltiness I'd come to expect from Cooper's, but a slice of brisket was so underdone that it fanned out like an accordion when I tried to pull it apart, while the rib meat held on to the bone for all it was worth. I was hoping for better barbecue just on the other side of I-10.

LUM'S BAR-B-QUE had been an unexpected favorite of mine on a road trip through Junction several years before, so I was anxious both to get back and to see how it had held up. As I said, I base most of my reviews on a single visit, so it's hard to tell if I'm hitting a spot on a bad, good, or average day. If I hit them on a great day and my blog readers then go out of their way to visit and it's no good, I get very frustrated.

It seemed that, at the least, Lum's own opinion of their work had not suffered over the last four years—their sign, which had read Go Band! now read Best BBQ in the World. All signs pointed to hopeful as I watched the meat being cut. Even though the meat was lifted from a steam table tray (this is generally bad given that the meat continues to cook on the side in contact with the warm metal), everything had a great black crust on it. I was looking forward to getting a respite from direct-heat cooking, too, as Lum's was running a true offset smoker in front of the building, though, of course, they used mesquite.

By the time we got to our table, my hopes had been dashed. It looked like a fan had been blowing over the meat. In just a minute the surface of the brisket had gone from glistening to looking like a shag carpet of curled meat fibers. The ribs hadn't dried out quite as much, but their edges were showing some age. The sausage link was sliced, but the knife hadn't gone clean through. As I pulled them apart I could see why. While sitting on the steam table the bottom edge of the link had dried to an inedible crisp. The knife couldn't slice through it easily because it was stiff. It simply should not have ended up on the plate in that state. I left a bit dejected. At least the deviled eggs were superb.

From Junction the road became considerably more curvy and hilly. The rolling landscape of the Hill Country north of I-10 was giving way to the mountainous region south of the interstate. The AC worked overtime as we made our way up the steep slopes. Even though it was January, the temps displayed inside my car were reading as high as 89 degrees. For the next sixty miles there were few signs of civilization along US Highway 83, which runs the entire north-south length of Texas, from Perryton, on the Oklahoma border, to Brownsville, on the Mexican border. I imagine that when 83 came through the western edge of Kerr County in 1952, the folks running the **GARVEN STORE** thought it would bring prosperity or at least more people to the area. Sixty years later, however, the store still sits on a very lonely stretch of 83 where it intersects State Highway 41.

Keith and Jackie Dowdy were running the tiny store when we arrived, just as the sun was setting. They are the most recent standard-

bearers in a long line of Dowdy family members who have had a hand in operating this place since 1932. The store is chock-full of what you'd expect from a convenience store, along with a room full of leather biker wear and an extensive line of jerky. I tried a few varieties and they're all incredible, but we were there for the brisket and home-made sausage. The thin brisket slices were respectable enough, with a bit of smoke and subtle seasoning, but the star here was the German sausage, a fifty-fifty beef-and-pork mixture seasoned with salt, black pepper, red pepper, and something else that was hard to identify. When I went back inside and guessed ginger, I got a forlorn look, as if they weren't too happy that I guessed it. Not only was the flavor top-notch, but the casing had a good snap, and the link was just juicy enough without dripping with fat. Keith joked that they'd only been doing barbecue for eighteen years, so they're still trying to figure things out. I'd say they've got the jerky and the sausage down pat, but the brisket needs some perfecting.

That's more than can be said of the **HOG PEN**, in Leakey, where a last grasp for barbecue before the sun went down resulted in a smoked boudin that was so oversmoked it provided an aftertaste similar to a cigar.

From Leakey we were headed for a cabin in Bandera, the Cowboy Capital of the World and our home-away-from-home for the night. I'd planned the route so we would weave our way through the hairpin turns and rapid elevation changes of Ranch Road 337, which snakes through a picturesque section of the Hill Country referred to by some as the Swiss Alps of Texas. Popular with motorcyclists for its twists and S-curves, *Texas Monthly* called it "one of the seventy-five things to love about Texas." It's the sort of drive that I—and my Audi Quattro—dream of, as long as we don't have to do it in the dark. But we had spent too long eating barbecue, so it was going to be white knuckles for the next hour and a half. The gruesome scene of a riderless motorcycle and emergency vehicles along the side of the road at the bottom of a hill did nothing to ease my nerves.

The lights of **KEESE'S CAFE & BAR-B-QUE** were a welcome beacon in Medina. An unplanned stop can sometimes be the best one, and the worst of the curves were behind us. As we enjoyed a hefty plate of meat and pie on the picnic tables outside, the owner and pitmaster, Keith Keese, joined us along with his only server, Missy. Missy had sold us on a slice of their excellent Cedar Bark Pie, which featured walnuts and coconut mixed with a sugary filling, much like a pecan pie. We ate it first. The brisket slices were commendable, given the late hour.

The meat had a good crust and was plenty moist, but could have used more seasoning. Thick and tender spareribs had a subtle, sweet glaze and were thoroughly enjoyable. Keith has been cooking barbecue for fifty years, and he built his own pit for this joint. Coals

···SMOKE··································

Smoking meat isn't really about an active cooking process. Once the meat is seasoned and on the pit, there really isn't much reason to poke, prod, flip, baste, mop, spray, wrap, or even look at it. The only active part of the barbecue process is with the fire, so good barbecue is an outcome based more on proper fire-tending techniques than the act of cooking. Properly controlling the fire isn't just important in maintaining a consistent heat. As wood burns it creates smoke of varying quality. In the research for *Modernist Cuisine* they noted that the optimal temperature for your fire is 750 degrees. Positive flavoring attributes of smoke don't even begin to develop until the fire is at least 570 degrees, and temperatures above the optimal level still drive off negative flavors. When wood is starved of oxygen and smolders on the fire—or when wet wood is used, choking out a hot fire—then off-flavors are developed and released in the smoke. Undesirable flavors like creosote cling to the meat and cause it to taste like ashes or a telephone pole. The creosote will provide a numbing sensation on your tongue, and in extreme cases will cause intestinal distress. Keeping a hot fire with good-quality smoke is key for great barbecue.

· ·

burned down from 100 percent live oak provide the heat. Keese's was one of only two places in the state (the other being the Salt Lick in Driftwood) I had encountered that used live oak solely, and this was the only place I knew of that used live oak coals for direct-heat cooking. Outside of brisket and ribs, Keith's specialty is cabrito. His customers won't pay the twenty dollars per pound that he'd have to charge for this expensive meat, so he only cooks it for the volunteer fireman's barbecue in November.

We drove slowly into Bandera. After stowing our bags in our rented cabin down by the river, we hit the well-known OST (Old Spanish Trail) Restaurant to grab a seat on one of the saddle-topped stools that line their bar. Only problem? They didn't sell booze. Back outside, we followed the sound of a live band to the nearby 11th Street Cowboy Bar, where we chatted up the attractive bartender before she got bored with the two bald thirty-something dads. Arkey Blue's Silver Dollar on the other side of Main Street was more our speed anyway, though they're a beer bar that doesn't have a license to sell hard liquor. A few beers into it, the live band called it a night. Hankering for bourbon, we set off on foot for the local liquor bar. Sadly, it had been shut down, so we opted for one last beer at the wine bar a block away. What were we thinking? There was bourbon, good conversation, and reasonably safe pecan cobbler from earlier that morning back at the cabin.

The next morning, fueled with caffeine and Tylenol, we retraced our steps along Ranch-to-Market 337 to take the long way around to Kerrville. After a quick stop at the Lost Maples Park (quite a dud in January) we made our way up to Ingram to see the cheesy Stonehenge replica. The accelerator and my reflexes got a workout along State Highway 39 as it swept along the banks of the Guadalupe River until we saw Pit Bar-B-Q on the sign of the **HUNT STORE**. With a clear head, I left the Audi in the parking lot to rest like a sweaty horse. That morning's scone was no longer cutting it. I was hungry. The smoked-meat menu at the Hunt Store was sparse—only brisket and pork. The brisket sandwich that I unwrapped on the trunk looked promising enough. It wasn't a revelation, but it was fine brisket, with a well-seasoned crust and a few wisps of smoky flavor. There was no time to lose now. We had several stops left for the day and a firm deadline in place for that night's Charlie Robison show in Luckenbach.

Poor planning and no cell signal meant we were searching blind for a joint called **BILL'S BAR-B-QUE**. Coming in from the west we drove right past Bill's along the Junction Highway (State Highway 27). A quick U-turn, and we were first in line. In addition to the ubiquitous brisket and ribs, they also had pork rump roast on the menu. With a plate full of meat, we retreated to the picnic tables outside by the pits. The aroma coming from the pits was unmistakably the result of cooking with wood

coals. A guy manning the pits said they were using mostly live oak with a bit of mesquite mixed in. The previous night I had been surprised that Keese's, in Medina, used lived oak, so it was extra odd to find it twice in two days. The coals I smelled were only there to cook the ribs and chicken; the brisket and pork were done in a large steel indirect smoker, also using live oak.

I must admit that the brisket didn't look like much; it didn't have either a well-defined crust or a smoke ring. One bite eliminated my preconceptions. A deep smokiness permeated even the lean slices. The moist and perfectly tender meat touched off all the sensors in my brain that adore salt. The supercrisp bark held a layer of intense rub. It was actually reminiscent of commercial fried chicken. Tender chunks of pork shoulder hadn't really been pulled or chopped, so the edge pieces on the plate had large portions of the flavorful black crust, which normally gets chopped into the meat. I was happy to have a few decadent bites of the fatty-crispy crust as it played against the ridiculously juicy meat. Owner Joe Marino has been running Bill's Bar-B-Q since 2005, when he took it over from his folks, who bought the joint from the joint's namesake thirty years prior. With such a long history and such good meat I was surprised I hadn't heard about Bill's before. We promised Joe that we'd help get the word out. He was curious about our reaction to the meal, but less curious about Nick's very large camera. He mentioned that a few other folks had been in recently snapping photos, so I guess he was just taking it in stride.

Meandering into Kerrville we found **BUZZIE'S BAR-B-Q**, which I was familiar with only from having tried a few bites of their excellent brisket at a festival in Austin. Nick's camera provoked the weirdest response here it had met with yet: the guy manning the register started geeking out with Nick about camera lenses and zoom capability. A net covered his long hair and an apron barely covered the Boston Bruins logo on his shirt. Beside him, the guy plating the meat had a Steelers cap on. I was starting to get worried until a larger guy with a camouflage hat emerged from the back door and a rush of aroma from burning wood trailed him. As I waited for our food, I spotted a notice that trimmed lean brisket was three dollars per pound extra. This was my kind of place. The plate we were presented with was heaped with three thick spareribs with bark the color of a well-oiled saddle. Hidden beneath them was a smaller stack of fatty sliced beef that was chewier than I remembered from my sample in Austin. The end of a sparerib had two meaty sides separated by a line of thick fat that ran from the cartilage out to the edge. When I see a rib like that, I like to start by pulling off the top end, which I call the knuckle. If it comes off easily, I know the rib is cooked right. And if it's a well-smoked rib, then I know that will be the best bite, too. It was a damn fine knuckle of pork rib meat. The rest of the bone wasn't bad, either.

Mark, the guy in the cammo hat, offered us a pit tour. It was essential we make good time to

Fredericksburg, because the new joint there that I really wanted to try was only open until midafternoon, but when someone offers me a pit tour I don't say no. Mark took us back to the large cabinet smoker in its own remote enclosure beside the restaurant. Even in January it was uncomfortably hot, and he laughed, noting that it reached about 120 degrees in there during the summer. There was a mix of oak and mesquite in the middle of a low firebox, and I'll be damned if there wasn't more live oak in the wood pile. The trend was growing with every stop. He explained how they cook the ribs closer to the middle of the smoker since they can take the high heat, while they keep the briskets toward the outside. The result is a smoked flavor on the briskets and a direct-heat flavor on the ribs. As we gazed into the flames, Mark told us about a recent grease fire that had been quickly contained. The same couldn't be said for the fire that destroyed their original location in Comfort (hence the separate enclosure for the smoker here), but the barbecue was certainly fine at this newer building. When the conversation turned toward old legends about

· · · **PHOTOGRAPHY** · · · · · · · · · · · · · · · · ·

As we took more barbecue trips, I became more and more interested in the various reactions proprietors and employees had to Nick's camera. Some seemed to assume it meant good things for business and left us alone. Others outright asked us to stop taking photos. Mostly, people were just shy about being the subject of a photograph. It helped when I got people talking about their place, because it made it easier for them to ignore the incessant snapping of the shutter. Nick is relentless, and he grew bolder as the days and miles wore on. When we started out he had mainly taken architectural shots and snaps of willing subjects like family and friends. It was personally satisfying for me to see him get more comfortable with his role as the sole visual record keeper of our adventures. Every night we could see the fruits of his boldness on the computer screen. By the time we got to Bill's, he was capturing the essence of these places in ways that let me understand them better.

· ·

crazy residents of the nearby area and tales of wild animal maimings, I found a break in the conversation and took it. Fredericksburg was just a half hour away.

Fredericksburg's Main Street was buzzing with plastic-cup-toting tourists. I felt at home. It's legal to drink beer on the streets of Fredericksburg, and I was warmly reminded of my college years in New Orleans, where you can imbibe without fear just about anywhere. Nick and I were on the hunt for a restaurant called **SUGAR & SMOKE**, which we found tucked into a courtyard off Main. You couldn't really call it a joint: the well-heeled crowd noshed on expensive desserts trimmed with fancy garnishes, and smoked meat comprised only a few lines of the three-page menu. This was a fine-dining establishment, complete with exposed wood rafters and a stone fireplace. I could have been in Telluride, but I think the clientele were mainly from the tonier parts of Austin and Dallas.

Always willing to dive into a barbecue plate with an open mind, I asked for a meat sampler, which wasn't on the menu. After clearing the order with the owner, our waiter brought out a shiny, paper-lined tray piled with neat stacks of gleaming meat. Given the clientele, I was expecting overly trimmed brisket, but the brisket slices had a thick line of nicely softened and crisped fat. The thin layer of finishing sauce on the brisket was welcome and not overwhelming. Even with the handicap of a gas-fired Ole Hickory pit, there was plenty of good smoke on these tender slices, too. I had to confirm that the pork was from the shoulder, because its richness made me think some belly had been mixed in. Served presauced with a peach barbecue sauce, the meat was both smoky and sweet.

The one meat that did not work with its sauce was the lamb. The mint vinaigrette belonged on a salad. The otherwise delicate meat was moist, tender, and barely gamey. It lacked the good smoke of the other two meats, but was certainly enjoyable. No matter how good the meat was, this place just couldn't survive in the competitive Fredericksburg market and has since closed. Pitmaster Nicole Davenport plans to take her concept to San Antonio for another try.

Since we had seen the bevy of plastic cups upon arriving in town, beer was the real dessert we craved. The Fredericksburg Brewing Company—and its brew pub—was our first and obvious choice. Don't make the same mistake. Simply enough, if I don't finish a beer, then it's pretty bad. Besides, Franziskaner was on draught at a German bar just a few doors down. Even with a buzz it was hard to get into the Fredericksburg scene. The gift shops, antiques stores, bad bars, and kitschy restaurants seemed expressly designed for tourists. We walked down to a barbecue joint at the end of town looking for another taste of F'burg smoked meats. As we waited to be seated we watched plates full of pale and dry-looking meat arrive at the other tables. Nick and I exchanged a knowing look and left—we had our own bottle of bourbon back at the Motel 6 and a night of country music awaiting us in Luckenbach.

Our pitiful intake of healthful nutrients was weighing on Nick. He was done with alcohol for the day and needed something fried, so the local Dairy Queen was our pit stop before heading south. By the time we pulled into the dance hall parking lot in Luckenbach, darkness had fallen and the night had grown chilly. The wooden doors into the old dance hall were still closed and a line for the good seats was forming. Despite the cold, a good number of the anxious female attendees sported cutoff jean shorts, cowboy boots, and plaid. The adjacent concession stand, the Luckenbach Feed Lot, opened first. An all-business lady with a German accent handed me a pulled-pork sandwich and some fried potatoes. I was glad I had abstained at DQ. The shredded pork came together with onions, pickles, and sauce on a grilled bun. After spending the day consuming so much naked meat, the sandwich was a welcome change in flavor and texture. Even better were the crisp, spiral-cut fried potatoes covered in spicy seasoning. Newly fueled by the food and a couple of Budweisers, I was ready for the show.

Charlie Robison, the country music troubadour we were there to see, grew up just an hour away from Luckenbach, in Bandera. He was one of the first Texas country music stars I couldn't get enough of when I moved to the Lone Star State. I didn't think I could top the time I had met him after an incredible show a few years back, but seeing him onstage in Luckenbach, in his ripped denim, with a lit cigarette perched in the strings of his guitar, was special. His voice had filled the car speakers for many miles of my and Nick's trip, and when he drifted into his West Texas anthem "Loving County," I could barely control my excitement. After my fair share of longnecks I was feeling about as high as Elton John's "Rocket Man," for which Charlie provided an excellent cover, and to top it off one of the plaid-clad beauties asked me to dance. Between my poor coordination and her inebriation it was pathetic, but I had a blast. Luckily, stone-sober Nick was there to drive us back. We stayed up for a couple more hours admiring the video he'd captured of Charlie and the band. We could sleep in tomorrow.

Luckenbach was a much different place in the morning. We couldn't resist a return visit to see what the town looked like illuminated by the sun. The morning was surreal; the town was so quiet, almost as if it had been abandoned. We felt like we were trespassing, but a voice from the bar welcomed us in for some free coffee. A few chickens pecked at the ground as we meandered toward the door. In the corner of the bar sat a figure with a lit cigarette and a steaming cup of coffee. Lifting his black cowboy hat, he greeted us with a welcoming smile and introduced himself as Cary Windham, a musician who loves playing Luckenbach but lives in Lockhart, the Barbecue Capital of Texas. He relayed his insider's opinion that Chisholm Trail Bar-B-Q was the joint Lockhart locals prefer over the other three more famous places. As we made our exit toward an early lunch in Sisterdale, Cary offered us one of his CDs for the road, and asked us to make sure and return for the annual Luckenbach Hug-In, in mid-February.

Scrubby trees and rocky soil flanked the route to Sisterdale. I imagined the hardships the German immigrants who had walked this unforgiving terrain must have experienced as they trekked from the Texas coast at Indianola to Fredericksburg. If they survived the hunger and exhaustion to make it to Fredericksburg, they were in for a further rude awakening when they discovered how poor the farmland was there. The lack of arable topsoil would leave them hungry even after reaching their destination, but enough of them toughed it out for us to still enjoy the fruits of their labor today.

Our prospects for barbecue on this day were a bit better. Our first stop was at **MAYWALD'S SISTERDALE SMOKEHOUSE**, which John Maywald opened in 2011, almost against his will. For four years, Maywald had been unable to lease the building that now houses Maywald's, so he finally decided, along with his spouse and some friends, to fish rather than cut bait. Still an accountant by day, John only opens this secluded barbecue

joint two weekends a month. An old Oyler pit that John picked up secondhand sits in a trailer out back of the joint. Hickory is the only wood that goes in, and what comes out is brisket with deep smoke and a perfect, meaty texture. The silky-soft fat had sucked up any remaining smoke that the meat itself had missed, resulting in an otherworldly flavor. The rub had a lot going on, but the high salt and sugar content kept the brisket's surface from getting gummed up with powdery ingredients. Tender but meaty

ribs were coated with the same rub, but it seemed to have more punch, maybe from MSG. I had to fish out the lonely link of sausage from under the pile. It was hiding from embarrassment. There was nothing that could redeem that limp precooked link. It was meant for an oblong white bun, not butcher paper. It honestly had me a bit depressed about the plate as a whole until I bit into the chicken. I can say without hyperbole or any self-doubt that this was the finest smoked chicken thigh I have ever consumed. Nothing is worse than chewy chicken skin or dry meat, but this thigh had a perfectly paper-thin, crispy skin that came away cleanly with every bite through the lusciously moist and tender meat. Smoked chicken is not something I'm used to gushing about, but this was poultry paradise. If John keeps this up he can kiss his day job good-bye.

That was some high point, so it would be a challenge for **FRITZE'S BBQ** in nearby Boerne to match it. We ordered a plate of St. Louis ribs and they arrived with a dark crust glistening from a sweet glaze. The smokiness went deep into the meat, and the rub, heavy with black pepper, played well with the sweetness. The pork was perfectly tender, without any sign of storage fatigue. The brisket was equally tender, but there was nothing to distinguish it from plain old roast beef. No crust, fat, or smoke flavor existed in those monochromatic gray slices of meat. It was as if Fritze's had forgotten to put the brisket in their Southern Pride smoker, as it didn't have any of the smoke wood flavor. A dip into their sauce, which tasted of Campbell's tomato soup, didn't help any.

We got back on the road for the long drive through the southern end of the Hill Country to get to Kyle. **MILT'S PIT BBQ** is the closest to the Central Texas style of barbecue that you'll find on the west side of I-35, but then it sits right on the interstate's service road. Milt Thurlkill was born in Texas but moved to California for work. After having enough of the West Coast, he headed to DFW and soon tired of the treeless landscape. After reading an ad for a defunct barbecue joint in small-town Texas, he moved his family to Kyle to try his hand at smoking meat. After several research trips to Lockhart and a few years of practice, Milt has it down—or at least I'd say so.

Milt follows the Central Texas tradition of smoking tender, peppery briskets with a midnight-black crust. Our plate of beef was piled with supple slices of fatty brisket stacked one atop the other. A line of smoke-tinged fat lined the top of every slice, and each bite nearly melted on my tongue it was so tender. It was some great brisket. The turkey breast, which I've found to be near perfect on previous visits, was a bit dry by the time of our late-afternoon visit, but its signature deep, smoky flavor was there. The pork ribs managed to have a well-formed crust despite the substantial rub that had been applied to them. A too-heavy rub can result in ribs with a gummy

···PORK RIBS ···········

Let's talk pork ribs. There are three kinds. Baby back ribs are further up on the rib cage—literally "high on the hog." These ribs are easily identifiable by the severe curve in the bone and they usually have a good amount of meat left above the bone. They don't come from baby pigs, either. Spareribs are lower on the rib cage. They can be very long and are sometimes confused with beef ribs because of their size. At the tip of a sparerib will be a large knob of meat separated from the long bone by a mass of cartilage. This meat is harder to extract, but is a favorite of the rib connoisseur due to all of its flavorful fat. When the butcher cuts off these tips, you get rib tips, which are a popular dish on their own in Chicago and can be found on some Texas barbecue menus as "regulars." After the tips are separated, the remaining bone is relatively straight and is called a St. Louis–style rib. This moniker has nothing to do with the style in which the rib is prepared, but simply the way it is butchered. This bone is flatter than a baby back and usually has a thinner meat profile. In Texas barbecue joints you are most likely to find spareribs, with St. Louis ribs coming a close second. Baby backs are scarce, and when they do appear on a menu in Texas, they are usually offered alongside spareribs or St. Louis ribs.

texture, but these were crisp and bold. The tender meat came off the bone with little effort. We had to restrain ourselves from cleaning off the whole tray, as we had one last stop for the trip, and it was a biggie.

Retreating from the interstate, we went headlong back into the thick of the Hill Country. The winding roads tested both the car's suspension and Nick's stomach. With civilization safely behind us, we took a turn toward Driftwood, home of the **SALT LICK**, and not much else. The Salt Lick has different meanings to different folks. A New York magazine editor once insisted it be a stop on the smoked-meat itinerary I was compiling for an article on Texas barbecue. "It's the most well-known Texas barbecue in New York," she told me. It's true that those who have their first Texas barbecue experience at the Salt Lick are generally stunned, and for good reason. If someone has been suffering through barbecue in the Northeast and came to Texas for the weekend, then this probably is the best barbecue they've ever eaten. The trip to the Salt Lick usually begins with a forty-five-minute drive from the congested city of Austin into the wide-open and beautiful countryside. The waits for a table are notoriously long, but the management encourages a party atmosphere with a BYOB policy and a patio full of picnic tables, where revelers can enjoy predinner drinks and live music. Once seated, most meals are served family-style. Huge bowls of potato salad and slaw, along with plates piled high with saucy meat, are lowered onto tabletops accompanied by involuntary ooh's and ahh's from the lips of the famished. As an introduction to barbecue, the experience certainly makes an impression, and the food's not bad, either. Even so, the Salt Lick draws the ire of most every seasoned smoked-meat fanatic. Spite-filled and hateful comments quickly follow the release of any article or best-of list that touts the quality of their barbecue. In my view the Salt Lick *is* highly overrated, but it does put out good barbecue. Overrated in the fact that every few months you'll find a new article from someone outside the state saying it's the best barbecue they've ever eaten. On my first trip to the Salt Lick, when I had only been in Texas for a month or two (and never to the Hill Country), I too thought the food was phenomenal—it was an incredible experience further improved by the fresh plate of family-style meats the server provided when she brought out the to-go containers. It was Southern hospitality at its best.

But after eating my way through the best joints in Texas, my return trips to the Salt Lick haven't been as impressive, of course. That's not because of diminishing quality on their end, but rather because of how high my personal bar had been raised when it comes to barbecue.

The Salt Lick has been barbecuing the same way for years, but they've kept their method a bit of a mystery. Not long ago Scott Roberts, the owner of the Salt Lick, did an interview with *Texas Monthly*. The interviewer asked a simple question: "Do you or have you ever used a gas-fired or electric smoker?" The interview was for a piece highlighting the Salt Lick's involvement in the *Texas Monthly* Barbecue Festival. Knowing that the article's readers were likely to be 'que-heads he crafted his answer accordingly. "We had some smokers that we put in that were

gas-fired, but we don't really do those anymore because they have a drier heat than the wood does." When you enter either of the enormous dining rooms at the Salt Lick, a stone-lined open pit, metal grates heaped with all manners of meat sizzling over burning coals, greets you. These pits give the impression that the meats are all cooked here, but that's not the case. On a visit several months earlier I had inquired about the actual cooking methods from a man who appeared at the kitchen's back

door to grab a few logs of live oak. He told me that there were a number of stainless steel gas-fired rotisserie smokers back in the kitchen, and that the show pits out front were really just used to finish the meat. With this information in hand, I wrote a positive review of the joint, but I also called out Scott Roberts for dissembling during his interview and denying that the Salt Lick uses gas smokers—basically, I called him a liar. His response was that of a seasoned businessman—he invited me back for a full tour of their operation.

I was looking forward to that tour, but Nick and I both wanted to eat first—a tour of the operation would have been torture to our hungry stomachs. As the food arrived at our table, late-afternoon sunlight poured into the dining room, and the sauce-covered meat glistened. The thick slices of smoked brisket had been spared the sauce treatment at my request, and these end cuts had a deep, black crust with plenty of smoky flavor. The sausage needed more smoke and cooking time to tighten up the chewy casing, but the pork ribs were phenomenal. Basted with sauce during the finishing phase, they had developed a sweet crust that required no additional sauce. I was pleased with how great the food was so far, but it was all just a buildup to the beef ribs. My favorite beef ribs in the state are thick and meaty short ribs, but the Salt Lick uses what most consider a poor man's rib: the beef back rib. This rib is part of the prime rib rack. When the prime rib portion is removed from the bone and sliced into rib eye steaks, the butcher has two options: leave plenty of meat on the bone and sell it cheaply at beef rib prices, or cut the meat tightly to the bone and get more weight on the rib eye portion. It's a no-brainer that leaves back ribs with a pitiful amount of meat on the bones. A normal order of these huge ribs is mostly bone, but at the Salt Lick they have a little trick borrowed from the competition circuit, called the Hollywood cut. It's when you cut the ribs so that every other bone is thrown out and each remaining bone essentially has double the meat. This way, when you bite into a back rib you actually get a mouthful of meat. The sauce at the Salt Lick is almost as famous as the meat. It has a cottonseed-oil base, so it pours more like salad dressing. When it's poured onto a hot beef rib, it really seeps into the meat without coating the meat in a thick, sweet tomato-based sauce. As a result, Salt Lick beef ribs might be the best combination of meat and sauce anywhere in Texas. But I'd still take a well-smoked and naked short rib over a sauced back rib any day.

Our repast complete, it was time for Scott to pull back the curtain and show us around the kitchen—the whole kitchen. As we stood beside towering Southern Pride and Ole Hickory gas smokers, Scott explained their system: smoke briskets for twelve hours, flash-cool them, coat them in sauce, Cryovac them, rest them overnight, unwrap them, place them on the show pits out front and baste them with sauce for a few hours. Then they're ready to serve. Scott didn't seem at all uncomfortable showing me the whole process, so I asked him why he had answered that interviewer's question the way he did. He chalked it up to a misunderstanding of the question, which he said the interviewer had phrased differently than what had showed up in print. Either way, I felt satisfied with Scott's tour and was happy he was willing to take the time to show us around. It may not be how I'd do it, but the Salt Lick has their system, and it keeps plenty of folks coming back.

The Salt Lick also offers something wholly unique for a barbecue joint, which gives their customers another reason to stick around on a pleasant evening such as this. They have a full wine-tasting room serving their own labels. Nick and I enjoyed a glass of the Salt Lick's new Tempranillo with Scott. He shared his passion for wine making, his plans for expanding the Salt Lick empire to the Dallas–Fort Worth Airport, and some history about his family, the site on which they chose to build the Salt Lick, and the innovations the location had required. Out in the middle of nowhere, you have to be resourceful. Even today the Salt Lick captures all of the water from their condensate drains and ice machine runoffs and uses it to irrigate the landscaping. They compost their massive amounts of vegetable trimmings and use it as landscaping fertilizer. Since refrigeration wasn't available in Driftwood when Scott's dad built the Salt Lick in 1967, even the recipes were developed with this place in mind. To prevent spoilage, the slaw and potato salad contain no mayonnaise. The sauce was purposely made with an oil base so it would be shelf-stable in the high heat. These were literally dishes that were made to last, and it gave me a new appreciation for the sides even though I don't really care for them. I also had a new appreciation for Scott Roberts. Although I wouldn't replicate his preferred smoking methods, I only hope that I could emulate the graciousness he showed me if anyone ever calls me a liar.

The sun was setting on the weekend and on our trip. We wolfed down some creamy coconut pie from the Monument Cafe as we barreled back up the highway. By then, it was too dark to admire that familiar limestone escarpment to our left. With the eating complete, our focus grew singular. Maybe the two dads would make it home for bedtime.

4 Days, 1,192 Miles, 23 BBQ Joints

CHAPTER FOUR

A LONG SEARCH THROUGH EAST TEXAS

An oppressively thick, gray haze hung over Interstate 30 on our way out of Dallas. It was Valentine's Day, so it was fitting that Nick and I were together, given that we would spend more waking hours in each other's company in the coming month than we would spend with our families. Our wives, jaded by too many years of marriage, didn't seem to mind a bit. They knew it was just barbecue that we were courting. The

first point of business was to get off the interstate, so we took the long way to Tyler along US Highway 80, the old road that had once provided the only connection between Dallas and Shreveport before the construction of Interstate 20. Interstates are the worst way to immerse yourself in a place, and we might just pass an unknown barbecue joint or two along this route. About sixty miles east of Dallas, in Grand Saline, I spotted what I had thought was just a legend: the Salt Palace, a bungalow made entirely of blocks of local salt. The wall of the salt palace would be the first thing with which I'd swap some spit that day—I needed to have a lick, just to see if it was really real . . . and it was. It was also just as awful as you might imagine.

Thankfully, **MR. B'S BARBECUE** just down the street in Grand Saline was open, so I could cleanse my aching tongue with a barbecue breakfast. Okay, so it wasn't *quite* open yet. A woman named Cheryl unlocked the door and escorted us inside. She shuffled back and forth between the steel barrel smoker outside and the dining room, as she explained that since they're closed on Mondays, I would be getting Sunday's brisket on this dreary Tuesday morning. She apologized that it hadn't yet been warmed through in the oven, but quickly reassured me that the microwave would fix that problem. I was appalled but didn't let on. Microwaving brisket is about the worst way to warm it. Believe me. I've had lots of leftover brisket to deal with, and it's better cold than nuked. Before she commenced slicing the beef, she slid her knife across the surface of the brisket, removing the entire fat cap—and any flavor that the brisket might have once had. She was doubtlessly just performing a task expected by a finicky clientele that demanded lean, lean brisket. I was getting a bad feeling about East Texas. Apparently, it was acceptable to microwave brisket here *and* strip it of all its fat. In my relationship with my mistress, smoked meat, I had found that fat is the sweet perfume that enhances her beauty, so the next several days held the possibility for heartbreak at nearly every stop.

We rushed from Mr. B's to what we hoped would be a source of solace. As Tyler's South Beckham Avenue descends into the town's medical district, it takes a sharp double curve. **STANLEY'S FAMOUS PIT BAR-B-Q** sits in the bend of one of those curves, its prominent roadside position further emphasized by a badass neon sign. Owner Nick Pencis is a tall, handsome man with terminal bedhead and a laid-back demeanor that is disarming. You'd never know from his humble and amicable nature that his pork ribs have been voted best in Texas for two years running, against some pretty stiff competition. I wasn't surprised, because I know Nick strives for constant improvement. See, Nick and I have a history. I first visited Stanley's a few years back. The review I posted on my blog was middling but mostly upbeat and hopeful. Shortly after the review posted to the web, I received a sincere e-mail from Nick. He said he was working to make things better, and he wanted to know if I could offer up any leads on a good sausage supplier in the area. It was the first time I had ever received a reply from an owner who was sincerely seeking to improve.

This visit, being my third, certainly showed many of the improvements I'd been hoping for. There was a little fat left on the brisket slices, which were well smoked, as evidenced by their black crust and bold, hickory-smoke flavor. All the brisket was missing was a good dousing of salt and pepper. As far as the sausage went, well . . . teaching an old dog new tricks isn't easy, but Nick had finally convinced the old codger

...FAT.....................................

The value of well-smoked fat cannot be understated. It is particularly heartbreaking to watch someone carving a brisket scrape off a beautiful layer of well-smoked fat and throw it in the trash. Fat deserves more respect than to be treated as little more than a sacrificial layer of beef protectant. Fat is flavor. Fat is a *vehicle* for flavor as well. Just like your body, meat is made mostly of water. Therefore it is a great place to store water-soluble ingredients like salt and sugar. But many spices, such as black pepper, contain essential oils that are only fat-soluble. In other words, as the spices dissolve in the fat, they release flavorful essential oils—so removing the fat from the meat prematurely will also rid it of some very basic flavors. But even more important than fat's ability to deliver the complex flavors of a rub is its unparalleled ability to capture the flavors of wood smoke. Next time you have a nice slice of brisket with a good layer of fat, remove the fat and take a nibble of it, then take a bite out of the lean beef. As the fat melts on your tongue, the smokiness will linger nicely, while it will only be a subtle flavor in the beef. Fat is *the* vehicle for smoke. Do not discard well-smoked fat.

The presence of fat is also important to help determine the quality of the barbecue. I often say that if the fat's done then the meat will be, too. The fat is "done" when you can hold a thin slice of brisket to the light and see light shining through it. Properly cooked fat should be translucent from hours of smoking. On the other hand, a layer of opaque fat will tell you immediately that the beef isn't done yet, either. Pinching the fat on a slice of brisket will also tell you if the beef has been adequately smoked, since if cooked correctly, it will offer little to no resistance.

Of course, too much fat on a brisket can also be detrimental. A usual packer brisket (whole and untrimmed) from the butcher or the grocery store will have more fat on it than anyone wants to eat—even a fat-lover like me. You want to trim that fat *before* you season the brisket, otherwise when the brisket is done, you'll still need to trim the excess fat and you'll lose all of the flavor the rub imparted. A good rule of thumb is to trim away all but a quarter-inch layer of fat on the brisket. Throw away the fat you don't plan to eat before you put the meat on the smoker.

....

who owned the local meat market to help him create a custom sausage blend. The fresh sausage, pork mixed with garlic and black pepper, was a revelation. The natural casings gave the links a bit of a rustic look, and the smoker gave that casing a great snap. The links had a gray center and a pink ring surrounding the perimeter. You don't usually see a smoke ring like that on a sausage link, because most sausages contain nitrates, which act as a preservative. The nitrates turn the meat red, which is why every shrink-wrapped link you've ever bought has a red tint to it. Nick's sausages were all-natural and nitrate-free, not to mention fantastically flavorful and smoky. Nick needed no outside help with the ribs. A thick, sweet glaze, heavy with cumin and herbs, finished off his baby backs. Don't smirk at this innovation until you try them. He has convinced this barbecue purist.

The purist in me was about to be tested again. I pride myself in striving to appreciate most any type of meat the barbecue world throws at me. And few items are so distinctly a part of the East Texas barbecue tradition as the local hot links. These aren't just any hot links. First, they're tiny and rarely sold fewer than a dozen to an order. Second, they typically gush with grease, their unctuousness matched only by their gamey aroma. Third, though filled with beef, you probably wouldn't recognize any of the cuts unless you were a butcher—they're ground from offal and scraps. When folks say you don't want to see how sausage is made, they mean these sausages—East Texas links, or ETL in menu shorthand. East Texas links are always paired with salty soda crackers and hot sauce, similar to how cheap tequila can be stomached only with a preparatory lick of salt and a tart lime finish. I'd only had East Texas links in Dallas, so it was with an open mind that I approached them in their native environment.

We weren't going to stop for any East Texas links until later in the afternoon, but Nick Pencis pointed us to an authentic joint in Tyler that made their own. Following his directions, we parked beneath a yellowing acrylic sign bolted to a rusty steel pole. It read simply **RHEA'S HOT LINKS**.

The interior was about as fancy as the sign. An order of four links was the smallest you could get, and we only wanted a sample. These links weren't smoked; they were quickly roasted in a small oven. The all-beef links had pork casings, and when I cut into one with the plastic knife provided, the chewy casing couldn't contain the loose filling. *Strong* is not a descriptor that does the flavor of these links justice. The iron-rich offal flavors coated my mouth while the visceral aroma of cow guts clogged my nostrils. More hot sauce, please. A Coke, too. Not to be dissuaded, we kept the other hot link joints on the day's itinerary hoping for a better payoff.

Driving east out of Tyler, the flora began to thicken. The piney woods of East Texas seemed practically claustrophobic when I compared them to the openness of the Panhandle. It was hard to spot a random barbecue sign among the growth, but we happened upon **SMOKEY'S BBQ** just outside of Tyler. The stop was unplanned, but we pulled off the road and down a curving driveway that led back to a small single-story house. What looked like a small guesthouse sat to the side and we walked through its side door. A low counter separated the small dining area from a kitchen that contained just a stove and a refrigerator. Oh yeah, and a microwave. An older lady named Leesie, who had an attitude that wouldn't quit, gave us what she called a sample of barbecue. Since it was a sample, she wouldn't charge us, so we bought a few personal-sized pies that she baked herself. They were the only good thing that came out of the kitchen. Pictures were not permitted. Not to be taken and not to be hung. "This isn't a place for lookin' at pictures, it's a place for eatin' food," she instructed. To further underscore her point, she told us she had even recently removed the photos of her grandchildren. All of the meats came straight from the fridge. She stood a cold rib on end so she could shave the meat off. She chopped the brisket and sliced a cheap commercial sausage. Finally, she dumped it all into a Styrofoam container, bathed it in a sweet sauce, then heated it all in the microwave. Man, that pie was good.

Not far down the highway, but still on the near side of Kilgore, is the famous **COUNTRY TAVERN**, something of a Texas legend. The shell of an old liquor store sits next to it, marking the edge of the county line, making Country Tavern the perfect destination for folks from dry Tyler to come over to wet Kilgore for a drink and a rack of ribs. Inside the tavern, a pool table took center stage and a long bar flanked one entire side of the room. The whole dimly lit place was bathed in neon beer signs and country music played over the stereo system. There was a cowboy at the end of the bar smoking a cigarette. Country Tavern was feeling more and more like a beer joint that happened to serve barbecue rather than a barbecue joint that served beer. When our food arrived, a few bites of the mediocre brisket and jalapeño sausage made it clear we should save ourselves for their heralded baby back ribs. The ribs were coated in a glaze that was grainy with brown sugar, which almost entirely overpowered the hickory smoke. The glaze was studded with cracked black pepper that helped temper a strong cumin flavor. There was some smoke there, but it was mostly an afterthought. The meat came cleanly from the bone with little effort— these ribs exhibited exemplary texture. From the photos on the wall, Larry Hagman and Robert Duvall clearly agreed that the Country Tavern has been a noted destination for ribs for good reason. It was

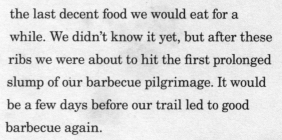

the last decent food we would eat for a while. We didn't know it yet, but after these ribs we were about to hit the first prolonged slump of our barbecue pilgrimage. It would be a few days before our trail led to good barbecue again.

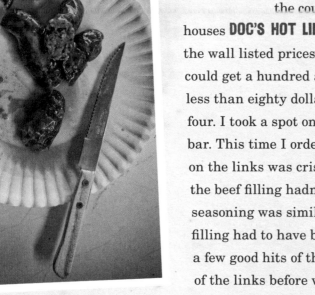

Turning toward points north along US Highway 271, we drove a half hour or so to Gilmer. The oldest building in Gilmer is the courthouse; the second-oldest building houses **DOC'S HOT LINKS**. A handwritten menu posted on the wall listed prices for up to twelve dozen links. You could get a hundred and forty-four of the tiny links for less than eighty dollars, but I was only going to order four. I took a spot on the long, U-shaped, Formica-topped bar. This time I ordered a Coke straightaway. The skin on the links was crispier at Doc's than at Rhea's, but the beef filling hadn't improved in quality. The links' seasoning was similar to a breakfast sausage, but the filling had to have been made of about half fat. I needed a few good hits of the hot sauce to eat a polite amount of the links before we could push off to Pittsburg—Pittsburg, Texas, that is. No *h*.

Pittsburg hot links are the original ETL. Pittsburg butcher Charlie Hasselback first brought the hot link recipe to Camp County, Texas, in 1897. More than one hundred years later they're still the standard-bearer for all East Texas links and hugely popular with the locals. While waiting in line to order at the **PITTSBURG HOT LINK RESTAURANT**, we noticed a few families, their tables full of plates piled high with these links. Even the toddlers were wolfing down these suckers. Once again, I ordered four. This was the mecca of the East Texas link—the originator. If they weren't

any good here, then I was going to give up. Cutting through just one link brought out enough grease to turn clear the solid square foot of butcher paper in front of me. The snap to the casing was similar to Doc's, but it retained a solid chewiness. They were the same pork casings with beef filling, and the flavor wasn't any more pleasing. When I had been placing my order, I'd mentioned that we were on a barbecue tour. The woman at the register had quipped back that this wasn't barbecue. Thank God.

Nick and I had some time on our hands and were now searching for anything worth eating. A few days earlier I had announced our upcoming East Texas barbecue trip on Twitter. @RearoftheSteer tweeted back "We serve Hot Links on Fri & Award Winning BBQ daily! Must try the Brisket if in the area. See http://rearofthesteer.net. Safe travels!" Since they were polite and ambiguously "award-winning," we drove to Omaha, which isn't on the way to anywhere, to check them out. **REAR OF THE STEER** is a curious name for a barbecue joint considering I've never had smoked rear, but it became even more confusing once we were staring at the enormous menu that read more like it belonged to a Dairy Queen. Burgers, chicken sandwiches, salads . . . I couldn't find the barbecue until I turned my head to a marker board that listed a few smoked meats. We took a seat and a plate of meat came out soon after. It was hard to see anything we'd ordered beneath the lake of dark, sweet sauce that tasted like a KC Masterpiece rip-off. I tried to salvage an untainted slice of beef from the bottom of the pile. It actually had a good crust and well-rendered fat but was so overcooked that I couldn't grip even a fingerful of meat. A cheap commercial sausage tasted like little more than fat and salt; the pulled pork was sawdust-dry. Nick was more offended by the burned onion rings. The search for a good dinner was still on.

Our hotel for the evening was in Jefferson, so we drove south. The light was still on at **OUTLAW'S BBQ** in Daingerfield. The optimistic masochist in me pulled over, knowing we'd get the end-of-the-day scraps, but hoping for good meat nonetheless. Even with an empty dining room and the chairs already stacked on the tables, they were happy to have us. We soon learned that Outlaw's was part of the Bodacious Bar-B-Q family, but in a roundabout way. Bodacious is a chain of barbecue joints located mostly in East Texas, but outposts can be found as far west as San Angelo. Almost every location is individually owned and operated. At Outlaw's they buck Bodacious's trend of using gas-fired smokers and instead use a hickory-fired Bewley pit from Dallas. A thick and meaty St. Louis rib was well smoked with a good bark and a thin, sweet glaze. The meat came away nicely from the bone. The hickory smoking had done wonders for the ribs, but the brisket still needed some work. I cut them some slack given the late hour, but the soggy brisket really showed its age. The crusty end bits held plenty of concentrated flavor and smoke, but the overdone texture was hard to savor. One of the employees brought over a plate of turkey saying it was by far his favorite. I was thankful for the gift, but found it hard to fathom that someone working at a barbecue joint could gush about processed, precooked deli turkey warmed by a smoker. At least we were able to cap off the day with a couple of great ribs. Beers were in order, but a long and curving road—not to mention the pitch-black country night—required the utmost attention from this weary driver. The Jefferson city limits sign was a welcome sight.

The next morning we walked up Polk Street to get some breakfast. As we passed the burned-out shell of a building that had been Riverport Bar-B-Cue, I felt a sting of disappointment. This joint had been on my to-do list for a couple of years, but less than a month before we'd set out for East Texas it had suffered a devastating fire. I'd been getting some very promising feedback about the work of owner and pitmaster Stephen Joseph, and he agreed to meet with us and discuss the restaurant's future. We found him and his father, Ed, seated inside Beje's Diner. Making Stephen relive the fire sounded cruel, but he took the lead and dove right in. A bad electrical connection had caused the catastrophe, not a pit fire. But by the day we were in town, Stephen had already had a new concrete slab poured and a steel delivery sitting on it. He's a forward-looking guy.

Stephen started his barbecue education working the pits at a Bodacious Bar-B-Q in Jefferson, which became the old Riverport Bar-B-Cue. He bought the place and moved it down the street to its current location. His first order of business as the man in charge was to change up some of those tired Bodacious recipes. He wanted the smoke from his wood-fired Bewley pit to be the star, not overpowering rubs or sweet sauces. As we stood on the empty slab surveying what would become the new building, more than a few cars stopped, including the sheriff, to remind Stephen that they missed his barbecue, but I don't think anyone in town was as anxious to see the place open again as Stephen was. We chatted for a while longer and he shared with us a few of his cooking tips, like his tried-and-true test for doneness. Wearing insulated gloves, he shoves his thumb into the fat cap of a brisket. If his thumb sinks in up to the knuckle, then he knows it's ready. He considers it worthless to keep track of a brisket's cooking time, which he compared to a gestation period. "Just because two women get pregnant on the same day doesn't mean they'll deliver on the same day" were the simple and memorable words of wisdom he left us with.

Sad about Riverport and ready for some good barbecue, we lit out for Caddo Lake. The highway out of Jefferson loosely follows Big Cypress Creek as it runs into the heart of Caddo Lake, the only natural lake in the State of Texas. All other Texas lakes are actually reservoirs created by man-made dams. On the edge of Caddo Lake, in the midst of a moss-draped cypress forest, sits the town of Uncertain, Texas. Many legends abound as to the origin of its name, but I can tell you from personal experience that if you spend any time there you'll mostly feel uncertain that you're still in Texas. The moss, the trees, the fan boats, and the pelicans feel a lot more like an episode of *Swamp People* than of *Dallas*. Most of the cottages in town are owned by weekenders, so it was particularly sleepy when we got there. A few of the full-time locals were hanging out on the deck of the **CADDO GROCERY**, which was partially obscured by a banner reading Bar-B-Q in bold red letters. Say no more. The "vittle menu," written on the marker board leaning against the wall, included pork ribs, sausage, pulled pork, and a two-dollar bottomless bowl of beans. Out of respect for my captive passenger, Nick, I opted to skip the beans. The sausage was a commercial variety, so I skipped that, too, and ordered a pulled-pork sandwich and three heavily rubbed St. Louis ribs. The sandwich came with home-made barbecue sauce that was just fine, but the spicy mustard sauce had much more character and made for a perfect complement to the smoky pork. The addition of some celery seed–flecked slaw to the sandwich made it a real winner, though hardly recognizable

as traditional Texas barbecue. The ribs had a rub that was too heavy with powdery spices to allow for good crust formation, but the pecan smoke was good and heavy.

The workhorse at Caddo Grocery was an unlikely and diminutive electric Smokin' Tex cabinet smoker in the back room. All in all, Caddo Grocery was better than I expected, and I couldn't blame these folks for

·· **RUB** ···

Television shows and food magazines have erroneously granted barbecue rubs a cultlike status, behaving as if some secret rub recipe will catapult merely good barbecue into the realm of great barbecue. The truth is, the best briskets I've eaten have a rub that consists of only two ingredients—salt and pepper. The coarseness and proportion of these two stalwarts may vary, but simplicity usually pays off. If you plan to use a commercial rub, look at the nutrition label before you buy it. If the first ingredient is a powder (most often paprika) put it back on the shelf. If the first ingredient is salt, then it's a keeper. Take it home and never open it. Use it as a reminder that there is no need to pay eight bucks for someone else's container of mixed spices that is mostly salt.

Salt draws the moisture out of meat and that moisture in turn dissolves the salt. As the meat cooks, the dissolving salt penetrates the meat, adding flavor. Furthermore, the moisture the salt drew to the meat's surface provides "grab" for all the smoke particles. Without salt, the surface of the meat would dry out, leaving nothing for the smoke to cling to. A rub that consists of mostly fine powder (think paprika, garlic powder, onion powder) not only dries out the surface of the meat from the beginning, but it keeps it dry throughout the cooking process by soaking up any potential surface moisture. These powders, being fat-, not water-, soluble, will also never dissolve. Think of adding cinnamon to a French toast batter. Try as you may it will never get incorporated fully. A dry layer of rub spices on a brisket will provide some flavor for sure, but it will also create an unappealing gummy texture in the meat. Worse yet, it will keep a good layer of tasty bark from forming on the meat's surface.

···

taking the easy route with an electric smoker, given the small demand for barbecue in this town of roughly one hundred permanent residents. The hospitable nature of the owner and the regulars, who were happy to help offer smoked-meat leads in the nearby towns of Marshall and Longview, was even more enjoyable. In gratitude, I grabbed a bottle of the spicy mustard sauce and a jar of Caddo's home-made mayhaw jelly (the mayhaw is a small fruit that resembles an apple and grows in the wet soils around Caddo Lake) on our way out.

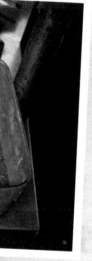

The boys back at Caddo Grocery hadn't sounded too taken with any of the barbecue options in Marshall, and Nick and I soon found out why. Our first stop, Ezell's, was closed when we arrived. Thick moss grew over the building's swayed-back roof and the entire structure looked in need of some major repairs. We wondered if it was closed for good. We left the car in the Ezell's parking lot, and walked up to the abutting property: **PIC-N-PAY DELI**, which advertised hickory-smoked barbecue on a sign out front. The folks at the counter acted as if they'd never heard of Ezell's though it was literally only a few yards from their parking lot. Back at the car trunk, the to-go container's contents didn't look promising. The fatty ribs were coated in a supersweet rub reminiscent of Asian flavors. They hadn't taken on much smoke and tasted more like candy than barbecue. The brisket had a hint of smoke in the crust, but the meat was chewy and underdone.

A few blocks away on a residential street we found **BBQ EXPRESS**. Their wide menu included smoked Pittsburg hot links—maybe it was the smoke all the hot links I'd had so far were missing? Nope. Still awful. A Hot-Hot Link was nothing more than a spiced-up hot dog. The crusty and saucy ribs were much better, though. The meat was tender and the relatively mild sauce, though generously applied, didn't obscure the smoke. The chopped-beef sandwich wasn't scooped out of a prechopped steam table vat. I watched as the knife man took a fresh brisket, sliced it thick, then chopped the slices on a wood block. The knife man told me it was a lean sandwich, but I had just watched him chop some fatty slices from the point end of the brisket. The meat was well smoked and the fat well rendered. The texture of the sandwich was silky, and the hickory smoke was prominent even with the heavy amount of spicy sauce.

At BBQ Express we were told to go try **PORKY'S SMOKEHOUSE AND GRILL** down near the Interstate. Just barely beating the rain there, we grabbed a table and ordered up a simple plate of brisket, ribs, and onion rings. Unfortunately what we got was the aforementioned and dreaded accordion brisket. The lean slice of brisket was so underdone that the collagen, which should have broken down, was still clinging to the meat fibers. When I pulled the slice apart, it remained intact but stretched out like an accordion. This was not a

good sign, and this wasn't good brisket. Not a hint of the hickory smoke could be detected. The light smoke, the heavy black pepper, and the dry texture of the thin St. Louis ribs were oh-so-familiar—they had Bodacious Bar-B-Q written all over them. At least the onion rings were good.

I wasn't sure if this joint had ever actually been in the hands of the Bodacious chain or if the owners once worked there, but the parallels between the two were unmistakable. I was beginning to wonder if every white-owned barbecue joint north of Interstate 30 in Texas either came out of the Bodacious bloodline or tried to emulate its product. It seemed to be the local gold standard—one I didn't find so golden. On the other hand, our previous stop at BBQ Express, which was black-owned, served—more than any other joint we'd found up to that point—barbecue that matched my admittedly preconceived notions about East Texas–style barbecue: hot links, supertender and saucy ribs, and a chopped-beef sandwich. In the early 1800s, before Texas became a republic and later a state, it was a favorable place to migrate for freed blacks and slaves seeking freedom. The laws created after Mexican independence in 1821 were even more favorable to black citizens who were either free or had escaped from southern plantations. By 1830 Mexico had abolished slavery in the territory that would become Texas and blacks were treated (in a legal sense anyway) as equals to all other citizens. Blacks didn't exactly flood into the territory, but those who did came mainly from southern states, so it made sense that they settled in eastern Texas. But the vast majority of black people in Texas were brought there as slaves, and this population increased after 1836, when Texas gained independence and reinstated the institution of slavery. Many enslaved people brought with them barbecue traditions that favored the use of sauces. The meat that a slave might get, if he or she received any, was certain to be a poor cut of meat and quite likely spoiled. The tough meats and their off-flavors required slow cooking and more heavy sauce to cover the taste of spoilage. While the barbecue that grew out of that history has come to incorporate beef, pork is the meat of choice in this tradition, which black-owned joints throughout East Texas and the Gulf Coast (and most of the black-owned joints in Dallas and Houston) keep alive today.

After three stops in Marshall, we felt like we'd given it a good shot and were ready to move on, when, on our way over to Longview, we passed a wooden sign in the shape of a dancing pig. **NEELY'S SANDWICH SHOP** is a small and understated place along busy Grand Avenue. A simple brown awning crowns the

unassuming concrete building. No less than five Open signs were hung in the thirty or so feet of its glass frontage. Despite the heart-shaped wreath pinned to the door, Nick and I decided to order from the outside window. A hand-painted sign near the window demanded "Try our delicious Brown Pig sandwich." So I did. What came through the window was a package of history wrapped in pale yellow paper. Inside the paper, a soft grilled bun was piled with hickory-smoked pork butt, chopped fine and mixed with a thin red sauce, and topped with shredded lettuce and mayo. After just a few minutes the shredded lettuce had already wilted. The tender and finely chopped meat, lettuce, and sauces combined for a singular soft texture, and this odd (to modern-day Texans) combination of ingredients worked well together. There was little about the sandwich recognizable to me as traditional for Texas, but Neely's itself is definitely part of a Texas tradition, the pig stand—the precursor to fast-food restaurants. The first pig stand opened in Dallas in 1921, when an entrepreneur named Jesse Kirby noticed that with the rise of the automobile people were seeking increasing speed and convenience in all aspects of their life, including food. The pig sandwich first served there had a pickle relish and barbecue sauce. You can still find similar sandwiches at chains like Van's Pig Stand in Oklahoma and at local pig stands around Texas. Neely's itself has been open since 1926, and their Brown Pig sandwich is so popular that most folks just refer to the place as Neely's Brown Pig. On any other day I might have eaten a couple of them in one sitting, but we had a few more stops to get through.

An odd bunch of tiny holes perforated the large blue canopy that covered the entrance to **CARTER'S BAR-B-QUE** in Longview, leaking rainwater on Nick and me as we entered. When we inquired about it inside, the answer we received was very matter-of-fact: the owner had dropped his shotgun while getting out of his truck, and it had discharged into the canopy. A huge black smoker on display behind the counter belched out hickory smoke just like every other East Texas joint we'd been

to, but, unusually, they had "boudain" on the menu. Why *boudin* is spelled with an *a* by many of the joints in Texas, I'm not sure, but I use whatever the joint I'm visiting uses. Boudin is a traditional Louisiana sausage. Robert Carriker is an expert on the subject and in his book entitled *Boudin*, he provides this succinct description of how it's made: "The pork meat is braised along with a concoction of onions and bell peppers while the rice is cooked using liquid from the braising. After the meat is put through a meat grinder, it is mixed and re-ground with the cooked rice before being stuffed into natural casing." Boudin is usually steamed or boiled, even grilled sometimes, but many East Texas barbecue joints choose to smoke it for a truly unique Texas take on the Louisiana dish. At Carter's you can get it by the link, or as part of an unholy concoction called the Carter's Special—chopped brisket and chopped boudain topped with sauce, chopped onions, and beans. I gave the Carter's Special a test run and decided its components tasted better individually. While the chopped beef in the Carter's Special was moist and smoky, the sliced brisket was some of the driest I've eaten. I could just see the juices evaporating as the very skilled knifeman worked his way through our half-pound order. The ribs were a bit better than the beef, with a tender texture and smoky flavor—but their surface was gummy. Soggy deli turkey and a cheap, fatty commercial sausage had good smoke and no other positive attributes. The links of boudain had taken on the smoke well, and were the best option. Still, it was good to see someone not trying to be Bodacious.

I tried to act forlorn when we pulled into the parking lot of the original Bodacious Bar-B-Q in Longview and found it closed. No matter, we needed to get a move on if we were going to make Nacogdoches by evening. I pointed the Audi south, setting our sights on Henderson, Texas. Passing up another Bodacious location in the middle of Henderson that I'd visited previously, we hit up **BOB'S BAR-B-QUE** just down the street. This family affair is run by Bob Allen, his wife, and his son. A fence hid their steel wood-fired pit, and they weren't willing to give us a tour. Bob assured us that "there's no gas up on this hill" and that "it's all hickory that runs these pits." I took my order to the far end of the dining room. The ribs were thin and on the dry side, but not too much so. The subtle seasoning didn't overpower the smoky flavor of the tender meat. Their hot boudain link lived up to its name, with plenty of spice and a good, snappy casing. The last cut I tried was the brisket. It was so sad-looking. All of the crust and fat had been chopped off. All that was left were uniform rectangles of gray beef. When I bit into it I was surprised by the moist meat and the hint of smoke that remained. Maybe there was more to this brisket than I suspected. I walked back to the counter and asked for some dark and crusty end cuts. They were happy to oblige and handed over some ridiculously good brisket. The fat had melted into the subtle salt rub like meat candy, and the deep, black crust crackled a bit in my teeth, releasing an all-consuming smokiness. "Why were you holding out on me?" I asked Bob. He told me that his customers don't like crust and fat. According to him, 99 percent of the customers want lean slices, which leaves all the good stuff for the chopped beef and for the staff, who know better. The difference between the two briskets was incredible, and I was sad to know that folks who prefer the first version consider

themselves barbecue fans. Now that I knew how to order the brisket here, I grabbed a couple of pounds to go. Some friends in Nacogdoches were going to be very happy.

Nacogdoches is the oldest town in Texas. It was the first city in Texas with its own newspaper and was also the site of Texas's first oil well, which went up forty-odd years before Spindletop and the Texas Oil Boom. A town of this importance in Texas's history should be well known to any Texan, but many folks in Dallas have a hard time distinguishing between Nacogdoches and Nachitoches, its sister city in Louisiana. The El Camino Real, also known as the Old San Antonio Road, connected the two cities—it was the road on which Stephen F. Austin first crossed into Texas. On this day, we were just hoping the road could lead to some good barbecue.

My friends James and Josephine Wise, who were hosting us, are natives of East Texas. As the local, James led the way out of Nacogdoches in the morning. A slight detour off of State Highway 21, which pretty closely follows El Camino Real, brought us into the parking lot of **MR. WILL'S RESTAURANT**. The characterless metal building had gas pumps out front, and inside it felt like a sterile sports bar. There was absolutely no one around. We didn't see a single customer or a waiter. Sure, it was early for lunch, but where was the staff? I paced around the register, my idle whistling growing louder. A full ten minutes later, someone came out from the kitchen. She informed us that they were out of sausage, which seemed odd given that it was 10:00 on a Thursday morning. I settled for brisket, ribs, onion rings, and a biscuit—to go. It was all prepared out of sight in the kitchen, so I steeled myself for a surprise when I opened the container.

The surprise was that they weren't out of sausage after all. Too bad it had just been sliced lengthwise and microwaved to its current tepid state. The brisket was sliced with the grain. Anyone who has sliced more than a couple knows to slice against the grain, but an amateur might not. There was definitely an amateur in Mr. Will's kitchen that morning, and the brisket slices were tough because of it. The brisket turned out to be better than I expected, though; the meat was well smoked and plenty moist. A salt-heavy rub was pleasing and the fat was tender and well rendered throughout. It was even better between two halves of a hot, greasy biscuit at this early hour. Yesterday's ribs were large and meaty but dry and still a bit chewy. They hadn't warmed up well. The hot and crispy onion rings were fresh, though, and a guilty pleasure for breakfast.

Continuing down the historic road, we followed State Highway 21 into San Augustine, which is almost as old as Nacogdoches. San Augustine's town center boasts an impressive collection of historic buildings, but we headed for the edge of town. There, at the bustling intersection of SH 21 and US Highway 96, sat a food trailer named **COWBOY CHUCKWAGON BBQ**. Since food trailers—which are essentially mobile—don't mess with big commercial gas ovens to cook their barbecue, I usually approach them with a hopeful attitude. This small trailer advertised bar-b-que, hamburgers, and boudin (they spelled it right). We placed our order, grabbed our food, and headed back across the soggy gravel parking lot. We took our normal position at the trunk of my car, despite the drizzle, and ate under the watchful eye of the food truck's aged proprietress. The brisket was nothing more than poorly seasoned roast beef. Ribs weren't even on the menu. The unnaturally red hot links tasted like liver and were absent even a hint of smoke. The boudin also seemed to have missed its appointment with the smoker, but the casing was taut and the pork and rice were well seasoned. It and the creamy mashed potato salad would make a fine meal, but it was barely barbecue.

From the soggy parking lot we could see smoke pouring out of the chimney of a small metal building up the road. We soon learned it was hickory smoke, coming out of a big steel barrel smoker in the front room of **WATTS & WATTS BAR-B-QUE**. The interior of the joint was Spartan to say the least—metal folding chairs and tables on a bare, poured-concrete floor. More boudin was on the menu, and again I had to wonder if maybe they were just putting the tip into the smoker. It was well cooked, but the smoke roaring out of that smoker should have provided it with a more distinct flavor. Thick ribs with visible fat and meat striations had good smoke, but little bark, and their poorly rendered fat made them hard to finish. A thick slice of black-crusted brisket was far superior. The tenderness of the meat made up for the slices' being carved with the grain yet again. The deep smokiness and the perfectly rendered fat more than made up for it here. Too bad we had only one slice to share.

Smoke seemed to be an afterthought at **BO-BO'S B-B-Q**, on the opposite side of town, where a sweet rub dominated the flavor of the ribs and the outline of the brisket slices could hardly be discerned under a pool of cloying sauce. It shouldn't be surprising that Bo-Bo's cowboy chuckwagon BBQ didn't survive. East Texans now have two fewer options for bad barbecue.

My first step after a barbecue meal out on the road is to pull out my iPhone and record my tasting notes. As I listened to my notes on the four joints so far on this day, I found myself reaching for positive things to say. It had been a while since we'd had a plate of really good smoked meat, and some of the mediocre barbecue we'd been having was starting to stand out just because it wasn't awful. East Texas was starting to wear on my palate.

After a long morning filled with plenty of meat, James called it a day and headed back home. Nick and I needed to be in Beaumont by nightfall,

but we had plenty of time for the drive and a few hours to kill before we'd get hungry again. We decided to take a scenic route and play tourists among the pines. Defunct gas pumps complete with abandoned, decades-old cars, Tyson chicken farms with ominous Keep Out signs on their gates, and picturesque churches dotted State Highway 21. We were nearing the Louisiana border when I saw a sign that looked more like a prop than an actual road marker. It read: Farm Road 1.

More than a decade ago when I moved to Texas I was confused about the FM and RM roads. I saw the signs everywhere once I left the big cities, but had no idea what they meant. I soon came to learn that an FM road is a "farm-to-market" road and that an RM road is a "ranch-to-market" road. Designating roads as farm-to-market or ranch-to-market is unique to Texas. These roads were built to quite literally connect rural farms and ranches to markets in the cities. The rule isn't strict, but US Highway 281 serves as the general dividing line between RM roads to the west and FM roads to the east.

The journalist Paul Burka wrote, "The farm-to-market road couldn't keep Texas a rural state, but it could keep alive the notion that the soul of Texas still lies Out There, waiting to be discovered." Nick and I both gained a new respect for the FM and RM roads on our trips. Because of the FM/RM system, one can literally cross the state on paved roads without needing to drive on a single interstate. This intricate system of roads allowed us to create more direct and more interesting routes that had far less traffic than the traditional arterial routes—and to discover the soul of Texas.

After World War II, the building of FM roads began in earnest, but it was a few years earlier, in 1941, that the first numbered FM road was built, starting at Ford's Corner along SH 21. It received the rather logical name of Farm-to-Market Road 1. After seeing countless FM signs and driving along so many miles of these narrow, two-lane roads, I was giddy to have happened upon the first one.

We were so close to the Texas-Louisiana border that we decided to cross into our neighboring state just for the hell of it—and to get a few snaps of the Welcome to Texas sign on the way back. Only a quick stop at **HEMPHILL BAR-B-Q** was needed to deem the spicy boudain the only menu item worth stopping for. Heading south, trees lined the highway all the way through the Sabine National Forest. Somewhere in the trees we passed the marker for the Old Beef Trail, the road ranchers used to use to transport cattle from Texas to eastern markets in the years before the northbound cattle trails like the Shawnee and Chisholm were established. Not even a slight clearing in the thick trees marked the former trail these days.

Though my research hadn't turned up anything notable about the barbecue served in Jasper, I had still jotted down a stop there in our itinerary: **LARKIN'S BAR-B-QUE & CATERING**. The barbecue trailer sat on a

concrete pad. Smoke streamed out from under its metal canopy. We waited for our order at one of two picnic tables sitting in the grass. Owner Michael Larkin came around from the smoker to have a seat and chat with us while we waited. He uses red oak, which is an oddity in the region and the state. A pile of the red oak looked damp and had clumps of dirt stuck in the thick bark. It would have made a wood connoisseur cringe a bit, but it didn't seem to faze Michael, who had likely just split it from one of the logs resting nearby.

I do not have a poker face when it comes to tasting barbecue, so it was unnerving to have the owner sit down to watch me eat. I went from one meat to the next looking for something positive to say. The brisket was overcooked. It had the texture of a roast

beef, a result of being wrapped during the cooking process. Wrapping the meat had also caused it to retain a great deal of moisture, making it spongy. The flavor was fine, with a decent level of smoke, but the texture was so unpleasant—like the bottom bun beneath a juicy burger—that it was hard to enjoy. The ribs, which were the owner's favorite, were my least favorite. Their surface was gummy from a powdery rub that didn't have enough salt. The ribs hadn't soaked up much smoke, and the chewy layers of unrendered fat didn't help any. Zummo's, out of Beaumont, made the hot links, which had good seasoning and great smoke. They paired well with the beans, which were mixed with chunks of onions and sweet sauce before being generously smoked. The stunningly good beans were what I would have remembered most about this joint, until Michael brought out his most prized menu item—a home-made link unlike any I'd ever seen. The casing was inflated from a shot in the microwave, but they were never packed too tightly to begin with. The casing was to be cut open and disposed of to enjoy the loose chorizo-like filling. A thin sauce of Italian dressing and a few other mystery ingredients verged on creamy and was poured over the meat. It didn't need the extra fat. The smooth texture of the finely ground meat created an odd mouthfeel, but the nuttiness of the heavy seasoning made these links both memorable and enjoyable, however odd the disparate components might sound on their own. Michael said they were his own creation, and they were truly unique.

From Michael's we headed south to the Lazy H Smokehouse. The beef jerky at Lazy H is legendary, and we needed legendary. Alas, we couldn't find it (we later learned it had been closed permanently). Our spirits flagging, we were about to lose hope when, on the south side of Kirbyville, we passed a sign that said BBQ. We pulled into the gravel driveway of **BELLI DELI BBQ** hoping to cap the night off right with some impromptu roadside smoked meat. We got some smoke, all right. I caught the first whiff on the small porch before I opened the door—it definitely wasn't woodsmoke. Inside we encountered an unmanned ordering window on one side of a small vestibule and a closed door on the other side. I heard some stirring and then the door opened. Nick and I both experienced a contact high.

An older man named John talked up the brisket in a gravelly voice as he sawed a few slices from the cold slab of meat. He urged me not to worry because he was only going to just *slightly* warm it in the microwave. Very reassuring. He put a couple of ribs on the plate and, with his back turned, sneaked on a ladle of sauce before serving. The meat had been smoked with oak, pecan, and some fruitwood. The brisket had a solid smokiness, but had been overcooked to the point of crumbling. It might have been pretty good about ten hours earlier. The huge spareribs probably hadn't been good at any point on that day. Way oversmoked and soaked with the flavor of creosote, they were also dried-out and chewy with lots of unrendered fat. There just wasn't much to like there, and the ding of the microwave only added insult to injury.

Still looking for some decent barbecue, we drove to **WEST TEXAS STYLE BAR-B-QUE** in Silsbee, which we knew had late hours. We pulled up just an hour before closing, but after the meal we had, I wished they had closed early. In short, it was awful. I've had pork cracklins that were less crunchy than the edges of the ribs they served us, which looked like they'd been sliced hours earlier. The banana pudding was a gritty mess of sickening sweetness. The chunks from a cold brisket were nuked to lip-singeing levels. Before this trip, I had encountered microwaved barbecue only three or four times *ever*. In our last three days in East Texas, I'd run into it five times.

I was beginning to take the shabby treatment of smoked meat in these parts personally. It was late, we'd enjoyed very little passable barbecue in the last few days, and I was hungry. Poor Nick was my only company, and he received the brunt of my rant. How could people spend so much time smoking a brisket only to microwave it to order? Why did everyone slice the brisket with the grain? Why was there such an overabundance of bad ribs? Then it hit me. Good barbecue begets good barbecue. When a community is exposed to good barbecue they begin to expect it. If another joint opens, then it better be as good as the last one. If the places with shitty smoked meats don't improve their game, they'll lose their business to the folks who barbecue with care and skill. But if everyone's barbecue is average or just plain bad, then the stakes are low. Mediocrity becomes the target. And when mediocrity is the benchmark, the low end can be as low as it was at West Texas Style Bar-B-Que and so many of the other joints we'd suffered through.

Finally in Beaumont, I was able to cool down at the hotel. Just down the street was a historic but defunct pig stand. Nick wanted to put his camera to the test at night, and the blinding spotlights of the Family Dollar across the street from the pig stand provided more than enough light to capture the wide cantilevers of its curved roof and the undulations of its crinkled canopy. Called Pig Stand No. 41, the flying saucer–shaped takeout joint had opened in 1943, but had been closed since 2006, awaiting a date with the wrecking ball. A group of preservationists had succeeded in staving off demolition of the city landmark thus far. Standing there surveying the still life that was the restaurant, I had an odd feeling of tranquillity. I was able to savor the feel of the place and its history without having to worry about another plate of bad barbecue. A handwritten note in the dusty window read "In pig we trust."

Three years earlier, I had downed forty-three shots of barbecue sauce at the Austin event Getting Sauced, a—you guessed it—barbecue sauce competition dreamed up by the guys behind the fantastic blog *Man*

Up Texas BBQ. Across the table matching me shot for shot was Chris Reid, a food writer from Houston who seemed to know his way around a smoked brisket. Chris and I became friends and he quickly earned my respect for his knowledge of smoked meat, his love of his city, and his unquestioning willingness to eat at eight barbecue joints in a single day. Later that year I took him up on an offer of a guided tour through the best barbecue that Houston had to offer. His buddy Michael Fulmer, a veteran of the Houston service industry who ate like it was his job, came along for the ride. (Midway through our crosstown barbecue adventure Fulmer had to scoot, but I forgave him since he was going to join a full-city wing crawl. Bowels of steel, I tell you.) A year or so after that, over an epic dinner in a tiny Dallas dining room, I learned that Chris originally hailed from Beaumont. I barely got the request out of my mouth before he agreed to guide me through yet another city's worth of barbecue. Now Nick and I were in Beaumont, and Chris and Fulmer, who wasn't about to miss out, were meeting us there to make good on Chris's possibly drunken promise.

We started the next morning at the site of many grade school field trips for Chris, the old Spindletop oil field. We crossed some train tracks and parked by a wooden platform that overlooked the site where the Texas Oil Boom began. On the morning of January 10, 1901, a Lucas oil derrick hit a gusher here so ferocious it took nine full days to cap the well. Spindletop became the world's most productive oil field, and within a year there were five hundred oil companies in Beaumont. The boom would end with the onset of the Great Depression, but the world's energy economy would be forever changed.

A train now sat on the tracks we'd just crossed. It was moving, but *very* slowly. We were trapped, but we still arrived at **BROUSSARD'S LINKS + RIBS** just early enough to beat the Friday lunch rush. Nearly everyone takes their order to go, but our group, which now included Chris's sister Ann, took up residence at a picnic table on the side deck. A long, slow-moving line had formed as I waited to retrieve our order. I was shortly rewarded

with a thin plastic bag that barely contained a teetering tower of Styrofoam boxes. Our feast was soon laid out from one end of the picnic table to the other. A diner who shall remain nameless asked for plates and forks, but this request was rebuked with a collective dismissive stare. Who needs plasticware when you have the forks that you're born with at the ends of your arms?

A link of boudain had good seasoning and a pronounced smokiness, but wasn't exactly unique. I was getting tired of the lack of variation in the boudain across the state. What was unique here at Broussard's was their great ribs. Their use of red oak was also a regional outlier. Though they were doused in a thin, sweet-and-spicy sauce, the smokiness of the dark-hued ribs shined through. The meat was ultratender but still stayed on the bone. The fat throughout was well rendered, and every morsel from rib to tip was worth savoring. I can't say the brisket here was equally good. It was commendable for the region and a welcome change from the awful stuff we'd gotten used to. The crust provided a nice, smoky flavor, but the lean and somewhat chewy meat dried out quickly. Chris made us pay special attention as he introduced us to the beef links, which hold a special place in his heart—as evidenced by the article he'd written, which was taped to the pickup window. The meat, the fat, and the casing are all bovine at this joint. The links had a bit more girth than your normal pork-cased links, and the casing was noticeably tougher, but the links had been smoked to a point of crispness that made it easy enough to bite through and chew. The links dripped deep red paprika stains as we bit into them and were pungent with garlic. In one breath,

Chris praised the sausage for its flavor and its connection to the old beef link recipes of the region, but in the next he bemoaned their lack of fat. He said that the authentic, old-style links had been so bolstered with beef fat that they ran red when sliced and that streaks of fat would course so swiftly down your arms you'd be wiping your elbows before you had a chance to swallow. According to Chris, links like those were a thing of the past, lost on a fat-averse generation.

A few minutes earlier, a man I'd been chatting up in line directed me further east along Washington Boulevard toward a new place selling home-made links. I shared the lead with the group, and the search party mounted up. A few blocks away we saw a Grand Opening sign out in front of **PATILLO'S BAR-B-Q**. The building itself definitely wasn't brand-new, nor was its cratered parking lot, which the unceasing drizzle filled with

puddles. Inside, the place looked more like an old-time New Orleans bar than a Texas barbecue joint. Red-and-white-checkered cloths that stood out against the dark wood paneling covered the tables. A smattering of neon signs above the bar were probably the least aged relics in the place. Turns out they should have called it a grand reopening. Hurricane Ike had shut this joint down in 2008, so the Patillo family shifted their focus to their 11th Street location. They later sold the 11th Street location and moved the business back into this building, where Patillo's had originally opened in the fifties. This was just another chapter in the long history of Patillo's. Not one of us had even heard of the name until today, but Patillo's opened their first barbecue joint in Beaumont one hundred years prior to our visit. A flood in 1925 and the recent hurricane were the only events that had broken the string of continuous operation. This was astounding news to some of us there who fancied ourselves experts on Texas barbecue.

We ordered a plate of pork ribs, beef brisket, sliced pork, and a side of jambalaya. The menu also listed links, and when the waitress confirmed they were home-made, they became a mandatory addition. Each meat got its own plate. The thinly sliced brisket swimming in a rusty brown sauce looked more like beef and broccoli—sans the greenery—than it did smoked beef. The sauce was more like a chile powder–spiked gravy than it was traditional barbecue sauce, but as the family recipe hadn't changed in at least sixty years, it definitely belonged to a deeper tradition than almost any sweet bottled sauce out there today. I appreciated the adherence to the family recipes, but I didn't particularly care for the tough beef. The pork shoulder slices were tender and had some good, crusty edges peeking through the same sauce. The ribs had the best smoke of any of the options, but their bones held tightly to the tough meat. We saved the beef link for last. It sat alone on a white side plate. The browned casing had wrinkled and collapsed onto the loose filling inside. A puddle of glowing red liquid had already begun to pool around the edges of the U-shaped link. Strings as brown as the casing held the ends tight, a sure sign of hand-crafted sausage. I cut into the tough beef casing and held either half of the link aloft above the plate for effect. How long would it continue to drain? The juice threatened to crest the edges of the shallow plate. I squeezed the loose filling out onto a slice of cheap white bread. Instantly, the bread was saturated. I folded the slice over and took a bite.

The fat that coated the inside of my mouth was the perfect vehicle for the sausage's intense spices: I tasted the bite of garlic and the heat of chile powder and a slight nuttiness I guessed came from nutmeg. I soaked a new piece of bread in the liquid gold left on the plate. As I did I saw Chris's face break into a grin. "This is it!" he exclaimed: the elusive all-beef link still made with a healthy fat content. We sat there, pleased with the success of not only having found a new joint worthy of return visits, but also of having discovered an endangered species. The real old-time fatty beef link, the juicy link of East Texas, had escaped extinction and was alive and well in Beaumont.

We were just about to leave when Robert Patillo invited us to see the kitchen. His brother, Frank Patillo IV, was manning the steel-and-brick pit, which had been built at the same time as the building itself, back in 1950. A tall man of few words, Frank sported a worn fedora and a graying soul patch, neither of which was tainted with even a speck of hipsterism. His handshake was memorably firm. Robert then showed us the other side of the kitchen. As luck would have it, they were stuffing some of those home-made beef links. We stood in silence while the kitchen staff cranked out ring after ring. They would stuff a thousand or so pounds of links that week alone. By this point, Ann was also stuffed, and she bowed out as the men continued the quest.

Fresh off the high of discovery, we journeyed on along Washington Avenue to the newly opened **SONNY'S BBQ II**, where we found more lackluster brisket and ribs and another stellar version of those same spicy beef links.

After the embarrassment of fatty beef link riches, it was time to hit **WILLY RAY'S BAR-B-QUE CO.** on the north side of town. As recently as 2008, Willy Ray's has made it into *Texas Monthly*'s annual issue devoted to the fifty best barbecue joints in the state (their carrot soufflé received special mention). Our waitress appeared confused when four grown men ordered a single three-meat plate to share, but she brought it out without a question, along with some banana pudding. The excellent but supersweet carrot soufflé would have made a better finale than that awful bowl of fake banana-flavored pudding. Of the meats, the thin-sliced brisket was probably the best, but not an overwhelming smash. Little of the oak smoke clung to the overtrimmed slices. The chicken had so little smoke it barely tasted like barbecue, and the rubbery skin didn't make it any better. The ribs were overcooked and coated with a powdery rub. All in all, food not worth coming back for—but the

diorama was. Diorama? you ask. It surprised the hell out of us, too. Above a narrow door at the back of the dining area hung a small sign that read Museum. Inside the door an even narrower walkway ran the length of a deep glass case. Inside the case was a series of tiny hand-painted dioramas depicting the entire life of Jesus Christ. There must have been more than

.... BARBECUE DESSERTS ....

There is nothing better to counteract a protein overload than a bite of something sweet. A bit of sugar can ease a stomachache, so a joint with a solid dessert or two is a welcome sight when evening closes in on the barbecue trail. Cobblers with peaches, blackberries, and even pecans are common, and buttermilk pie is a slice of Texas on a paper plate. But my personal favorite is banana pudding. At its best, banana pudding is simplicity in a bowl. Sliced bananas, vanilla custard, and a topping of Nilla wafers are all that's required, but as with Texas brisket, this simple dish gets mangled in myriad ways. The most common problem I've encountered is the use of flavored instant pudding. I can almost forgive the use of instant vanilla pudding in cases where there are enough bananas to counterbalance it, but banana-flavor instant pudding is a soulless, noxious abomination. It is counterfeit banana pudding and should be outlawed.

a hundred little boxes in the thirty-foot-long case. Without a doubt, we had found the oddest sideshow in any of the barbecue joints we'd see on this series of road trips. You can still visit the diorama these days, but the ownership has changed the name of the restaurant to JACKK'S Diner and the concept from barbecue to an '80s themed diner. Seriously.

Sometimes taking the interstate is inevitable, and the drive from Beaumont to Orange, Texas, is one of those times. We headed due east for thirty miles on Interstate 10 until we found **JB'S BBQ** near the Louisiana border. Their stenciled sign had the curious tag line "It's better than you like it." A pile of smoked meats topped with a generous ladle of sauce came out on real china. A request for some sauceless burnt ends was fulfilled for free, which *is* better than I like it. The chunked and sauced brisket was fine, but the fatty ends, with their crispy edges and silky texture, were much more enjoyable. The ribs had a decent smokiness to them, but the fat spares were a bit tough. The sausage wasn't memorable. They had just cracked open a newly smoked ham as we were about to leave. As it was a specialty of the house, they insisted we try a few slices, then they handed us a bottle of soy sauce. The thin slices were about half fat. The saltiness of the soy sauce was more than the already salty meat needed, but the fat was so well smoked it melted before it reached the back of my throat.

If you want to stay in Texas, then there's nowhere to go but west from Orange. Chris had promised us an unusual barbecue feast in Nederland.

The highway rose like a roller coaster out of the swampland as we crossed over the Neches River on the Rainbow Bridge. Refinery smokestacks belched gray smoke against an equally gray sky. We were early for dinner, so the small parking lot at **SARTIN'S SEAFOOD** was empty. A crab on the Sartin's sign hinted at what we were in for. Barbecued crabs have little connection to actual barbecue. They aren't smoked or even grilled. Instead, the raw crabs receive a heavy spice rub all over their shells and in every available crevice and are then deep-fried. I was looking forward to a crab feast.

The Gulf had just been opened for oyster harvesting a few days earlier, so we started with a half dozen sweet bivalves. If it hadn't hit me that the piney woods were long gone, that first briny bite of oyster placed my senses firmly on the Texas coast. We let the hot crabs cool a bit as we downed a few perfectly golden and crispy onion rings, along with some deep-fried boudin balls, a coastal delicacy. When we were ready to dig into the crabs, our server warned us to be careful of the sharp shells. My fingers had mastered the art of peeling crawfish while living in Louisiana, so I wasn't worried. I took to the sport like an old pro. Despite the mounds of meat we had ingested previously in the day, we all found our zone as we devoured the seafood in front of us. It wasn't really barbecue, and I didn't have time to care. There was another crab to dismantle.

Nederland also had some Texas barbecue to offer. A stop at **BUTCHER'S KORNER** right at closing time didn't allow for their best effort, but I'll be back for some of their fresh-smoked sausage.

The sun was setting as we finished our meal and it had started to pour. Nick and I had planned this trip partly around the Mardi Gras festivities in Port Arthur. The big parade and live band were scheduled for that evening, rain or shine. Chris and Fulmer had hung longer than I ever expected, and though they had no desire to watch a family-friendly Mardi Gras parade in the rain, they were up for one last barbecue stop. The bare fluorescent lights illuminating the exterior of **COMEAUX'S BAR-B-QUE** were a stark contrast to the overcast sky and the block's burned-out streetlights. It had probably been some time since four white guys had walked into this joint with cameras blazing, but Mr. Comeaux took it all in stride. A plaid, plastic tablecloth covered the lone table, which was snug against the wall under a boarded-up window. Wood paneling covered the walls and decorative latticework framed the ordering window. Above a Coke machine from the Carter administration, the plaster peeled from the ceiling.

The ribs were gone, so we settled for links, brisket, and "bones." "Pig spine" would be a better name for bones. These nearly meatless nuggets offer plenty of heft but little substance. They are sometimes called regulars, which most likely started as a mispronunciation of *irregulars*. Bright-red slices of brisket were sliced with the grain. Not only were they beyond chewy, they tasted oddly of cured meat. It was as if the meat had been rubbed with curing salt before being smoked. But inside the container that held the beef link, we got what we were hoping for: an authentic fatty beef link. The beef casing here was too tough to eat, but the filling was excellent. The link was a bit less fatty than Patillo's, but nowhere near as firm as Broussard's. The spice mix was bold, but not as spicy Patillo's. We ate every bite, and ended the day on a high note of continued discovery.

Nick and I bid our friends good-bye and drove down to Procter Street to take in the rain-soaked parade. A palm tree provided some cover as adolescent revelers wrestled for beads in front of us. When the streets had cleared, we drove down the parade route, thousands of deserted Mardi Gras beads glistening in our headlights. Ahead of us, the glowing towers of an industrial facility lit the foggy night sky. Nick suggested we find a spot to park so he could get some proper photos . . . and that's how we ended up on the Port Arthur terrorist watch list.

I had been sitting in the driver's seat of the idling car for no longer than a few minutes when a truck pulled up behind me, its headlights flooding the car. I sat there, tweeting calmly, until a private security guard came to my window. I told him that we'd seen some pretty lights and wanted to photograph them. By this point Nick was walking back toward the car. Another rent-a-cop cornered him, demanding that he admit to a juicy terrorist plot against the city of Port Arthur. We both told identical stories of a barbecue road trip, confounding the security drones. The first guard countered that it wasn't a very good idea to photograph the largest refinery in the country under the cover of night. "Is that what that is?" I replied. We don't have that kind of stuff in

Dallas, but I was going to have to explain that to the Port Arthur PD. Shortly afterward, an actual police officer appeared at the driver's side. He had a good laugh at the situation and waved us on. Beers and dry clothes were in order back at the hotel.

Yet another gray morning greeted us. It was day five of our East Texas trip, and I hadn't seen the sun shine since I don't know when. It began pouring again as we left Port Arthur. I left the windows up as we snapped a few photos of the Valero refinery—just for spite—on our way out of town. Chris had given us a lead on a promising joint at an interstate gas station northeast of Winnie. There wasn't a dry spot to be found under the gas pump canopy and all my plotting about how to make it to the front door of the **BAR-H COUNTRY STORE** and remain somewhat dry was for nothing. I had to clean my glasses and wipe my generous forehead dry before I could even read the menu. The joint was a convenience store with half its space given over to tables and booths. Alternating beer signs and deer heads were mounted on the rustic wood paneling that lined the walls above the coolers and counter. The cashier yelled back to the kitchen to confirm that all the meats in our order were ready, and soon we had a plate of brisket, pork ribs, and sliced pork to share. I was pleased that they hadn't even offered barbecue sauce, until I lifted the slices covering the plate and found that the plate itself had been sauced and my meal was sitting in the pool. All the meats were lean and tasted like the heavy rub. The pork ribs were overtender but at least had a mild smokiness. The brisket slices were undercooked and lacked even a mild amount of smoke, while the thin-sliced pork was dry and flavorless. By adding the sauce they were telling me they knew better. The meat needed it.

A couple exits away in downtown Winnie we met Chris and his girlfriend, Tamara, at another gas station. This one served piping-hot boudin balls filled with processed cheese. Given our general poor luck with barbecue, I was looking forward to our destination. **STINGAREE RESTAURANT**, midway down the Bolivar Peninsula in Crystal Beach, which specializes in Gulf seafood. Some of the clouds had started to lift as we pulled into the Stingaree parking lot and though they continued to thin as we watched the barges pass from the upstairs dining room, we never did see the sun. The Stingaree menu was huge, but Chris was a pro. He took care of the seafood orders, while Tamara made sure to get us each a famously strong frozen Stingarita. Course after course of seafood filled the table. We sucked down more fresh oysters from the Gulf, some of which were so giant they required two bites. Crawfish season had just started up along the Gulf Coast. Nick had never had a mudbug, so we ordered plenty of those, too. And since this was a barbecue trip, after all, a stack of barbecued crabs made their way to our table. They lacked the addictive spiciness of the crabs at Sartin's, but they were still hard to put down. We consumed a raft of fabulous fried shrimp with admirable speed, but the coup de grâce were the pan-fried oysters. Lightly breaded and fried in a butter-filled shallow pan, the oysters were still tender, not cooked all the way through. Some butter vats remained on the table, which had been meant for dipping crab, but we had a

gluttonous idea. Butter-fried oysters dipped in butter were richer than any dessert we could think of.

Chris and Tamara headed back east and Nick, the Audi, and I loaded onto the ferry over to Galveston. Once on the island, we drove over to the corner of Broadway and 55th, the home of **LEON'S WORLD FINEST BAR-B-QUE**. Leon O'Neal himself was loading trays of meat onto a pickup truck as we walked up. He was clad in a red apron over a stark-white V-neck T-shirt—the low neckline showed off a gold lion's-head medallion on a gold chain. His gray hair showed in his thin mustache and short sideburns, which were just visible beneath his black felt cowboy hat. He wondered aloud why we were tooling around outside his restaurant when there was good food to eat inside.

Inside, a woman named Anita displayed both a stunningly bright smile and an in-depth knowledge of the menu. Although it was tough not to order the Link du Jour, she steered us to the Downtown Link. Ribs and brisket were required, of course, as well as a link of smoked boudin. Leon's charged more for lean beef than

it did for fatty brisket, a practice I, of course, found admirable. "Oh, you want the Mr. Leon cut!" was Anita's reply to my request for said fatty beef. As the food came out from the kitchen our table soon filled. The thin St. Louis ribs had a deep red crust; the smoky meat was pink throughout and a bit on the dry side, but in a good way. The meat came away from the bone cleanly, and boy those bones were *clean* after we'd polished off a few. They were the best ribs we'd had so far in East Texas. The quality of the fatty brisket varied between the slices. Some had luscious borders of fat, while others had intramuscular fat that could have used a bit more cooking time. All of the meat had great seasoning and a deep smokiness. The boudin was pretty much the same as most of the other links we'd had, but this one had a definite smokiness and a crisp quality to the casing.

We were almost done eating when Mr. Leon strolled over to check on us. I was diving into the home-made Downtown Link and grease had breached the corner of my mouth. Leon's round spectacles rode low on his nose as he explained the genesis of the link, while I munched away contentedly. He had started making it almost twenty years earlier, based on old-time recipes from the twenties and thirties. He was proud of the fatty links, as well he should have been. They had a texture somewhere between the firmness of Broussard's and the loose quality of Patillo's links and were straight-up spicy. The fat didn't run quite as freely from the Downtown Links, but they were decadent as they were. We'd yet again found another home-made all-beef link done in the old style. With all the bad barbecue, this trip had been a tough one to endure—but there we sat, fat and

happy. The world of barbecue taketh away, but mostly it giveth. This stop was going to be hard to surpass.

When you're near one of the greatest monuments in Texas history on a tour like this one, you need to stop. An impressive stone tower rises 570 feet in the air above the San Jacinto battleground, where Santa Anna was defeated and Texas won its independence. As our luck would have it, the view from the top was completely blocked by thick cloud cover, so our visit was short.

Much to the detriment of Nick, I was always looking for another barbecue stop along our route, and most of the time it ended with another mediocre meal. **KING'S BBQ** in Deer Park, just south of LaPorte, was one such stop, and my better judgment told me to drive on when I spotted the gas-fired smoker on the side of the building. My better judgment rarely wins out in situations like this, and therefore my taste buds rarely win as well. My taste buds didn't leave King's victorious.

The only task left on the itinerary was a stop at **GILHOOLEY'S**, in San Leon. They're as famous for their no-kids policy as they are for their wood-grilled oysters. Neither Nick nor I would normally be able to stop here, but on this childless night we could—and we were looking forward to it. It was dark as we searched the obstacle course that passed for a parking lot at Gilhooley's. The lot was only the first sign that Gilhooley's isn't a great place for folks who need to be accommodated. Three signs painted on the backs of used license plates were tacked to a tree by the entry. The first listed the hours, the second advised No Pets, and the third No Kids. (I think the reasoning for this exclusion has less to do with their hatred of children and more to do with the fact that it's a bar. The signage eliminates the gray area that all parents who enjoy having a drink with their meal have had to agonize over. Will people judge me if I take my kids in there? You don't need to question it here.) Furthermore, cash is the only acceptable currency at Gilhooley's; and a trip to the

bathroom convinced me I might as well have pissed on the floor, since it seemed everyone else had. Again, Gilhooley's: Not for those with delicate sensibilities.

The menu was huge, but it took little time to zone in on our order. Oysters Gilhooley were described as "roasted on our open-pit wood fire of pecan and oak." That was enough explanation for me. We had no appetite left, but anything less than a dozen seemed criminal. What arrived at the table was a tray of oysters still on the half shell, their flesh just slightly shriveled from the hot fire. Melted butter still bubbled around the buds of meat and Parmesan cheese sprinkled over the surface was burned and crisp in some spots and gooey in others. Nick was at his limit after two. I gulped the rest down like I hadn't eaten in a week. I then scraped the remaining butter and Parmesan onto a few saltines and ate those, too. Those oysters might not have been barbecue in the strictest sense, but they were simply seasoned meat transformed into something heavenly with just the aid of a wood fire. I'd gladly leave my kids in the car for another plate.

Our final stop was unplanned. Prompted by a call from Texas food historian and fellow barbecue fiend Robb Walsh, we stopped in Houston. Robb was holding court at the refurbished movie theater that now houses the **EL REAL TEX-MEX** restaurant, which he co-owns with his business partners, Bill Floyd and chef Bryan Caswell. In between glad-handing customers all over the dining room, Robb sat with us to direct our selections from the multipage menu. He said he had spent too much time developing the perfect enchilada to let us get by without trying one, but the truth is, I was more interested in the fajitas. I knew from reading

Robb's book *Tex-Mex Grill* that he takes his fajitas seriously. I had no idea how seriously addictive they'd be. El Real cooks the skirt steak for the fajitas over mesquite on grills manufactured in Mesquite, Texas, at J & R Manufacturing. The platter of meat came out with a bowl filled with a mysterious frothy concoction, which turned out to be melted butter seasoned with garlic and lime. Robb instructed us to dip the meat into the bowl before placing it on the house-made tortillas. As with great barbecue, the simple pairing of the buttery meat and the warm tortillas needed no further accoutrements. My stomach had been bulging when I walked in here, yet somehow I'd still managed to consume a third of the steak fajita platter—a testament to its quality. It was a reminder of how good simple food can be when care is taken to do it well.

There had been very few rays of sunlight over the last five days in East Texas, either in the weather or the food. By and large, the barbecue had been subpar. Our most memorable meals had included barbecued crab, grilled oysters, and mesquite-grilled fajitas. I don't envy the likes of Nick Pencis at Stanley's, in Tyler, or Stephen Joseph at Riverport Bar-B-Cue, in Jefferson. They are the real prophets of smoked meat, striving to create disciples from a complacent population. I know they'll keep preaching good barbecue until the folks in East Texas begin to demand it. Until then, tread cautiously through the Piney Woods.

5 Days, 1,257 Miles, 32 BBQ Joints

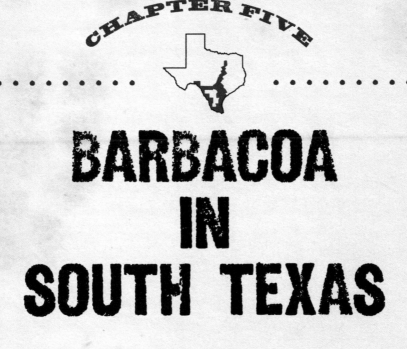

CHAPTER FIVE

BARBACOA IN SOUTH TEXAS

It's all about perspective. Dallasites will tell you that anything below San Antonio is in South Texas. Folks who live in Brownsville, almost three hundred miles south of San Antonio, laugh at the idea of including points as far north as the Alamo City in South Texas. The cities along US Highway 90 at the base of the Balcones Escarpment still consider themselves part of the Hill Country, although they're only two hours north of Laredo at the US/Mexico border. This may be good marketing for those towns, but it's not geographically or geologically correct. Geographic elements define the southern edges of South Texas: the Coastal Plains are, well, along the Gulf Coast; the Rio Grande valley comprises the communities that lie along the Rio Grande River between the Falcon Reservoir (about fifty miles south of Laredo) and the river's mouth at the Gulf of Mexico. Between the Coastal Plains and the Rio Grande valley is the unforgiving and desolate no-man's-land referred to simply as the South Texas Plains. The northern border of the plains is hard to define, but most agree that it's somewhere south of San Antonio. General opinion of the South Texas Plains holds that there's nothing to see there, an attitude that merely strengthened my yearning to experience it firsthand. I'd witnessed the plains' dust storms years before from an airplane window midway from Dallas to Los Angeles, but on this trip I would have a ground-level view.

Like the borders of South Texas, the definition of one of its famous dishes, barbacoa, also shifts depending on one's own perspective. The English word *barbecue* actually derives from *barbacoa*, but traditional barbacoa doesn't have much in common with the rest of Texas's smoked meats. A few South Texas barbacoa joints advertise barbecue on their signs—for the benefit of gringos such as myself, I'm guessing—when in fact they serve barbacoa. I think this creates more confusion than clarity, but then again, I'll stop just about anywhere serving any form of barbecue, regardless of the language on a sign. The meat used in barbacoa could be any cut of smoked lamb, mutton, goat, or beef, but most of the time when you find barbacoa in Texas it will be cabeza de vaca—cow's head—and it will rarely be smoked. If at this point you are either a hopeful or disgusted Chipotle customer wondering what *they* serve as barbacoa, pay no mind to this discussion of cow heads. Chipotle uses beef shoulder, or clod, as their preferred cut of beef. But all along the Rio Grande valley, you can safely assume that most any place with barbacoa on the menu will be serving you some portion of beef head, even if it's only the cheek or tongue. Across the border in Mexico, barbacoa is traditionally slow-cooked over coals in a maguey-leaf-lined pit in the ground. On ranches and in backyards of South Texas and northern Mexico, the term refers to this process of cooking meat in the ground. This can mean the use of cow head or, just as commonly, a whole goat or lamb, but rarely (if ever) pork. On this trip we were in search of beef, preferably from the head, and more preferably cooked on the skull. Before leaving for South Texas, all of the barbacoa I'd eaten in my life had been steamed or roasted in an oven, a far different method from the traditional coals in the ground. Meat prepared without a splinter of wood can hardly count as barbecue, so I was also hoping to find some examples of wood-cooked barbacoa that belonged in a conversation about Texas barbecue.

Before we'd need to practice our restaurant Spanish, we had a few detours planned for our drive down from Dallas. A stop in downtown Belton brought us to **MILLER'S SMOKEHOUSE**. It was a true small-town joint that served smoked meats on a strict Monday-through-Friday schedule (though they've since added Saturday hours). In true Central

Texas fashion, they offered home-made sausages along with deer processing and taxidermy. Thankfully, they did the latter two in a building next door.

Ribs were a Friday-only special at Miller's, so since it was a Wednesday, we ordered some brisket and all three of their home-made sausages. Just looking at the brisket, I knew it would be good. The fat was translucent, the crust was black, and the smoke ring was pronounced. With the first bite, my taste buds were enveloped in oak smoke, and I was in heaven. This was some of the most deeply smoky brisket I'd had, but it didn't cross the line into oversmoked territory. The fat was buttery, and the meat came apart with ease. The seasoned salt, garlic powder, and black pepper rub added restrained but necessary zip while still allowing for a crackling bark. The pulled pork was a letdown in comparison. A sweet, tomato-based sauce had eradicated most of the meat's character. The sausages as a group had rather limp casings and could have all used more smoke and seasoning. Their flavor varied only subtly from one to the next; each one had the same beef-and-pork mixture and a similar seasoning base. My visible disappointment at the news that their ribs were available only on Fridays led our server to offer us two pork spareribs that had been "rescued" from a catering order. They'd been wrapped with foil toward the end of their cooking, so condensation had ruined their crust, but the smoky flavor was deep in these ribs. A rub heavy with black pepper and garlic created some bold flavors in the nicely cooked meat, though the very ends suffered from a bit of dry stringiness.

At this point we were doing the exact opposite of pacing ourselves. When Dirk Miller, the owner and pitmaster, asked us to try some burnt brisket ends, we couldn't resist. Nick and I split a large chunk of the rich, fatty meat. The intensity of the rub and the smoke were magnified but still delicious. We let our stomachs settle as we toured the joint with Dirk. There was a larger dining room at the rear of the building, which we'd missed. A huge steel smoker, belching oak smoke and filled with wrapped briskets, sat out front. A couple of smaller vertical smokers, about the size of water heaters, sat idle, but had been used earlier that day for the sausages and chicken. These smaller smokers were fueled with coals and utilized direct heat for cooking. I thought a little more heat in those suckers would have delivered the nice crispiness that I sought in the sausages, but who could complain when eating brisket like Dirk was dishing up? A fellow connoisseur of the smoked-meat arts, Dirk shared his desire to get to Austin. He'd seen Franklin Barbecue and JMueller BBQ on the cover of *Texas Monthly* and wanted to try both. When I asked if he'd be seeking out any tips during those visits, Dirk said "I just make what I like, and hopefully other people like it, too."

A late start, large lunch, and Austin traffic now had us uncomfortably delayed. Our planned late afternoon stop turned into an early-evening visit to **HAYS COUNTY BAR-B-QUE**, in San Marcos. It was nearing dinnertime so, as I expected, some of the meats showed signs of fatigue. A pork chop was a bit dried-out and the remaining crust was probably never as crisp as I'd prefer. A couple of sad, dry ribs had been hacked apart from what remained of an old rack, but as an employee named Josh rang up the order he noticed the ribs, and without a word or extra charge brought out two new, thick, moist ribs to our table and apologized. A thick bark of salt and black pepper provided a smoky burst on the ribs that was lacking in the chop, but the meat could have come off the bone a bit more easily. The fatty brisket was admirable at this late hour. Plenty of silky fat had created a moisture shield, so the meat

beneath hadn't dried out too much. With an exquisite crust and smoke ring, these slices were perfectly smoky and well seasoned. Slices of real turkey breast had somehow survived the whole day unscathed. The exemplary meat was moist and tender. The simple seasoning of smoke, salt, and pepper let the poultry shine. Sausage making is an art practiced by an ever-shrinking list of barbecue joints, but their home-made links were a high-quality mix of mostly brisket, some pork shoulder, and a seasoning mix high on the black-pepper quotient. The links were excellent on their own, but a swipe through the sweet and mustardy sauce brought them to a new level. I could imagine how good the food must have been about five hours earlier.

Unbeknownst to Nick and me, while we had been eating, Michael Hernandez, the owner of Hays, had been freaking out. He had e-mailed me several months earlier and offered to give me a personal tour of the operation. I hadn't bothered to explain that a planned meeting wasn't part of the process for a proper review, but I wrote back that I had the place on my radar and would stop in at some point. Since then I'd heard good things about Hays, so it was an easy decision to make the visit. Michael wasn't there when Nick and I arrived, so I'd given my card to Josh as we were finishing up and asked for a tour of the pits. As Josh showed us the unique half-barrel steel smokers in the back, another employee walked in with the phone. It was the owner, and he wanted to talk to me. Michael apologized frantically for not being there (he had business to attend to in Austin) and, curiously to me, apologized for the meat. Neither apology was necessary.

I have had the benefit of working with and befriending some great folks in Dallas who, sadly for me, moved away. Luckily, Jessica and Ryan Soliz had moved to a convenient spot just north of San Antonio, into a house big enough for Nick and me to each spend the night in our own bedrooms. Jessica had helped lure me to my current architectural office, and Ryan had convinced me to buy the car I was driving on the trip. More important, they both love barbecue, so it didn't take much convincing for them to join us at **CBQ EATERY**, in Schertz, just outside of San Antonio.

Whenever a barbecue joint adds a word like *eatery* to its name, my expectations for the smoked meat drop substantially. Unfortunately,

CBQ Eatery met my low expectations. The bone-dry brisket sandwich tasted of burned sauce. It could have used some of the moisture from the waterlogged pulled-pork sandwich. A rack of baby back ribs were basted in sauce and sprinkled with diced chives. The meat was tender but any smokiness was covered up by the flavor of burned sugar, which results when meat basted with sugary sauce is exposed to the direct heat of a grill. The best dish was the one that didn't pretend to be authentic: house-made, thick-cut, barbecue-flavor potato chips topped with saucy chopped brisket, blue cheese, and chives could have been a meal for two.

Back at the house we shared a few beers. Ryan had given up beer for Lent, but wasn't off to a good start on Ash Wednesday. He promised to stay sober on Easter to make up for it, but I didn't check up on him. We needed *something* with which to toast the news of Jessica's pregnancy, after all (she toasted with water). We said our good-byes the next morning and made our way to Castroville, a historic Alsatian town about twenty miles west of San Antonio, where—for the first time in my life—I'd eat raw beef for breakfast.

Tejanos may be the strongest cultural influence in most of South Texas, but in 1844 Henri Castro and a group of French immigrants settled Castroville. The Alsatian sausage taking up prime real estate in the **DZIUK'S MEAT MARKET** meat case reflects the cultural legacy of those settlers. A fresh pork-and-beef sausage with a fairly fine grind, seasoned with coriander and stuffed into hog casings, its delicate flavor is

nothing like the links of aggressively seasoned and smoked beef sausage that you'll find in Central Texas. It's not really meant for smoking, either. Unfortunately Dziuk's only sold it raw, so we'd have to keep a cooler packed with ice for a couple of days before we could dig in. Another raw item in the meat case needed no cooking. I'd read about parisa and knew it was like a cross between beef tartare and ceviche: finely ground lean beef mixed with diced onion, shredded cheddar, salt, and pepper (and in this case diced jalapeño) "cooked" in acidic lemon juice. We were assured that it had been freshly ground that morning and needed only a saltine for accompaniment. They kindly offered us a sample before we purchased any. I'd compare it to my first sushi experience. Nothing about the flavor was unpleasant, but the unexpected and thoroughly yielding texture on my tongue was telling me that something was different about the meat. It didn't offer the resistance of cooked beef, but it was still tasty enough for me to make a purchase. The parisa wasn't going to travel well, so Nick and I finished a quarter pound of the stuff during a car-trunk picnic. Unlike the sausage, I could find no connection between this raw meat concoction and the town's Alsatian roots. Some Castroville residents I talked to who were familiar with the area's history confirmed that parisa is a Medina County creation (specifically in the towns of Hondo and Castroville) as far as they could remember, and that these days it's only available at Dziuk's and another meat market, in Hondo. We washed it down with some of Dziuk's famous jerky and dried sausage. The dried sausage was fine, but the jerky was something special. Dziuk's makes their jerky by taking a large hunk of beef and covering it liberally with barely cracked pepper corns before drying it. They then take the chunk of meat to the deli slicer and slice it across the grain. The resulting texture made for the tenderest jerky I'd ever eaten.

Westward, toward Hondo, we could see the Balcones Escarpment on our right, dipping down into the South Texas Plains. The utterly flat highway can lull you into speeding pretty easily, were it not for the famous sign in Hondo, which reminds you "This is God's country, please don't drive through it like hell." I hit the brakes just inside the city limits at the sight of a new barbecue joint.

There were only a couple of customers in line at **HEAVY'S BBQ** when we made our way inside. This can be a bad sign at 11:30 A.M., but before we'd finished the meal there was a line of folks out the door. I guess the lunch bell rings no earlier than noon in Hondo. We got a sampling of meats that included sausage, pork loin, ribs, and both fatty and lean brisket. As I watched the black-crusted brisket relax onto the cutting board I knew I was in for something good. Heavy's knife glided effortlessly as each slice fell gently onto the next. The beef neither quivered nor bounced, which are both bad signs of underdone brisket. The fat melted onto my fingers as I brought a few fingersful to my mouth. I braced in anticipation, and it didn't let me down. Even the thick fat that remained was good to the last bite, holding tightly on to the

smoke. The beef was buttery-tender, no matter if it was from the moist or lean end, and every slice had a deep, smoky flavor from the mesquite in the smoker.

The sausage was gray, indicating fresh sausage made without preservatives. It was smoky, juicy, and perfectly seasoned. I thought it might be home-made, but it turned out Heavy has fresh, uncooked links delivered from Pollok's, in Falls City, twice a week. It's worth the shipping cost. Pork loin is a lean cut that's apt to dry out, but this one was juicy, with a deep smokiness. The simple seasoning of just salt and cracked black pepper served it and the other meats well. The spareribs were perfectly tender and had a nicely rendered fat layer. The bark gave them a deep smokiness. The tomato-based barbecue sauce had plenty of black pepper and vinegar, with just the right amount of sweetness. It was so good I was drinking it from the cup, but the irony was that I wouldn't dare use it on any of the excellent smoked meats.

To produce meat of that quality, a pitmaster has to perfectly manage a mesquite fire, which takes real skill. Heavy cut his teeth on barbecue at Bert's on the University of Texas campus in Austin, but moved his family out here for better schools and a country upbringing. Thankfully, he brought his smoked meats with him. Yet I write this now with a little embarrassment, wondering if I'd been duped. After Nick's and my trip, a friend stopped in Hondo on my recommendation and found the meats at Heavy's to be subpar. A quick look around the side of the building revealed a new Southern Pride gas-fired pit smoking away and the original pit sitting cold next to it. Who knows which of those smokers had held the meat that I ate.

The barbecue business is always changing, and often not for the better. Four years earlier I'd raved about the smoky meats coming out of the barbecue trailer behind **BILLY BOB'S HAMBURGERS**. Since then, I'd heard rumors about its declining quality. When I drove by on this trip, an empty patch of mud and grass was all that remained where the smoker and the trailer once stood. But the drive-through menu still listed barbecue, and the guy at the window insisted they still had a smoker. When I unwrapped the sandwich on the back picnic table, it was obvious things had gone terribly wrong in the last few years. The slices of brisket had a slick texture, as if they'd just done a round on the flattop for warming. The meat was chewy, with edges so crunchy I'd swear they were hung to dry before serving. Through the slats in the wood fence I saw the Master Range Smokehouse, a sad little gas-fueled cabinet smoker— essentially a gas oven with a small drawer for wood chips. It's a smoker in the same way your gas grill would be if you threw a small tin of wood

chips in it and provided more insulation. If anyone has visited Billy Bob's due to my recommendation, please take this as my sincere apology. What is served there now has little resemblance to barbecue.

It's a wonder that **EVETT'S BAR-B-QUE** in Uvalde is even still in operation. These days it's hard enough to find a family member, let alone a family friend, to keep a place going after the parents have had enough. Robert and Janice Gagliardi, the owners of Evett's, were friends of the Evett family, the original owners, who started the business in 1964. In 1992 Mr. Evett and his son died in a tragic car accident, and Robert and Janice took over, keeping the business alive. Janice was our host on the day of our visit, and she showed Nick and me around back, where hulking concrete pits spewed mesquite smoke. I've seen horizontal concrete pits with metal lids that lift from above, but these were cabinet smokers with concrete on every side but the front, where a huge metal door offered access to the meat racks and another door just below it offered access to the fire pit.

Back inside we enjoyed a plate of brisket, ribs, and sausage. The sausage came from the HEB grocery store next door. In the past, Janice and Robert ordered their sausage from a local meat market, but the market routinely shorted Janice by seven or eight pounds for every fifty-pound box. The market refused to address the issue

to her satisfaction, so off to HEB she went. It was a fine rendition of commercially made sausage with a good black-pepper kick, but I bet that meat market stuff would have been worth the extra money. The thick slices of brisket were smoked beyond integrity, with the resulting texture of mushy roast beef, though its fat was well rendered. The overpowering smokiness came through the thin, sweet sauce with which Janice had doused the meat when I wasn't looking. While I had been placing my order, I had happily noticed the absence of the usual vat of sauce with a ladle sticking out. In the time it took to turn my head just to see the drink options, Janice grabbed the hidden vessel of warm sauce, which was camouflaged as a coffee pot, and sneaked about a cupful on my plate. A gasp escaped me as I looked down, but it was too late to do anything other than reinforce the mental note: *Always* ask for sauce on the side.

Luckily it was a good sauce; the ribs that had been so good on a previous visit were dry this time and definitely in need of it. As for the sides, the beans tasted like they came straight from a can, but the mashed potato salad, with a hint of red pepper and sugar, was enjoyable. The sauce that had migrated onto the potato salad didn't harm it a bit. I would have savored the smoked meat a bit more if I had known that I wouldn't get a decent rib or a well-smoked brisket for a few more days.

Past the Nueces River we crossed the Kinney County line. Although it takes more time to traverse this county than it does the state of Rhode Island, it only contains two towns of note: the tiny county seat of Brackettville; and Alamo Village, where the John Wayne movie *The Alamo* was filmed. The gates to Alamo Village were closed, and there wasn't any smoked-meat action in Brackettville, so we moved on to Del Rio. A sign outside of town warned drivers of low-flying aircraft. I nearly drove off the road as a fighter jet whooshed overhead right on cue. It might have been a T-6 Texan II, which fly routinely out of Laughlin Air Force Base.

Del Rio necessitated only a quick drive-through. I just needed to scan the town to see if any new joints had opened up—I had no desire to return to the ones I'd been to before. Nothing doing. I put the hammer down as we tried to make Langtry before sunset—we wanted to check out the town that was essentially created by the infamous western scoundrel Judge Roy Bean, known as the Law West of Pecos. I assumed we'd breeze through the Border Patrol stop just outside of Comstock, but the drug-sniffing dogs had other ideas. It seemed obvious to me that a carful of jerky and leftover barbecue had lured the dog, but the taciturn agent thought otherwise. In the end he blamed my prescribed cholesterol medicine (the barbecue lifestyle strikes again), but I think he was just trying to save face after coming up completely empty. We got the last laugh, though, as an unlikely vehicle approached the checkpoint: a full-size Oscar Mayer Wienermobile (one of only six in the country), piloted by cute coeds. They stopped for what amounted to more of a photo op than an inspection. They smiled and waved as we too snapped a few shots, but they didn't offer any tube steaks.

The South Texas Plains that we'd been so lazily driving through soon gave way to rocky, hilly terrain as we climbed up onto the Edwards Plateau. An hour outside of Del Rio, the elevation had increased about six hundred feet. We zoomed past semitrucks as the relentless inclines put them at what seemed like a standstill. The only flat stretch of road came crossing the bridge over the Pecos River. Langtry was drawing near.

Langtry is a small town that mostly serves as a historical marker for the life of Judge Roy Bean. Back in 1882 Judge Roy Bean set up shop in town, where he opened a bar called the Jersey Lilly Saloon, from which he dispensed his own corrupt brand of law and order as justice of the peace—he was known as the Hanging Judge, though in reality he hanged almost no one. Though various movies and television shows have mythologized the judge's life, Langtry itself is almost a ghost town these days. The main draw is a visitor center, operated by the state of Texas, which includes the original Jersey Lilly Saloon building, in which Judge Roy Bean died in 1903. He had no idea that one day a chain of kitschy barbecue joints bearing his name would sling mediocre barbecue around

the South. According to the online menu, the "Judge's favorite!" is catfish tacos. I'm glad the chain's Texas locations didn't survive.

We lingered a while to watch the sun set over the mountains west of Langtry. The sky was so clear that even the far eastern horizon was tinged purple from the setting sun. When it was gone, we drove back over the Pecos toward Del Rio. The Border Patrol officers sat idly as we passed. On the outskirts of Del Rio we pulled into a parking lot to admire a starrier sky than either Nick or I had ever seen.

Back in Del Rio we had a few drinks with a local reporter curious about our quest. I told him that previous experiences in town precluded any barbecue stops in the morning, but that I was on the lookout for good barbacoa recommendations. With every drink his insistence grew stronger that he'd find us a great barbacoa stop for the morning. Not a single actual recommendation came to the surface by the time we paid the bill, but it was time to turn in. My quest for knowledge in the world of barbacoa was a new one. I've spent years eating brisket and ribs but was hoping that a trip along the highway that hugs several hundred miles of the Rio Grande would offer some insights on beef cheek and tongue.

The next day was a Friday, but not just any Friday. It was the first Friday of Lent, so the entire observant Catholic population wasn't eating meat. Nick and I also got a crash course in the meaning of "Sabado y Domingo," as in Saturday and Sunday *solamente*. Most places served barbacoa on weekends only, and some only on Sunday. (If barbacoa is on a restaurant's menu every day, they're probably just steaming cheek meat, not whole cow heads.) Let's just say it was a disappointing morning on the barbacoa trail. I was able to tally up plenty of stops for a future to-do list as we meandered through Del Rio's old Barrio Chihuahua neighborhood on the south side of the railroad tracks, where the houses are diminutive, the streets narrow, and the historical markers frequent.

Circling back along Frontera Road, we got our first glimpse of the border fence. It was about fifteen feet tall, its steel bars painted black. A

dusty gravel road ran along the fence on either side. A block away from the fence, on the American side, a gas station called **BORDER STOP ONE** advertised barbacoa "todos las dias!!!" A few words of Spanish, and a few minutes later Nick and I were in possession of a very large, fresh, flour tortilla heaped with chopped cheek meat (which is nothing more than a fatty cut of beef). Because barbacoa traditionally receives no seasoning before or during cooking, I sprinkled on some salt and a little salsa verde. The meat was unctuous and moist, but though it was enjoyable, it wasn't earth-shattering. No matter, we had set a quality baseline to work from. As we paid the bill at the register, Border Stop One's owner, Sergio Garza, explained that they only use cheeks (cachete) and lips (labios) in their barbacoa, but that lips were becoming too expensive to offer. He used to use whole heads, but the space required to cook the skulls became too prohibitive. He eased the pain of our fruitless search a bit when he told us he didn't know anyone in Del Rio who still bothered with the head. This was a cachete town.

Between Del Rio and Eagle Pass, a border town and our next destination, we seemed to pass every type of vehicle in the Border Patrol fleet besides a boat. There were pickup trucks, SUVs, cars, and four-wheelers on the road and small planes and helicopters patrolling from the sky. Border Patrol agents drove slowly on unimproved roads running along both sides of the highway, keeping their windows down, looking for fresh tracks in the dirt. Driving through a perpetual crime scene alongside uniformed hunters searching for human prey made me more anxious than I'd expected. When a Border Patrol car lurched out from behind the bushes and sped right up on my ass, I imagined our wives engaged in a fruitless life-long search, seeking the truth about our disappearance. The car backed off, but the feeling that we were unwelcome strangers in our own country persisted.

After a few false alarms for barbecue along the road we pulled into **M & M CAFE**. Barbacoa was on the menu here, but we knew something was lost in the translation when gray slices of flavorless and tough baked brisket arrived. Out of politeness we covered the uneaten meat with paper napkins at our corner table, then tore into the excellent tortillas and lentils instead. Things didn't improve much once we reached Eagle Pass. *Day-old* would be an optimistic term to use for the sorry brisket and ribs at **WAGON WHEEL SMOKEHOUSE**, where the impressive, show-quality smoker out front was stone-cold; and another smoker in the yard of **CHARLIE'S B.B.Q.** further into town seemed to be for show, too, after we watched our meal being heated up in an oiled skillet. I was quickly discovering why barbacoa was more popular around here.

Eagle Pass is a border town, and the checkpoint is hard to miss, as the largest Mexican flag in the world is mounted on a four-hundred-foot-tall pole on the Mexican side of the Eagle Pass–Piedras Negras International Bridge. Fittingly, it was Flag Day in Mexico, and we stopped for a minute and watched through the chain-link fence as the futbol field–sized flag swayed slowly in the wind. The closest we'd get to crossing the border was a visit to the jewel of Eagle Pass—**PIEDRAS NEGRAS TORTILLA FACTORY**. We had choices to make at the counter inside: mixta or cachete? We knew we liked the cachete, and I was curious about the mixta, a gamy mix of head cuts that is both fattier and cheaper than cachete. We decided to get

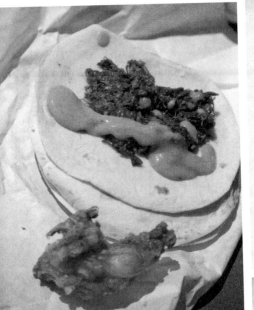

both. The friendly cashier told us that cachete is most customers' first choice, and that mixta is what they choose when the cachete is gone. I thought the mixta was a good sign that they were using whole heads, and the cashier confirmed this. Even on a Friday.

We feasted on the trunk of the car. Fresh tortillas and a salsa verde, made smooth with pureed avocado, were the perfect complement to the tender cheek meat. The mixta, with its gamy flavor and squeezed-from-a-tube consistency, took some getting used to. Cachete, on the other hand, was quickly becoming a favorite of Nick's and mine.

With full bellies we continued south. McAllen was our destination for the night and we had a long way to go. For miles the landscape beyond the windows was nothing but flat land and scrubby brush. After an hour or so, gas wells began popping up with increasing frequency along the highway. Semitrucks loaded with drilling equipment were the most common vehicle we passed. Texas was in the middle of another energy boom—we were driving right over the South Texas leg of the Eagle Ford Shale, which holds natural gas reserves out the wazoo. As we drew closer to Laredo, the traffic grew increasingly worse. So many trucks clogged the highway we slowed to nearly a standstill. Luckily for us we saw a trailer parked alongside the road, displaying a cardboard sign that read simply BBQ Plates. Waves of mesquite smoke came through our open windows as we pulled off the road. We learned from some business card we snagged that the official name of the operation was **TEXAS STYLE BBQ**. They'd set up shop here to serve the swarms of oil and gas workers. Everything was grilled over direct heat. The brisket was sold out. The meats were served sauced, with pickled carrot slices and whole jalapeños strewn over the top. Fluffy and well-seasoned rice came alongside a half ear of smoked corn. The chewy ribs and cheap sausage were forgettable, but the chicken took on the flavors of the grill quite well. It wasn't bad for a quick stop off the highway, but I wouldn't travel far to seek it out again.

After enduring more Laredo-bound traffic, we finally made it to the town itself—and to **BRISKETS & BEER SMOKEHOUSE**. With a name like that, I expected a beer joint that happened to serve barbecue, even though their sign did boast they were the Best Little Smokehouse in Laredo. There was a five-meat sampler on the menu, so we decided to try a little of everything. The brisket slices were overtrimmed and, weirdly, had either been brushed with or dipped into beef broth before serving. The chicken had flabby skin and little smokiness. Luckily, it got better from there. The beef back ribs had a thick crust and great smoke. The meat could have been a bit more tender, but they were respectable for back ribs. The pork ribs were superthick and the fat within nicely rendered. Big chunks of pork came easily off the bone, and all of it had good smoke. The sausage had good snap and some good seasoning, but it

was an appetizer that stole the show. Briskets & Beer had found some seriously large chiles for their jalapeño smokers—peppers stuffed with a mix of chopped brisket and cream cheese, wrapped in bacon, and smoked. I could have made a meal of them.

After we ate, we talked out back with Lisandro Moreno, Briskets & Beer's owner and pitmaster. He smokes with mesquite in an offset steel smoker. I asked him about other barbecue options in town, but the Rudy's chain was all he could think of. I asked about barbacoa, and he mentioned that it was on his menu but was listed with the Tex-Mex options rather than the barbecue, so I had missed it. Nick and I headed back to our table after confirming the need for an order of said barbacoa. A minute or so later, I unwrapped the foil package to find a freshly crisped flour tortilla filled with shredded meat with a nice reddish hue. Lisandro uses only cheek meat and smokes it just a touch before wrapping it tightly and cooking it in the oven overnight. Unlike all of the other unseasoned barbacoa we'd eaten, this cachete was salted and seasoned with garlic and cumin. It was a bit addictive. Nick was pretty full by that point, so I polished off the rest of the taco, pleased enough with our barbacoa-tasting progress. It was time to move on to the lower Rio Grande valley.

Just south of town, our progress came to an unexpected halt. Over the sound of our own radio playing Marty Robbins, we heard thumping bass emanating from a spot called **MAMI CHULAS DRIVE-THRU**. Out in front of the drive-through, three women in high heels were giving it their all, dressed in as little clothing as possible. At that very moment Nick got thirsty. I whipped the car around and pulled up into the beer barn. My German sedan didn't seem to cause as much excitement in the ladies as the big trucks in front of us did. I ordered two very large cans of beer and promptly parted with twenty dollars. I'd been ripped off for sure, but the photo Nick snapped of the cute redhead in a purple lace bra was priceless.

With beers in hand, I put the hammer down as we headed south on US Highway 83 so they might stay cold enough to drink once we got to McAllen. A light sprinkle had just let up, giving way to a full-on double rainbow. Life was good. An hour later we found the house that would be our base camp for the next three days. Nick had kind relatives in McAllen who were letting us stay in their multibedroom house while they were on vacation. While setting up the itinerary for the next day I realized just how large the lower Rio Grande valley actually is; I had planned to have breakfast in Brownsville, our ultimate destination for the next day, but we were still an hour's drive away. We would need breakfast before Brownsville.

The next morning we stopped in Harlingen for a barbacoa breakfast at **CAPISTRAN'S TORTILLAS & BBQ**. The two ladies filling orders didn't speak English. Nick pointed to the camera, then to the women, an

inquisitive look on his face. They shook their heads. When the food arrived we pointed to it and the camera again. Yes, as long as it was just of the food. I was over feeling like an insecure gringo who had to order the "authentic" mixta. It was early and the cachete was plentiful. The meat was rich. Despite the BBQ on Capistran's sign, there was no smoked meat there, but a heap of fresh tortillas and a container full of chopped onions, cilantro, and lime wedges provided all the distraction I needed. The large chunks of onion were a nice textural counterpoint to the silky meat, and the lime juice brightened it. After a few bites I remembered the salt shaker. Even better. I tried to ask, in my mangled Spanglish, if they used the whole head. No clear answer was forthcoming. I later learned that the tiny building is actually a satellite location of the original Capistran's Tortillas & BBQ in Brownsville. In Brownsville they cook whole heads on the weekends, so maybe some of the meat had been shipped to Harlingen. None of that was clear at the time. But despite the language barrier, our clean plates and full bellies made it clear we had enjoyed the food.

A few streets away we stopped at a barbacoa joint I had received a tip about. We were thwarted before we walked in the door: Barbacoa de Cabeza los Domingos. We'd have to wait until tomorrow. A block away, at Lara's Bakery, we could see a solid line of customers through its glass facade. We had some time to kill, so we took a spot in line. Fifteen minutes and $1.35 later, we had five pig-shaped cookies and a front seat full of crumbs. It was time to make our way toward Brownsville, where the Charro Days Fiesta and its Grand International Parade awaited us.

We followed Route 281 as it hugged the Rio Grande. A border fence paralleled our course. I was surprised that there were so many large holes in the fence. Tempting detainment, I drove down a gravel road through one of the tears in the fence. The road snaked around the other side of the fence and continued along the top of a levee. The next opening we saw looked like it dead-ended at a gravel pit so we kept driving, slowly. Another opening looked more promising. There wasn't anyone else around, so I turned the car sideways in the fence's gap for a photo op. We drove nervously back toward the highway. They are always watching. No less than five Border Patrol vehicles waited at the intersection up ahead. One flashed its lights and pulled up alongside us. Another blocked our exit path. An officer motioned at me to roll down my window. I cracked it in the drizzle and explained our

intentions with an utter honesty that must have sounded too deranged to be a lie. With a stern warning never to do that again, they let us drive on. Nick and I were two guys from Dallas on a barbecue road trip who drove through the fence because we thought it was humorous that we could. Most important, we were US citizens. Despite my carefree explanation, it would take a few miles for the nervous shaking to subside.

Even with our delays, we arrived in Brownsville with more than an hour to spare before the parade. I couldn't take it any longer. I was still full from breakfast, but the object of my desire was near. I had spent a lot of time reading about and researching this particular restaurant—the only one of its kind in Texas. My pilgrimage had led me to the doorsteps of the legendary **VERA'S BACKYARD BAR-B-QUE**, where cow heads are still cooked over a mesquite fire in an underground pit.

Vera's is an endangered species. No other commercial operation in Texas—and thus probably the country—cooks barbacoa in the traditional way. Barbacoa connoisseurs are well aware of this fact, as are those who

have read Lolis Eric Elie's *Smokestack Lightning*, which contains a detailed account of Mando Vera's cooking methods, but Vera's hasn't seemed to capitalize on this popularity statewide. Only a faded line of script on their hand-painted sign advertised the fact: Barbacoa en Pozo con Leña de Mezquite. The unassuming yellow building topped with a simple hipped roof wasn't flashy on the outside, and its interior was equally modest. Over the next two days we spent several hours at Vera's, and we never saw another customer use one of the tables in the dining room. Either from the counter or the drive-through, this place was built for takeout. The menu was a bilingual lesson in beef head biology:

     Cachete—Cheek
     Lengua—Tongue
     Mixta—Mixed
     Jeta—Lips
     Ojos—Eyes
     Paladar—Palate
     Mollejas—Sweetbreads

As I ordered, I could see through an open door into the kitchen. No one tried to hide or seemed nonplussed by the macabre nature of the

work being done there. As his wife and daughters took orders, Mando stood at a small prep table, meticulously stripping the meat from a few skulls in various stages of undress. We ordered cachete, a few flour tortillas, and a small plastic ramekin of house-made salsa verde. Smoked brisket was also on the menu, and as I am a man of unrelenting habit, I ordered it, but we won't talk about it. I was here for cheek, not breast.

I took a few fingersful of meat and ate. It was heavenly. It was really unlike any other barbacoa I'd eaten. The meat had been wrapped in foil during cooking, but enough smoke had seeped through the cracks to provide another level of flavor. The surface of the meat was also a bit dry, which gave it some textural contrast I hadn't encountered so far. I made a taco and scarfed it down. There was no savoring. By now I was miserable. It was hard to admit to myself, but I'd been gorging for days and was simply too full to enjoy Vera's to its full potential. We decided to come back the next day for a feast, but my journey was fulfilled. A budding relationship with real barbacoa had been consummated.

Back in the kitchen, Mando showed us the different cuts on the head. The sound of the camera's shutter snapping was perpetual as Nick shot away. As we talked, Mando occasionally looked toward us, but his hands never stopped peeling away meat. He didn't even have to look at the different bins as he separated cheeks and lips and . . . well, everything else, which went in the mixta. Nonchalantly, he pulled out an eye. It was larger than I expected. It was a quarter pound of meat the color of roast beef but with an unfamiliar white string of optic nerve hanging down. I knew that people really ate this, but I asked if folks really enjoyed it. He said that customers always asked for the price of the other cuts before buying any, but that they never questioned the price of ojos when available. They were at a premium, and like briskets, there are only two on every cow. When I questioned Mando's opinion on the eyes, his wife laughed. He had never eaten one. Without delay I asked if we could share our first eye if I returned the next day. He agreed. It was on.

Seventy-five was turning into Nick's and my lucky number. Back in August, we had attended the seventy-fifth XIT Rodeo and Reunion. This rainy weekend, Brownsville was hosting its seventy-fifth Charro Days Fiesta. The weekend-long celebration was created during the Depression to lift spirits and honor binational friendship with Brownsville's sister city, Matamoros. In past years, the international bridge between the cities was open during the festivities, and people from both sides of the border partied together. These days, the bridge stays closed. The mayors of the two cities meet in the middle of the bridge and shake hands, kicking off the festivities. Meanwhile, armed members of the military stand guard on either end of the bridge. We drove into the old section of downtown Brownsville just in time to catch the drizzly International Parade. Dignitaries and marching bands alternated with motorcycles and gaudily painted cars depicting scenes from *Scarface*. There were many men dressed as charros—the gentlemen Mexican cowboys who were heroes of the borderlands—dressed impeccably and mounted on beautiful horses. There were screams for the telenovela star Arath de La Torre, but the loudest cheers (other than those for the poor boy who was shoveling behind the horses) were saved for the Border Patrol. The crowd clapped and cheered relentlessly as Border Patrol cars, trucks, and boats passed. One trailer hauled a Border Patrol band. All the while a helicopter hovered directly above the Border Patrol floats as they crawled down the street. It was clear that the community here did not view the Border Patrol as an annoyance. They were obviously revered and respected, and they had a cool helicopter.

We were going to be back in Brownsville tomorrow, so we felt fine about ditching out early on the Charro Days festivities. We followed the old and scenic US 83 through a series of small towns. We had consumed enough barbacoa—it was time for brisket and ribs. Several smokestacks scented the air at a street festival in La Feria. We walked around and found table after table of prechopped beef in Crock-Pots. We purchased nothing. La Feria was a portent of things to come; the rest of the day's stops would run together in an unceasing chain of mesquite-smoked mediocrity.

The thick-sliced pork loin had been rewarmed on a grill and was dry as could be at **FAT DADDY'S BBQ & BURGERS**, in Weslaco. Nothing was terribly smoky, and little of it showed potential. The fatty brisket was chewy and poorly seasoned. The baby back ribs had been stored for some time before serving, and the meat was both dried-out and mushy. Luckily, a peach cobbler and Blue Bell Ice Cream made for a good ending.

The big beef ribs at **THE ORIGINAL WILLIE'S BAR-B-Q**, in Alamo, were well smoked but they lacked any sort of seasoning. A sweetish rub went on the crusty pork ribs, but the meat wasn't tender enough. The fatty brisket had gobs of undercooked, opaque-white fat running throughout the meat, and I could only stand a couple bites. Late in the day Nick had usually had enough of the whole eating thing. He'd look over at me for a visual cue that he should dig in, that it might be worth the stomach space. I had given him zero positive glances before I bit into the smoked fajita meat. A thick and pleasantly chewy exterior shielded moist and tender meat. Sliced thinly against the grain, the meat was in no way too chewy. The smoke ring was almost as thick as the meat. I gave Nick a look and took another bite.

At **UNCLE ROY'S BBQ**, in Pharr, we got the prettiest presentation of smoked meat that I've seen in a to-go container. An aluminum pan had dark slices of brisket stacked neatly in one corner and onions, pickles, and jalapeños in another. The black bark of the beef rib played against the crimson-red baby backs. A couple whole links of sausage and an ear of buttered corn dusted with red spices pulled it all together. It really was too bad that none of it tasted as good as it looked. The brisket was soggy and washed-out, as if it had sat submerged in liquid between slicing. The sad state of the brisket was even more lamentable, given its good smokiness and perfectly rendered fat. The cheap links of sausage were a bit chilly. The little pork ribs were good. A sweet rub covered the still-moist and plenty tender meat. Not much can help meatless beef back ribs, and these weren't a good version. Make a meal out of the pork ribs and the roasted corn here. Hopefully they won't be out of cotija cheese for the corn when you visit.

Sometimes you meet a pitmaster or an owner who is such a nice guy that you want so badly to like their product. Felix was one of these guys. He bought the land, out on the west side of Hidalgo County, which would become **FELIX MEAT MARKET** for thirteen hundred dollars in 1962. He opened up the meat market eleven years later in 1973, after learning butchery at the local HEB grocery, back when they had real butchers. Through the years he taught himself some barbecue skills. He preferred to cook with direct heat from mesquite coals, unlike most of

the other joints we'd encountered in the region, which used smokers for indirect mesquite smoke. He was nearly out of meat when we came in, but he had brisket and sausage left. I knew that it was Hillshire Farm sausage because I saw it lining the entire top shelf of the saddest butcher's case I'd ever seen. The overly trimmed and thinly sliced brisket reminded me of my bad brisket memories in Kansas City. Just as that city relies on sauce for flavor, so does Felix. No, really. In reference to the sauce he said, "That's where the flavor really comes from." If only the fajita meat had still been available. I bet it would have been good.

The mesquite wood they use at **LONE STAR BBQ** in McAllen was expected, but an item on their dessert menu was not a regional specialty—grapefruit pie, made from locally grown Rio Red grapefruits. Rio Reds, which are native to Texas and grow in abundance in the Rio Grande valley, are sweeter even than Ruby Red grapefruits—perfect for pie. And there it was, at the bottom of the menu: grapefruit pie. It was the first thing I ordered.

"We don't sell it here."

"You mean you're out?"

"No, we only sell it at our Mission location."

"Why is it on the menu?"

"I'm not sure. Would you like some cobbler?"

I didn't want cobbler. I sulked away with a container of brisket and ribs. I'd spend the rest of a fruitless evening searching Google for any restaurant in the area that served grapefruit pie. Nothing, and Lone Star's Mission location was closed the next day. I tried to drown my sorrows in smoked meat, but it wasn't worth more than a few bites.

The meat was rubbed with too much cumin and had lost its structural integrity. It was way overcooked. I needed a distraction. The *Bourne* something-or-other was on TV and there were High Life tall boys in the fridge. Good night.

It was before sunrise, but **LA EXCLUSIVA TORTILLA FACTORY**, in Pharr, had been open for more than an hour. We took barbacoa and

· · · SMOKING WOOD · · · · · · · · · · · · · · · · ·

On our South Texas trip, we encountered little variation in the wood used for smoking; it was almost always mesquite. Mesquite is one of the four native Texas woods that commonly appear in the state's barbecue pits, but it takes a special skill to harness the harsh smoke it produces. Mesquite is particularly high in lignin. Lignin is a complex chemical compound. When wood burns, its lignin releases two methoxy phenols—guaiacol and syringol—that impart the flavor and aroma of smokiness. All that lignin produces a harsher smoke from mesquite than most hardwoods. Next on the smoke scale is oak, followed by hickory and pecan, which impart a subtle and sweet smoke.

In the Hill Country, mesquite is also the wood of choice, but it is burned down to coals before use, thus eliminating any of the smoke flavor. Post oak gets the same treatment at a few joints in Central Texas. Indirect smoking using mesquite is prevalent only in South and West Texas, and it can easily go wrong, causing a particularly nasty creosote flavor. The creosote gets even worse if you find a pitman who thinks using freshly cut green mesquite is a good idea.

Milton Peikoff of M & M Firewood, in Alvarado, Texas, is a third-generation Texan. Milton's been working as a wood supplier to restaurants, barbecue joints, and competition cookers since he was fourteen years old, and he understands the smoking quality of various woods like none other. He sells mesquite, but only if it has been aged at least a year, guaranteeing that the volatile oils have leached out of the wood. Some pitmasters do use green hickory, oak, and pecan mixed in with drier stuff as a method of controlling fluctuations of heat or humidity in the pit. Because greener wood contains more water than dried wood, it provides more humidity as the water in it boils off and in turn lowers the temperature of the pit.

In my search I've found the most popular smoking wood in Texas to be hickory. There are many varieties of hickory. Pignut and black bark hickories are commonly found growing in East Texas and are na-

tortillas back to the car, hoping that some bracing salsa might do in place of espresso. The sign out front said they use barbacoa de cabeza on the weekends. It was fine, but once you've had Vera's. . . .

The sun was just up as we pulled into Vera's again. This time we were hungry and got some mixta along with the cachete. There were numerous salsas to choose from, and I wanted to try them all. This was

tive to the area, but the flavor of their smoke can go sour. For this reason, wood suppliers like Milton use hickories harvested in Oklahoma and Arkansas such as bitternut or mockernut hickory, which both age nicely, and also work well as "green" wood. Shagbark and shellbark hickories have a high sugar content, and thus create a sweeter smoke. All of the hickory varieties tend to create sweeter smoke as they age, according to Milton, so well-aged wood is usually preferred.

Along with its cousin hickory, pecan trees (the state tree of Texas) are found in the *Carya* genus. It is the fourth-most-popular smoking wood around the state, but I prefer it when cooking at home because it produces a slightly milder and sweeter smoke than oak or hickory. You'll also find the nuts of the pecan tree in pies and cobblers all over Texas. The Salt Lick even uses soaked pecan shells on the fire in their open pits.

Any kind of oak can be used for smoking; the most popular in Texas is post oak, especially in Central Texas. Post oak grows all over Central, North, and East Texas. Unless you buy your wood from an honest wood supplier like M & M, the post oak delivered to you may have some white and red oak mixed in. White oak and red oak might make fine smoking woods, but if it's the specific flavor of pure post oak smoke that you're after, then you may need to develop a keen ability to identify the species of already split logs. You have to have an eye for the bark and the grain to identify the different species if the leaves are gone. Post oak is so popular in part because it is an extremely knobby tree and therefore doesn't make for good lumber. A few places buck the post oak trend, though, and use red oak or live oak, which is a good dense wood that burns hot and clean and leaves little ash.

Milton offered a last valuable tip about wood quality, which had nothing to do with species: If wood is dirty or smells musty, then it's poor quality. Poor quality wood will only create poor-quality smoke, so you need to maintain a clean woodpile.

a meal to savor. With every taco, I assembled a new combination of salsa, lime, onion, and cilantro. I took a chilipiquin by the stem and ate it whole. Barely the size of a caper, these little suckers pack the heat of a whole jalapeño. It's the only chile to grow wild in Texas and unlike the jalapeño, the chilipiquin is native to the state. I'd like to see it on more menus around here.

After a few excellent tacos, there was a break in the line, and Mando came over to our table. As we had agreed the day before, he brought an eye with him. I envisioned us tilting back our heads and dropping the fatty orb into our waiting mouths simultaneously. Mando had other ideas. He wasn't going to eat this thing unless it was in a tortilla and covered in salsa. He chopped the eye and filled our tortillas. We gave a mock toast and took an optimistically large bite. Our feigned looks of enjoyment quickly turned to laughter. We both felt a palpable sense of relief the instant we finished the fatty tacos, but we had done it. A barbacoa legend and I had shared our first cow eye together. Touching, I know.

After our feast at Vera's, we didn't have the appetite we'd need for more smoked meats, so we took a drive from Brownsville to the end of the map. State Route 4, or Boca Chica Boulevard, reaches all the way to the beach, just a mile or so north of the mouth of the Rio Grande where it empties into the Gulf of Mexico. I parked the car and noticed what I thought were blue plastic bottles littering the beach. As we got closer, we realized that they were Portuguese man o' wars, which look like jellyfish, but are actually a kind of siphonophore. They

··· BARBACOA ·········

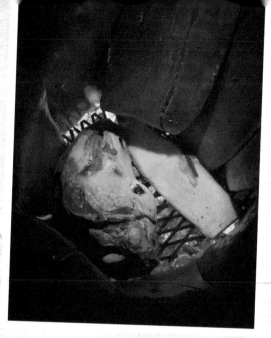

Some months later I would have the pleasure of witnessing the preparation of traditional barbacoa at the West Dallas home of my friend Cesar Coronado Jr. His father, Cesar Coronado Sr., was something of a neighborhood barbacoa king, and they offered to cook for my family and me. In return for the cost of the meat, I was able to witness and document a family tradition and a dying art form.

We met after dark the night before the barbacoa party. Flames were already emanating from the subterranean, concrete-lined pit in Cesar's backyard. The pit was at least four feet deep and about three feet across. A good amount of mesquite had been burning in it for less than an hour, but the heat was already noticeable from several feet away. A pile of soil and a large metal lid sat next to the pit. In between pulls from a Modelo, Cesar Sr. stirred the coals with a long metal pole. He was waiting for the flames to subside, leaving behind a bed of coals about a foot deep. Cesar Jr. acted as translator for his father and me as our conversation began to require more than simple questions and answers. Cesar Sr.'s English was good enough for the construction crews he ran in the Panhandle, but he didn't trust it around a couple of camera-toting gringos. When the flames were gone he lowered a metal grate directly onto the coals. He stacked the maguey leaves (from the succulent century plant, or *Agave americana*) waiting on a nearby table vertically around the wall of the pit. The coals' singed thick bases and peaked tips formed a star pattern in the dirt. He placed a few more leaves on the grate at the bottom of the pit, which he quickly followed with the meat. Cesar Sr. is from a ranch outside San Luis Potosí, in Mexico, where putting whole goats into a pit is the norm, but this would be an all-beef dinner. An entire cow head went in first, then beef ribs, chuck steaks, and rump roasts. None of it cost more than three dollars a pound. No seasoning was added. Cesar folded the leaves over the mound of meat and placed the large metal lid over the pit.

After the lid was secured, we each grabbed a shovel and spread the pile of dirt over the metal lid to act as an insulator. Cesar's little brother tamped down the dirt with a flat metal bar attached to a long handle. When the dirt placement was nearly complete, Cesar Sr. got on his knees and crawled around the pit's perimeter with a flashlight, looking for any escaping smoke and feeling for hot spots in the dirt with the palm of his hand. Another layer of dirt was placed on each of these spots until he was satisfied that the pit was well sealed. The only thing left to learn that night was a lesson from Cesar Sr. on opening a bottle of Modelo with a machete.

Cooking times were irrelevant here. We could have opened the pit as early as nine in the morning, but we were eating in the midafternoon. Cooking meat for that long in a sealed environment with steady heat renders its fat, resulting in incredibly flavorful, butter-tender meat. Once the cameras were ready, we cleared the dirt off the pit's metal lid, then Cesar Sr. carefully swept the top to prevent any dirt from falling onto the meat. With the pit exposed, we began peeling back the maguey leaves, which showed some serious fatigue. The meat mound had settled significantly, but we filled several huge pots as we emptied the pit, our fists full of meat. The lower jawbones from the skull were completely clean, and much of the skull was exposed. We nibbled a bit on the chuck roasts as the pit was emptied, but I wanted a look at the full head as it was removed whole into its own container.

Cesar's mother set a table in the backyard with fresh guacamole, salsas, and homemade tortillas. Salt shakers dotted the table, as it was now time to season the meat—just before eating. We all grabbed some easily tonged chunks of meat from the ribs or the chuck and devoured a few smallish tacos. Finally, the meat from the head had been separated into all of its different cuts and was ready to eat. The cheek meat was plentiful and had its familiar fatty quality. The meat wasn't sopping wet like you'd get from a steamed head, but it was in no way dry. I downed a few fingersful of the meat. It was superb and unlike any other barbacoa I'd eaten. The mesquite coals, the steam from the maguey leaves, and the insulated earthen oven had all come together to create something unique. I was on my fourth taco when Cesar Jr. peeled the tongue (*lengua*) and started slicing. Until my first bite I hadn't considered myself a *lengua* fan, but all that changed instantly. The only cut left to sample was one I had joked about before. *Ojos*. The eyes. These highly prized orbs are usually saved for the elders. Cesar Sr. agreed to split one with me. There were no other volunteers. We plopped the eyes into heavily seasoned tacos. This was my second time at the fair, and the first hadn't been pleasant. I could call *ojos* fatty bits of beef, but they are really beefy hunks of fat. These particular *ojos* weighed in at about a quarter pound per eye. They were not to be consumed like popcorn chicken. They required real chewing. Cesar Sr. and I exchanged a glance, each raising an eyebrow as if to say, "Yep, this tastes as bad as I thought it would. Another Modelo, please."

During this incredible meal, lovingly prepared over a night and a day, I realized how far commercial barbacoa has strayed from its artisanal past. If you check out the operation of most revered barbecue pits from here to North Carolina, you'll see that their process differs little from that of a backyard cook. The scale might be increased, but the methods are the same. The offset smoker you might find in a Houston backyard is hardly different from the steel smoker you'll find at the famous Snow's BBQ in Lexington, Texas. On the other hand, the world of commercial barbacoa is far removed from its roots—how that happened I may never know, but a cow head wrapped in maguey leaves and cooked over coals is so vastly different in flavor and texture from a tray of steamed beef cheeks that it can hardly be considered the same dish. It was that steamed meat that made me struggle with including barbacoa in a discussion of Texas barbecue, but what I ate in West Dallas should meet anyone's definition.

• •

stretched across the beach, their stinging tails trailing behind them. The further we walked, the further we could see them spread down the beach in either direction. There must have been thousands of them, still inflating and deflating as they washed up on shore. They looked like small, translucent blue balloons. The sight was eerie enough, but the popping sound was gut-wrenching. Driving is allowed on that portion of beach—trucks tooled up and down the shore. As they drove over the Portuguese man o' wars the animals popped like asphalt bubbles on a hot country road. Now I was really hungry.

Our next destination was South Padre Island, so we made a big loop back down Route 4 past the Palmito Ranch Battlefield, where the final battle of the Civil War was fought—a full month after Lee surrendered. Communication wasn't so great in those days. Outside Los Fresnos, we pulled over for gas. In the Dallas area you can't go more than a few blocks without seeing a 7-Eleven. In South Texas, the same is true for Stripes. They are everywhere, and most all of them have a **LAREDO TACO COMPANY** location inside. After seeing dozens of them, it was time to try one of their tacos. They had barbacoa. For some reason, Nick bought two. Well-seasoned and tender meat that wasn't too fatty was wrapped in a respectable flour tortilla. They certainly could have been worse, but I wasn't about to tear into the second one. We had some Los Fresnos barbecue to try out.

"Which blog do you run?" were the first words out of Abraham Avila Jr.'s mouth as we walked through the doors of **WILD BLUE BBQ**, in

Los Fresnos. Abraham is a classically trained chef trying to make it in the barbecue world of South Texas, with mixed results. In 2008 *Texas Monthly* had named his joint one of the fifty best in the state, but the customers weren't packing the place. In fact, a month before we left for the South Texas trip, Avila had announced he was closing Wild Blue, but then changed his mind somewhat by modifying the hours to weekends only. By the time I got around to writing this, he'd closed up shop for good.

We could see the gleam in Avila's eyes as he took note of the camera—he was intent on wowing us. It didn't take long for the Tour for Two to arrive at the table, along with some other assorted sides. I make a point not to announce myself in a barbecue joint, but the fact is, even if I am spotted, there's only so much they can do to the meat they've got. That brisket's already smoked, and it'll be another twelve hours before another's ready. Case in point: that day at Wild Blue even the best cuts from the marbled point of the brisket were chewy, with little smoke and too much opaque fat running through them. A line of thick and undercooked fat marred the dry slices from the flat. Luckily, the ribs made up for it. The smoky baby backs were tender and moist, with a nice, sweet glaze. The seasoning was a bit heavy and smacked of a chef's need for thirteen different herbs and spices, but the ribs were good overall. Dark-meat chicken was pleasantly moist and well seasoned—a counterpoint to the dry breast. The skin on both was flaccid. The chef couldn't help but form pulled pork into a cylinder, and it had great smoke and good flavor, but was dry from having been pulled long before. Links of peppery sausage had good smoke and a nice snap. But all of it paled in comparison to the sides and desserts.

Avila's training showed in his insistence on sautéing to order some of the finest green beans I've had anywhere. I also had a great macaroni and actual cheese and some savory corn bread along with it. Dessert was the grand finale. The banana pudding was some of the best I've had; all that was in it was ripe bananas, wafers, and a bit of toasted coconut, which sent it over the edge. How could it be topped? By the finest dessert I've had at *any* barbecue joint. The sweet potato flan was a lesson in restraint and simplicity. I've had yams as a Thanksgiving side dish that were far sweeter than this pie, which was its genius. Avila added just enough sugar to the sweet potatoes to coax out their natural sweetness without obscuring their flavor, which was further enhanced by its subtle spicing. The buttery crumb shell added textural contrast to the whipped, fluffy filling. It was so heavenly it almost made me forget about that brisket. Almost.

A couple of miles away, I'd come to understand why the barbecue they were putting out at Wild Blue was notable for this area. I peered through a sneeze guard clouded from the steam table where the presliced meats were unceremoniously aging at **JB SMOKEHOUSE** in Los Fresnos. The scene made me question my own mantra of trying any joint once. I was beyond full and the bite of rib I had just taken wasn't pleasant. We were out in the parking lot, so instead of risking regurgitation, I just spit it out onto the gravel.

There isn't any notable barbecue on South Padre Island, but I still

· · · **RANCIDITY** ·

How you store meat that's been cooked or smoked has a huge effect on its flavor. When meats, especially those high in fat, are exposed to heat and air for prolonged periods of time, it begins to oxidize. Eventually, oxidization will turn fat rancid. Fats higher in saturated and monounsaturated fatty acids don't oxidize as quickly, so they take longer to turn rancid, whereas fats high in polyunsaturated fatty acids oxidize more quickly. Pork, for example, which is three times higher in polyunsaturated fat than beef, begins to oxidize and taste old more quickly than beef.

Even if cooked meat is exposed to oxygen and heat, there is one sure way to slow its oxidation: Smoke it. Smoking meat has long been a traditional method for preserving it. Smokehouses served three purposes: flavoring the meat with smoke; preserving it by eliminating moisture in the meat; and discouraging flies and other pests from eating the meat by way of a thick cloud of smoke. While I don't advocate treating your meat poorly once it's cooked, you can at least have the knowledge that a hefty dose of good-quality smoke will help repel the elements determined to turn it rancid, no matter how poorly it is stored.

· ·

wanted to check it out since I had never been there before. Padre Island is the largest barrier island in the world, and just one of many that protects the majority of the Texas coast. The only item on Nick's and my agenda was to find a bar on the beach and get a drink. I don't remember the name of the place we found, but the rum punch was strong and the pours were generous. We walked it off along the beach, but if Nick was hoping for romance, all he got was an ass load of more dead Portuguese man o' wars. Leaving the island, we drove back over Laguna Madre on Texas's second-longest bridge, the Queen Isabella Memorial Highway, on our way to San Benito.

LONGHORN CATTLE COMPANY was situated along San Benito's highway service road. They tried hard to separate themselves from it and instead tried to emphasize a ranch-like ambience with a corral out back that held horses and cattle. In addition to mesquite-smoked barbecue, they offered mesquite-grilled steaks. This bit of fanciness required a waitstaff and an amuse-bouche of their "world-famous" pinto bean soup. The beans were good, as was everything that wasn't meat. A side of home-made potato salad, with plenty of egg and pickles, was great. The slaw was crunchy and had a pleasingly sweet dressing. But I expected more from the meat after seeing the all-wood-fired J & R smoker out back. But not even a smoker could have helped the sliced deli turkey or the Polish sausage that fell far short of memorable. The ribs were well cooked and didn't fall off the bone, but the smoke just didn't come through in the slightest. The brisket had picked up some of the smoke, but the meat was chewy and underseasoned. The overly lean slices were a testament to why I don't like a barbecue joint with a waitstaff. When you order your meat directly from a knife man, you can make specific requests he can grant in real time; a waitstaff eliminates that option. Otherwise, I could have steered clear of those dry lean slices and asked for something from the fatty end.

From San Benito we headed back to McAllen and hit up the home base, then headed right back out to meet a friend of a friend. Blanca and Tobin have a nice, large home on a cul-de-sac, and there's a Soccer Mom sticker on the SUV in the driveway. Nick and I broke the ice by pulling out a couple bottles of wine that featured a pig on the label, while Blanca fried and sliced some of the Alsatian sausage we'd bought back in Castroville and warmed a few tortillas. A dab of salsa verde topped off our multicultural snack.

We talked briefly about missed barbecue opportunities that we wouldn't have time for tomorrow and the quality of the spit-roasted goat in Reynosa. We had our passports, but they urged us that this wasn't a good time to cross, and that they hadn't ventured across in years. With daily news stories of violence in nearby border towns, they viewed the Border Patrol as a welcome necessity, not as the menacing figures we'd manufactured in our minds. The next morning as we drove north, we passed through the final Border Patrol checkpoint of the trip just south of Falfurrias. It was February 27 and their year-to-date seizures were already 71,602 pounds of drugs and 3,620 undocumented aliens. An impressive number for sure. It made me realize the real good done by the Border Patrol, but I still exhaled as we passed through the checkpoint without incident and left the occupied territories of South Texas behind.

Falfurrias was worth a look since we were passing through, but the only hint of barbecue we caught sight of was a hand-painted sign on Rice Street directing drivers to Rudy's Bar-B-Q (not an outpost of the statewide chain) a few blocks off the main road. The sign on the front door noted that it was open on Friday and Saturday only. It was Monday. I was especially disappointed, given that their sign also touted the best cabeza plate in town. My disappointment was short-lived, however, after a quick trek around the rest of the small town made it pretty clear that there wasn't any competition.

We continued east on State Highway 285 as we headed out of

town. Our route was a little out of the way, but it would take us to the southern border of the Santa Gertrudis Division of the famous King Ranch, one of the largest ranches in the world—and part of the enduring mythos of Texas. We hoped to get a look at some Santa Gertrudis cattle, the first US developed breed of beef, but we didn't spot a single head of beef. The King Ranch, which covers six counties, isn't contiguous. It's made up of four large sections called divisions, only two of which share a border. In the middle of all that King Ranch territory sits the town of Kingsville. In 1904, fifty years after the formation of the King Ranch, ranch manager Robert Justus Kleberg hired a surveyor to lay out a town site three miles from the main gates of the King Ranch. The town served mainly as a stop for the new railroad running through South Texas, but in time it became the location of a Naval Air Station and the campus of Texas A&M Kingsville. (And while you might think the school's mascot would be a Santa Gertrudis bull, especially given one of the campus's major thoroughfares is Santa Gertrudis Avenue, their mascot is . . . a javelina.)

CB'S BAR-B-QUE in the middle of town wasn't quite what we expected; the joint is housed, somewhat bizarrely, in a geodesic dome with a stone facade and brown-shingled roof. But when we pulled up, right at opening time, it was pumping out a steady stream of mesquite smoke, so I hoped for the best. Owner Jerry Miller built the joint seventeen years ago and has been smoking with mesquite ever since. A photo of Macho, the prize-winning twenty-five-hundred-pound King Ranch bull, hung on the wall, but Jerry wasn't cooking Santa Gertrudis beef. The fatty brisket on our plate had been sliced, sadly, with the grain—

making for some tough beef. The fat tasted oxidized, as if it were yesterday's brisket, but it was worse than that: they'd been closed the day before, so it was more likely Saturday's brisket (later, after our meal, Jerry invited us to the back, where we watched him slice some lean brisket for a customer's sandwich. The resulting slices were so dry they looked more like unsanded lumber than beef). Two big rib tips came on our plate. I'm not sure how, given all the smoke rolling out of the smoker, but the ribs lacked smoky flavor and they too were dry. The sausage casing was so dry it was nearly flaking off the filling, which crumbled as I cut the link. How the jalapeño-creamed corn turned out so bland, I'll never know. The baked beans, on the other hand, had plenty of seasoning, but they seemed mismatched to the dish—I prefer my beans not to taste like Christmas.

Having seen about all that Kingsville had to offer, we drove north toward Corpus Christi. We made an obligatory stop in Robstown to pay our respects to the site of Joe Cotten's Barbecue. A year earlier, Joe's had burned to the ground. An iconic barbecue joint renowned around the state since its opening in 1968, it should have been a must on our itinerary. I

was sad that I had never had a chance to try it. All that was left of the place was its old sign along the highway with a tattered banner that read Open Mondays and an empty gravel lot where the restaurant once stood. It was Monday, but we'd have to move on for barbecue.

A detour through the west side of Corpus Christi led us past a billboard for

LOU'S LANDMARK SALOON advertising
"Bar-B-Que, Etc." Although Lou's wasn't on our
itinerary, it was about lunchtime, and Nick and
I agreed that a drink to wash it down couldn't
hurt. A sign above the door claimed we were
about to enter the oldest establishment in
Texas. When I asked the bartender, Erica, about
the claim, she said it had something to do with
the owners' getting the first liquor license in
Texas about sixty years ago. No matter the
seemingly dubious claim, the bar definitely had a
lived-in, old-school ambience. The kitchen was
about to close up, but Erica brought us two
sandwiches to go with our cold Lone Stars. A few bites
of the crusty and dry sausage and mushy brisket was
all I needed. Nick was busy shooting photos and
returned to find a sandwich waiting for him. He gave
me an inquisitive glance and I shook my head. Erica
was happy to bring some peanuts to munch on. The
place alone was worth soaking up. A few rope lights
above the bar and some pool table lights seemed to be
the only sources of illumination in the bar. Although
smoking is banned in bars and restaurants in Dallas,
the smoke wreathing the air at Lou's seemed to go just right
with the sad country music playing on the jukebox. The wooden
soffit above the bar was covered in stapled photos of every
playmate from the late seventies and early eighties. Men who
looked like they didn't plan to be anywhere else this afternoon
were shooting pool. They gave us both some recommendations for
local smoked-meat joints and a bit of ribbing for taking photos of
the food and drink. It was a good reminder to just be in the

moment. Nick set his camera down and we sat at the bar enjoying our cold mugs of beer. Lou's was quite likely the coolest bar I'd ever just happened upon. I could have stayed there for the long haul, but Nick reminded me of the task at hand. We had barbecue to discover.

As we stumbled out of Lou's I noticed a Bill Miller BBQ location across the street. It's a well-known fast-food type barbecue joint complete with a drive-through that's based out of San Antonio. They're better known for their fried chicken than smoked meats, and I wasn't *that* hungry. **THE BAR-B-Q MAN RESTAURANT** was right down the street. The fenced-in parking lot was empty in midafternoon, but there was plenty of meat stacked up along the ordering line in anticipation of a crowd. There was a five-meat sampler plate on the menu, so we chose a little of everything. The deli ham and deli turkey weren't anything special, but the ribs were quite good. They had a nice bark, with good smoke, though they could have been a bit tenderer. The brisket had a good crust and smoke ring, but its fat was poorly rendered and the beef needed more time in the smoke to tenderize. The sausage was really good, though; the casing had a great snap, and the link was nice and smoky.

Malcolm DeShields, the Bar-B-Q Man's owner, stopped by the table to see how we liked the food and agreed to give us a full tour. He was an older man, neatly dressed in a crisp, short-sleeved plaid shirt tucked into

blue jeans and shiny black leather shoes. His hair, gray at the temples, was slicked back, and he showed some bold fashion sense with an orange feather extension that had been woven right in. At first the conversation was polite and reserved. He showed us his collection of Texas vanity license plates with all the variations of BBQ Man that can be imagined. Old wooden chairs salvaged from Joe Cotten's had "Cotten's-BQ" carved into the back, the "-BQ" an homage to the legend that the word *barbecue* came from an old cattle brand that used a bar (-) followed by the letters B and Q. According to *Legends of Texas Barbecue*, it was Joe Cotten who was partially responsible for perpetuating the myth that *barbecue* came from the French phrase *barbe à queue* (beard to tail), so I found it particularly ironic that his old chairs promoted a different etymological myth.

An antique US Border Patrol sign hung above the double Southern Pride smokers built into the kitchen wall. From the moment we stepped outside the doors to see the mesquite pile, there was a lit cigarette in Malcolm's hand. He became more demonstrative while talking about the old days with his friend Cecil Cotten, who had owned Joe Cotten's.

It seemed as if they'd shared a long friendship—and plenty of drinking stories. The huge pink pig out front had been a gift from Cecil, who had it delivered hand-painted with the Bar-B-Q Man logo. As for the rumors of a new Joe Cotten's joint opening in Corpus Christi, Malcolm had little hope (a takeout-only version has since opened). Other rumors abounded that the insurance money from the fire had gone to Cecil's ex-wife, which would make a rebuild tough.

We mentioned our previous stop, at Lou's, and he laughed—he and his dad started out cooking barbecue there. They grew too big for the place in 1977 and went out on their own, which was when they built the Bar-B-Q Man. Malcolm seemed like a person who offered honest opinions, so we asked him about a few of the barbecue joint recommendations we'd received at Lou's. He shot them all down, but mentioned a place called Sam's, out west of town. We knew we had to go, but would have to wait until the next day—they were closed on Mondays. Another joint we wanted to try, Mr. G's BBQ, which was being run by some Joe Cotten alumni, was also closed on Mondays. We marked it for a future visit.

We were going to spend the night in Corpus Christi, but we only had another stop or two on our itinerary. The rain was keeping us from seeing anything scenic, so we opted to take a little trek to **VAN'S BAR-B-Q**, an hour away in Oakville. The picturesque dump sat right along the Interstate. The dining room was half full in the early evening. A cordial woman waited on us. I sat down, eagerly anticipating a plateful of their highly touted mesquite-smoked meats, but disappointment lurked in my future. The ribs had no bark, little seasoning, and not much smoke. A nice link of

Pollok's sausage was barely warm, and it had no smoke and a limp casing. The brisket looked good, but the black crust was limp. The meat tasted as if it had been sitting around in its own grease for most of the day. The fat was poorly rendered and even stringy. It wasn't tender beef—not even the excellent sweet-and-spicy mustard sauce could save it. A home-made pecan pie could have saved the meal, but it came out molten-hot, its melted filling pooling on the plate from a too-long spin in the microwave. It was a long drive back to Corpus.

We hadn't had much good barbecue the previous day, so we woke ready to conquer the final leg of our South Texas trip. It was still too early in the morning for our ambition, though, so we drove downtown to walk along the Corpus Christi seawall. As we drove along Shoreline Boulevard, I cranked up Robert Earle Keen's "Corpus Christi Bay" to get our juices flowing. We continued out to the bridge over to Padre Island and drove to its northernmost point, Port Aransas. We'd been hoping to take in some great ocean scenery as we drove, but the fog was so thick we could barely see a hundred yards ahead of us. Fortunately, by the time we reached Port Aransas the fog had lifted, which made it easier to find **RUSTY JEEP HICKORY PIT B-B-Q**. We drove straight from Rusty Jeep's drive-through to the Port Aransas car ferry, where we would have to make a rapid assessment of the food: the ferry's quarter-mile route only takes about ten minutes. We didn't need much time, though: the dill and cucumber salad could have doubled for a

soup course; a cold, loose corn salad, with diced peppers and onions and a vinegar dressing, was much better. Huge ribs with a good level of hickory smoke were dried-out from being cooked the previous day. Even drier, the flavorless brisket wasn't worth the stomach space.

After circumnavigating the bay, we came all the way back into Corpus Christi just in time to arrive at **MR. G'S BBQ** as it was opening. It was only a few minutes after eleven, but the tables were already beginning to fill. Nick and I ordered our food to go. The man who took our order, Jesse Pena, had been a waiter at Joe Cotten's for forty years. After the fire he retired, but sitting at home didn't agree with him; he figured he would die sooner if he wasn't working, so he gathered up some of the staff from Joe Cotten's and opened Mr. G's BBQ. Jesse brought the sausage maker at Joe Cotten's, Carlos, along to Mr. G's and Carlos brought his sausage recipe with him. Jesse gave no word on where Cotten's pitmaster had gone, but Mr. G's used mesquite wood on an all-wood-fired smoker, just like they had at Cotten's. Though the brisket had taken up some of that smoke, it was a good two hours or more shy of being done. The ribs were decent; although the rub was too heavy on the powdery ingredients, the meat was tender and well cooked and the smoke level pleasing. But the truly excellent link of sausage delivered. Juice shot out of the link as I took a big bite from the end. The casing was taut and its juicy filling wasn't too fatty; a great seasoning mix, heavy on the cracked black pepper, heightened the savory pork-heavy mix. With sausage that good and their Joe Cotten roots, the place was definitely worth a return visit, even if the brisket and ribs hadn't blown me away.

Heading west out of town, we drove to Calallen. Smoke was billowing from a barbecue trailer at the corner of FM Road 624 and County Road 73. Out front, a metal sign incised with a pig announced **SAM'S BAR-B-Q/ LIDIA'S ROAD-KILL**. Two different people had recommended this joint, so we had high hopes. They were quickly dashed when we struck up a conversation with the pitman, who proudly showed us some cold bricks of brisket, which he was planning to warm up. They had been smoked

on Sunday. It was Tuesday morning. There certainly seemed to be an aversion to serving freshly smoked meats around these parts. We ordered a large combo plate anyway. I requested broccoli salad and Tex-Mex rice as my sides, but the person taking our order quickly warned us away from the rice. He explained that as it was the only thing the owner made himself, he insisted that it stay on the menu, but that it "sucked." Thankfully the pasta salad was a great replacement. The broccoli salad reminded me of home. Most every cookout back in Ohio includes a broccoli salad like that one: blanched broccoli mixed with sesame seeds, chopped red onion, and raisins and tossed with a sweet-but-vinegary mayo-based dressing. Sam's Bar-B-Q's was an excellent version. Of the meats, the V & V sausage was easily the best item. It's a beef sausage made in Central Texas that has heavy black-pepper seasoning, and this version had good smoke and a nice snappy casing. The three-day-old brisket was as dry as I expected, and the huge spareribs were about the same. Sadly, I could see the potential in both meats, so who knows what the stuff could have tasted like fresh.

In the town of Odem, we found the red metal building that housed **FERMIN'S SMOKED BAR-B-QUE**. Business cards on the counter served triple duty for the family trucking business, their Mexican restaurant, and the barbecue joint. The food was cheap, but that's about all it had going for it. Mesquite smoke rose from a screened-in pit room out back, which we could see from our trunk-side picnic, so it was puzzling how so little of that smoke got into the meat. More old and dry brisket was clearly yesterday's meat. I was starting to gather that the regional style was to let the meat rest for a full day in the cooler before serving it. The ribs were so underdone they were hard to chew. Although the V & V sausage was pleasing, its ubiquity was getting old. A side of Spanish rice was good, but the beans were startlingly bland. Until then I hadn't realized it was possible to make such flavorless beans. I've had tap water with more oomph.

Refugio offered us no refuge from bad barbecue—its lone barbecue joint was permanently closed. Although Goliad was also a barbecue-free  zone, we had to stop there. Though I've lived in Texas for twelve years, I still feel like I'm earning my Texas stripes. But even many natives don't have the Goliad pride they should. Any Texan who feels like more of a Texan after visiting the Alamo needs to make plans immediately to go to Goliad. The rallying cry we know so well today—"Remember the Alamo!"—is missing a crucial part. The Texan soldiers who defeated Santa Anna at San Jacinto were all yelling "Remember the Alamo! Remember Goliad!" It was the massacre at Fort Goliad, on Palm Sunday 1836, that cemented Santa Anna's reputation as a cruel take-no-prisoners leader. In late 1835, in the early days of the Texas revolution, Texan soldiers seized the fort from the Mexicans; the first declaration of independence of the Republic of Texas was signed there that December. The following March, the Mexicans recaptured the fort after defeating the Texans at the Battle of Coleto. Colonel James Fannin surrendered the fort after accepting a written agreement that he and his men would be treated as prisoners of war. But Santa Anna, then president of Mexico, ordered all the survivors executed. In all, 342 Texans would be massacred that Palm Sunday. Less than a month later Santa Anna surrendered to Sam Houston at the Battle of San Jacinto and the nation of Texas was born.

Just outside of Goliad, in Fannin, **MCMILLAN'S WORLD FAMOUS BAR-B-Q** is proud to announce, "Quality is our goal. Our aim is 98 percent of our goal, and we don't take shortcuts." They have a sign at the counter

that says so. I must have experienced that 2 percent sliver where their aim was off. I've said before that humility and good barbecue go together. There's little of it that comes out of Louis McMillan. From his restaurant's World Famous sign to stories of cooking for the world on the Washington Mall, Louis will talk about how good his barbecue is as long as you'll listen. When I opened our takeaway box on a picnic table outside, the brisket did look very promising. There was a black crust and a red smoke ring. Sadly, the sauce I'd requested on the side covered the meat. A thick line of fat had been left on the brisket slices, which was a good sign. I was still hopeful. I pinched a slice, and the fat was so undercooked that I couldn't even squeeze through it. The slices themselves took significant effort to pull apart. The brisket was at least a good three hours from its sweet spot in the smoker. The ribs had the opposite problem: they were overcooked, and the meat was falling off the bone. The meat did have a little of the smoke from the pecan, oak, and mesquite mix, but it was hard to taste the essence of it underneath the heavy sauce. A tepid link of sausage had barely been warmed through, rounding out a plate of decidedly poor barbecue. I hope he served something else on the National Mall.

One thing Louis McMillan did get right was that a stop at **MERLE'S**

BAR-B-Q on the south side of Victoria was not worth it. A few engraved silver-trophy platters adorned the walls, evidence of triumphs at past barbecue contests. They must not have competed using the oversmoked dry meats that I was served. I was sure it was yesterday's brisket. Chewy fat clung to every slice. The one rib I managed to get through tasted like an ashtray and the sausage was dried-out. The only redeeming thing at Merle's was the lemon bundt cake. On the way out, the owner made sure to tell us "I've cooked ten thousand pounds of brisket, so they say now that I'm a pitmaster." I'm not sure who "they" are, but quantity alone doesn't get you that title. I know the meat we got on that day didn't come from a master, and I guess the rest of the town caught on, too, since Merle's closed a few months later.

On the other side of Victoria, we encountered the lone bright spot in a couple bad days of barbecuing. As we walked up to **MUMPHORD'S PLACE**, I smelled the unmistakable aroma of direct-heat barbecue. We started our visit at the source of the smoke, with a tour of the pits from Bubba Barnes, who is one of a few pitmen there. There were several pits going, and each had its own given name, like Goliath and Chicken Smoker. A mix of mesquite and oak coals provided the flavor, and Bubba provided the know-how. When I asked him how he could tell when a brisket was done, he handed me his fork and told me to start poking the briskets from right to left. As we got to the briskets on the left side of the cooker the fork slid in

more easily. "Those are about ready," he explained. Who needs a thermometer?

A four-meat plate piled high with ribs, brisket, turkey, and sausage was soon in our grasp. Employee-recommended green beans and potato salad rounded out the plate. Direct-heat cooking doesn't make for incredibly tender brisket, but the meat wasn't tough. It had a pleasing chew, a simple seasoning, and great flavor from the coals. The ribs were thin on the meat and a bit dry in a good way. Their overall flavor from the rub and the smoke was excellent. A dip in their home-made sauce (the only secret they kept from us was this recipe), which I guessed was a mix of tomato, mustard, and maybe Italian dressing, took care of any moisture issues. But my favorite meat there, the turkey, needed no help. Mumphord's had started with a whole turkey breast, applied a salt-heavy rub, and laid it over the fire. The meat was perfectly tender, moist, and succulent. A German sausage, from Schulenberg, was nicely smoked, with good snap to the casing and a pleasing spice mix of salt, pepper, and garlic.

The fresh green beans, in a sauce heavy with salt and butter, were still crisp, and the potato salad, while obviously home-made, contained too much sugar. A better option for a sweet tooth were the desserts made by a woman from a local church. A slice of chocolate cake with cream cheese icing was perfectly moist. It was a great way to top off one of the best meals we'd had in some time. Our stop at Mumphord's restored my faith in the barbecue of South Texas, at least a little.

We were nearing the day's end as we closed in on Cuero. I consulted the map as we turned down tiny Taylor Road, thinking I must have misread the directions, but **STRIEDEL'S FINE MEATS** was right there. Roland Striedel, Striedel's owner, greeted us with the bad news that they no longer served barbecue. The work was just getting too hard, so they now offered only their house-smoked meats: bacon, beef jerky, and fresh and dried sausages. That was plenty for us anyway, so we grabbed a few items and started munching right there at the counter. One of the items,

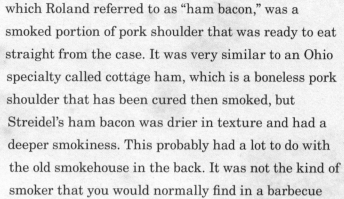

which Roland referred to as "ham bacon," was a smoked portion of pork shoulder that was ready to eat straight from the case. It was very similar to an Ohio specialty called cottage ham, which is a boneless pork shoulder that has been cured then smoked, but Streidel's ham bacon was drier in texture and had a deeper smokiness. This probably had a lot to do with the old smokehouse in the back. It was not the kind of smoker that you would normally find in a barbecue joint. In fact, it was more like a smokehouse. The small building was about the size of a generous walk-in cooler. A small cast-iron stove sat in the middle of the room, giving off more smoke than my lungs could take. Racks sat on either side of the stove, lined with various sizes of hooks for different meats. On our visit, the smoker was full of sausages.

As we enjoyed some summer sausage, Roland filled us in on the local history. Just down the road was the Taylor Cemetery, which was where Josiah Taylor was buried. He was the patriarch of the Taylor family who comprised one faction in the longest and bloodiest feud in Texas history. For ten years, from 1866 to 1876, the people of DeWitt County were forced to choose sides in an internecine feud between the Taylor family and the Sutton family, who made a habit of ambushing, lynching, shooting, and beating each other. Even the Texas Rangers were unable to put a stop to it. When the feud finally came to an end, it had claimed the lives of thirty-five men, some of whom were killed by the famous Texas outlaw John Wesley Hardin, whose sympathies were with the Taylor family.

The Goliad Massacre may have provided the rallying cry for the soldiers at San Jacinto, but the start of war for independence can be traced back to Gonzalez. In 1831 the Mexican government loaned Gonzalez a small cannon for protection against Indian raids. After the outbreak of hostilities between Mexico and Texan settlers, Mexican soldiers crossed the Guadalupe River to retrieve the cannon. In response, the feisty Texans raised a flag above the cannon, emblazoned with the taunt Come and Take It. The small-scale skirmish that ensued is considered the first battle in the Texas Revolution. The only thing that led us there was to come and take some lamb ribs from the **GONZALES FOOD MARKET**. It was getting late and the young employees staffing the joint were more worried about finishing up their cleaning than serving good barbecue. I should have known better than to order just a half hour before closing, but it was my only option. A girl stopped mopping long enough to compile my order, and Nick and I sat down to a few lamb ribs, along with some sliced brisket and house-made sausage. The lamb ribs were tasty but very dry. The brisket was about the same, but the considerable amount of well-rendered intramuscular fat kept it from being as dry as the lamb. A link of well-spiced sausage was easily the best item. The juiciness of the link was barely contained by the snappy casing. It had both good smoke and great seasoning. Next time I'll show up earlier.

Our trip was coming to a close. We'd had a fun seven days, but Nick and I were both anxious to get back home. Just south of Lockhart, the car's odometer ticked over two thousand miles for the trip. Still, I had to make a stop in Lockhart to see the square and the Caldwell County Courthouse at night, since I'd only been on the square during daylight hours. Just down from the courthouse, I noticed the lights were on at **BLACK'S BARBECUE**. It was still open. We may have found bits and pieces of some good barbecue on this trip, but I was seeking a full-blown smoked

reward. The oak-smoked beef rib they cut for me at Black's weighed in at around a pound and a half. With its peppery crust and lusciously rendered fat, it was barbecue heaven, and I ingested it with primal abandon. It was the sort of meaty manifestation I needed to keep holding fast to my belief in smoked Texas meat. The last week had been a long string of mesquite-smoked disappointments, but with that beef rib in my hand I felt restored. My words as a prophet of Texas barbecue couldn't fall on deaf ears while I wielded that divine beefy staff.

7 Days, 2,232 Miles, 30 BBQ Joints

CHAPTER SIX

WEST TEXAS: FROM FORT WORTH TO EL PASO

The draw of the open road, the possibility of seeing the Marfa Lights, and most probably the need for a bit of a break from his young and energetic toddler brought my friend Sam into the fold for this leg. El Paso was our westernmost destination for this trip, but we had to start where the West begins, as goes the official slogan of Fort Worth, Texas. Fort Worth is also home to the easternmost outpost of **COOPER'S OLD TIME PIT**

BAR-B-QUE, the chain famous for using direct-heat cooking. That Robb Walsh named this direct-heat cooking method the "West Texas Cowboy Style" in his book *Legends of Texas Barbecue* is a bit of a geographical misnomer. We *were* in Cowtown eating cowboy-style barbecue, but of the thirty joints that we'd visit between here and El Paso, we would find only two others using direct heat, and they were places owned by the same family. Smoking with indirect heat was the real theme of barbecue in West Texas, and mesquite wood soon became a constant.

Cooper's provided a fine spread of beef ribs, brisket, and another giant Big Chop, but none of it seemed to equal the quality we had found at the original in Llano. Knowing that this was an overgrown copy of the original meant to mainly serve tourists to the Fort Worth Stockyards certainly tainted my opinion, but Hill Country barbecue is just better in the Hill Country.

We did find a rare hybrid of the direct- and indirect-heat methods just a few dozen miles west of Fort Worth at **HOG'S HEAVEN BBQ** in Weatherford. Hog's Heaven bucks Texas tradition and uses a pit designed to smoke meats, but with a smoldering hickory wood fire (rather than hot coals) several feet below the cooking rack. It's odd, but then pitmaster Charles Huggins and his custom-made pit both hail from Alabama. After ten years running Pete's Boyz BBQ in Huntsville, Alabama, he followed his brother to

Weatherford to bring his version of southern barbecue to Texas.

Initially, Huggins's barbecue did not include brisket. Texas barbecue without brisket is nearly unthinkable, but Huggins just wasn't a brisket fan. After about a year of chiding from regular customers he finally added it to his lineup, but on the day of our visit it still hadn't made it onto the large menu tacked to the wall beside the counter. We were nearly finished with our pork and poultry meal before Huggins offered us a couple of slices. He said it was the fatty nature of brisket that he finds undesirable, so I immediately asked for some extra fatty slices from the brisket point. The slices had developed a thick, black bark and a deep smokiness over the smoldering hickory fire. The meat was a bit tired from being wrapped and stored for too long, but this was highly respectable smoked beef, especially coming from an Alabaman.

Showing its Alabama roots even more clearly, Hog's Heaven serves an Alabama white barbecue sauce alongside its smoked chicken. The white sauce tasted of buttermilk and Italian dressing, and it added a pleasant tang to the crisp and juicy chicken quarter. Pork barbecue in the South is a deep tradition, and the moist and smoky pulled pork at Hog's Heaven would have made Charles's daddy, whom he learned to cook from, proud. What was most surprising were the spot-on Texas-style ribs. Rather than cooking them to the point of disintegration and slathering them with sauce, these St. Louis–style ribs allowed for a clean bite through the meat. The bite took little effort to release, but the rest of the meat didn't pull away from the bone along with it. A subtle rub complemented the ribs' smokiness rather than overpowering it. Almost as an afterthought, I took a healthy bite from a cob of smoked corn. Juicy kernels popped in quick succession as a buttery sweetness tinged with more than a hint of hickory filled my mouth and nostrils. This wasn't some wimpy cob grilled with a protective husk wrapping. It was a naked cob that had been subjected to direct and aggressive smoke, and I wanted more.

It was a good thing I managed to hold off on that corn, though, because just twenty-five-odd miles later, we were chowing down on some great barbecue. Though it's not part of the Hashknife Ranch nor is it on the Chisholm Trail, the **HASHKNIFE ON THE CHISHOLM** in Peadenville still has the absolute best name of any barbecue joint I've encountered. It was especially easy to overlook the moniker's geographical inaccuracies when "Big Jim" McLennan, the Hashknife's owner, explained that his great-grandfather John N. Simpson had been the owner of the old Hashknife Ranch in Abilene, Texas. Back in 1880, along with a few other ranchers, Simpson convinced representatives from the Texas & Pacific Railroad to run their rail lines over land that they owned. A year later the rail lines came, and the city of Abilene was born.

The fact that the great cattle drive trails through Texas owed much of their demise to the new access to rail that Mr. Simpson helped usher in added a splash of bittersweet irony to the story, which Jim clearly appreciated. In just half an hour of conversation, Jim filled us in on the history of the isolated highway intersection that pretty much constitutes the town of Peadenville, the legends of Native Americans who were lynched on trees still standing within view of his front door, and a chapter in what was surely a full book's worth of oil-field stories. As we listened, we enjoyed a bevy of smoked meats.

Jim McLennan learned Cajun food techniques from the legendary Louisiana chef and food historian Poppy Tooker, and while he does griddle up chicken-fried steaks inspired by the legendary Mary's Cafe in Strawn, Hashknife is first and foremost a barbecue joint. Jim fed us thick slices of brisket with an unapologetic layer of fat still clinging to each slice. Each slice was eminently smoky from a mix of oak and pecan wood. The pork shoulder was pulled rather than chopped.

The moist mound of meat had a good mix of crust, fat, and meat, which made for an excellent combination of textures and smoky, sweet, and salty flavors. A few slices of overly salty and too-finely-ground Miiller's sausage from Llano, Texas, weren't impressive, but the ribs more than made up for it. The St. Louis–cut pork ribs had a midnight-black crust studded with black pepper and a subtle sweetness from the brown sugar in the glaze. We ended on an even sweeter note with a trio of fruit cobblers and a helping of Oil Field Pudding, a vanilla pudding fortified with Cool Whip and what Big Jim jokingly refers to as "gas drip" from the oilfields, which could have just been corn syrup, given how sweet it was. He wasn't willing to share the secret ingredient with us, but he was more than willing to show us around his smoker out back. It was a trailer-mounted Southern Pride gas-fired smoker, the likes of which experienced rural pitmasters don't normally use. Jim was going against the grain, and he wasn't apologetic about it.

To be fair, what Jim McLennan serves at Hashknife on the Chisholm doesn't resemble roast beef. His brisket is one of the few exceptions to the rule, which proves a Southern Pride *can* put out good barbecue. He makes no secret that his decision to use a gas-fired pit was due to its general ease of use. Given his age and the restaurant's small staff, he might not be able to continue smoking meat if he had to use a traditional, wood-fired pit. He also understands that his gasser, as some people call them, comes with built-in handicaps. There is no way to disable the gas burners, even once the wood is burning, and he burns plenty of it. Smoke came pouring out of the doors when he gave us a peek inside the pit, and his wood supplier makes plenty of trips out to his remote location. Also, once the smoke is created, it is recirculated within the cooking chamber rather than being drawn over the meat from the fire to an exhaust valve, which is the principal around which most wood smokers are designed. He mitigates

···· ROTISSERIE OVENS ···········

Stainless steel rotisserie smokers are finding their way into barbecue joints across the country. Like the labor-intensive steel-and-brick smokers found in most of the historic joints in the state, these commercial, gas-fired pits use wood, but their propane assist can do all the work of actually cooking the meat if you let it, turning them into nothing but a fancy Ferris wheel for meat housed in a large, expensive oven. Southern Pride and Ole Hickory are the two powerhouses of the industry, and the design of their pits allows for a set-it-and-forget-it attitude. Where a traditional all-wood-fired pit requires stoking in the middle of the night and a watchful eye during all other hours to maintain a consistent temperature, a gas-fired smoker can keep things humming along at 225 degrees with no attention required. Gas burners heat a chamber at the back of these pits, where wood can be burned to create smoke, but the wood in this case is completely unnecessary to cook the meat. I've heard barbecue joint owners brag about how little wood they have to use with these types of gas smokers, but funneling your money to the gas man instead of a wood supplier is not the way to produce well-smoked meat. These pits don't necessarily result in bad barbecue, but they can create the illusion for many inexperienced or unskilled pit minders that they're actually smoking meat properly just because the meat always reaches the desired temperature and the results are consistent. However, smoking cuts like brisket require that you smoke *beyond* doneness—that is to a point where the meat provides signs of completion that can't be measured by a thermometer, but only by the well-trained eye or feel of an experienced pitmaster. Smoking meat to a certain "magic" temperature might produce consistent results, but those results will most likely be nothing more than consistently mediocre. In Wyatt McSpadden's *Texas BBQ* (a beautiful collection of smoked-meat photography), John Morthland writes that "those 'exact same results' lack the deep, smoky, primal flavor of real barbecue—in fact, the stuff tastes suspiciously of roast beef." If it's roast beef you're after, then feel free to let some high school–aged part-timer set the wheels in motion on your rotisserie smoker. But if great barbecue is the goal, then you'll need a real pitmaster no matter the smoking apparatus.

the possibility of stale smoke by occasionally opening the smoker's doors to release the "used" smoke during the smoking process. No matter the cooking methods employed at the Hashknife, we were happy to have been fortified with such good barbecue, which would prove more and more elusive as we traveled further west.

As we pushed on toward Abilene, we stopped briefly at Fort Griffin State Park to take in the view of the park's grazing longhorns, which the state husbands as part of the official State of Texas longhorn herd. Did I mention that we take our beef seriously here in Texas? After the Civil War, many soldiers returned to Texas with no job prospects. They did find, however, an abundance of undomesticated longhorn cattle. It became lucrative to round up these wild cattle and drive them north to markets in Kansas, Missouri, and Nebraska, where they were sold, then taken by train to Easterners hungry for beef. Popular north-south cattle drive trails, such as the Chisholm or the Shawnee, became well worn across the state. The most heavily used of these trails was the Great Western Trail, which crossed the Clear Fork of the Brazos River right next to Fort Griffin as it made its long route to points north. We followed the trail along US Highway 283 for a bit, but had to reluctantly bypass the mesquite-grilled steaks at the Fort Griffin General Store. We were in need of mesquite-smoked brisket.

In a generic-looking strip mall just down from Abilene Christian University sits **BETTY ROSE'S LITTLE BRISKET**. It was one of three joints on the itinerary for Abilene, so we went with an order we could duplicate easily at all three: sliced brisket, ribs, and sausage—the holy trinity of Texas barbecue—along with beans and slaw. Only the pleasantly dry pork ribs and ranch beans, both heavily flecked with black pepper, were worth noting. The mushy brisket slices were light on flavor and had captured little of the mesquite smoke; the slaw, with a mayo dressing, was soupy; and the sausage was that abomination referred to as "German sausage" in these parts. Any German sausage artisan would take offense after tasting the salt-saturated slices dripping with fat, which exhibited a texture closer to a frankfurter than a good bratwurst. The same order at **SHARON'S BARBEQUE** provided marginally better meat, but at the bottom of the plate I found a seasoned and smoked rib bone that contained not even a speck of meat. The ribs that did have meat had a pale bark that highlighted the cracked black pepper in the seasoning. Moderately tender and adequately moist, they weren't bad. Both the sausage and the brisket were sad. A long tanning session under the heat lamp had caused the casing on the sausage to become brittle and crunchy. The brisket was so dry that it crumbled into a heap on the plate when I tried to pick it up. Its crust had also dried to a crisp, and the mesquite smoke was barely evident. Unseasoned beans and dripping-wet slaw did nothing to make up for it. A neon sign down the street led to Sharon's ex-husband's place, **JOE ALLEN'S** (they had an ugly public divorce that split the barbecue business into two nearly identical operations for each to run). Joe Allen's proved only to be the best of a bad bunch, and at least had flavorful sausage (though it's hard to argue that the flavor of maple is a positive attribute for smoked sausage in Texas) and a very good crispy chopped slaw that had a sweet-but-subtle dressing. Thick spareribs needed more time on the smoker. Since the recent and sudden demise of the storied Harold's Pit Bar-B-Q, there was no further reason for us to stick around town, so as the sun was setting, we made a trail to Buffalo Gap just south of Abilene.

We had little hope that the Bar BQ Barn, in Buffalo Gap, would be open at this late hour, but from their website we knew the mesquite and the neon would be glowing at **PERINI RANCH STEAKHOUSE**. After having hit six barbecue joints already that day, we opted to split a thick rib eye steak, along with some jalapeño poppers and a pork rib appetizer plate. I like a place where a half dozen mesquite-grilled, pepper-crusted ribs count as just an appetizer. The direct-heat cooking made for a sweeter flavor and slightly drier rib. They were easily the best we'd had in the Abilene area. Perini's signature sauce is nearly as famous as its steaks. Although it tasted like a compromise between steak sauce and barbecue sauce, we used it on neither, per the recommendation of our server, Jessica, who suggested we save it to dip the bacon-wrapped jalapeño poppers in. I'd forgotten just how much Sam could consume in a day, and he continued dipping until the plate was empty. We soaked in the last bit of a warm evening, then called it a night.

Two thousand twelve had been the year of no winter in Texas. At least it had been until March 8, 2012. At 8:00 A.M. the temperature was 45 degrees and getting colder. Gusts of icy wind buffeted Nick, Sam, and me as we descended the stairs of the Motel 6 in Sweetwater. We had been well on our way toward spring without so much as a hint of cold weather, but a massive cold front had come in from the west and covered most of Texas. The cold front would last for three days, erasing the vast blue skies West Texas is so well known for and replacing them with skies so overcast that the sun could not be located. The low temperatures transformed the rain to sleet. As the guy who chose the dates for this epic West Texas adventure, I was the one to whom Nick and Sam gave relentless grief as we weathered the storm and tried to imagine all of the stars we should have been seeing in that West Texas sky.

As we waited for the windows to defrost and the car to warm up, I questioned my decision not to pack a coat. My car's thermometer showed that it was 45 degrees outside as we reached the Interstate bound for Odessa. **MESQUITE BEAN BAR-B-Q**, in Merkel, opened early, so we made it our first stop. The joint wasn't registering on Google Maps, so

we drove through downtown Merkel searching for it. More than a few boarded-up storefronts flanked the empty IGA grocery store on Merkel's main street. Just like the rest of the still-viable businesses in town, we found Mesquite Bean out near the highway. Owner Urban Bright said he'd lived in the area for twenty-some years, to which I added that he must've seen the town change quite a bit. He nonchalantly replied it hadn't really changed, minus the Dairy Queen's moving out near the highway.

A short tour of the Mesquite Bean pit room confirmed we had just eaten yesterday's brisket, as Urban Bright was in the middle of wrapping a brisket to be placed in the cooler, which he would serve the next day. He

...DROUGHT ....

We encountered so many dying small towns in our trek around Texas that finding a rural town not in decline was an item of note. The phenomenon wasn't a recent development, however. The first "dying off" of the Texas small town had begun more than fifty years earlier, during the drought years between 1950 and 1960. In his essay "When the Sky Ran Dry" historian John Burnett noted that during this decade—the worst stretch of drought the state had ever seen—the number of farms and ranches shrank from 345,000 to 247,000. The state's rural population decreased from a third of the total population to just one quarter of it. The lack of viable grazing lands forced ranchers to sell off their herds and move back to the city, sometimes for good. The trend continues with Texas's urban population reaching eighty-five percent of the total per the latest census.

In 2011 Texas experienced the driest seven-month span in the history of the state. Decent cattle grazing land essentially disappeared, and the price of hay skyrocketed. Ranchers were forced to either invest more money in their cattle than they'd ever get out of them, or unload their skinny, malnourished cattle (which are sold by weight) at reduced prices, due to all of the other cattle flooding the market for the same reason. The worst of the drought has passed—for now—and there's finally some water, grass, and hay to feed cattle, but trying to get back in the game is tough. Ranchers who want to continue have to take the measly sums they received in 2011 and try to rebuild while cattle are going for close to double the average price at auction. It's a losing game that I fear many will choose to stop playing.

talked up the carne guisada breakfast taco more than anything else, and it was certainly more enjoyable than the cheap commercial sausage and thick-sliced deli ham. Mesquite remained the wood of choice. We warmed ourselves by the pit as Urban described his weekend-only "country club" steakhouse in nearby Trent and told sordid stories of Merkel's recent past. We were a day early for the Rattlesnake Roundup, which Urban blamed for decimating the local rattlesnake population, eliminating the main predator of large rats, which were rapidly proliferating, on his ranch. For the roundup, hundreds of snakes are literally rounded up from the surrounding ranches by hunters who get paid by the pound, and the snakes are then brought to Sweetwater for a grilled or batter-fried demise. I was happy to stick with brisket.

Access to early-morning barbecue is almost a right in Central Texas, where the meat markets serve smoked meats for breakfast, but in West Texas most places wait until eleven o'clock to open their doors. Sitting in the gravel parking lot of **BIG BOY'S BAR-B-QUE**, in Sweetwater, we cranked the car's heater until we saw the Open sign light up. Owner and pitmaster Gaylan Marth greeted us at the ordering window inside and quickly got to work on our meaty sampler plate. What came out were *two* plates full of brisket, sausage, and

ribs, along with a slice of his wife's home-made key lime pie.

Big Boy's served two kinds of ribs. My Ribs (the "my" in question being Gaylan) were slices of thick country ribs, which aren't really ribs at all, but are more like pork steaks. The meat was tender and the fat was soft, but the well-seasoned slices still offered pleasant resistance to my bite. Your Ribs were St. Louis–style ribs that had a thick, sweet glaze that had been applied after cooking. The meat was expertly cooked—it had just the right amount of give and the perfect level of moisture. The flavor of the mesquite coals was unmistakable, shining through the peppery glaze that added to the whole, rather than dominating the flavor profile of the meat. Slices from the lean flat of the brisket were on the overtender side, while the fatty

slices from the point were chewy. In fairness, Gaylan only served us the fatty slices because I insisted on it. He was reluctant to do so and up front about it, because he knew his hot-and-fast cooking method failed to render the considerable amount of fat in the cut, which he usually reserved for chopped brisket. An excellent peppery sausage came from Klemke's, just up the road in Slaton. Gaylan had kissed it with just enough direct heat to give it a nice, snappy casing, and the well-balanced seasoning blend of garlic and red and black pepper did the rest.

When I asked what wood he used to smoke his meat, he quickly rebuked me. He cooks meat, he doesn't smoke it. Smoking is a form of drying and preserving, so why smoke the meat if you're going to eat it today? That was the mantra he had learned from his German grandfather and father. Gaylan cooked all of his meat in steel cookers of his own design. In efficient German fashion, the small size of the pits had been determined by the size of the steel plate he could buy. They were designed to be put together with a minimum of cuts and without any wasted steel. The architect in me enjoyed the thoughtful design. When the tour was complete, we dove into the fluffy key lime pie, which had a thick, buttery, home-made graham cracker crust. The recipe certainly didn't hail from Germany, but it was a welcome bright spot on a very cold day.

For days leading up to this trip I had repeatedly described to Nick the unending fields of huge steel windmills we would encounter. Just west of Sweetwater, we veered off I-20 toward Roscoe, where a frenzy of windmill erection in 2008 and 2009 created a corridor along State Highway 84 where you couldn't look in any direction without seeing a windmill. I had witnessed the windmill forest months earlier on a road trip back to Dallas from Colorado, and I was anxious to get my friends' reactions to it. To my dismay and slight embarrassment, a fog thicker than the whipped cream on the key lime pie we had just eaten obliterated everything more than a few yards from the highway's shoulder. We could see just a few of the enormous windmills; their giant blades disappeared eerily into the fog as they spun. The crosswind became so fierce as we made our way further north that I had to steer into the wind just to stay in our lane. By that point the wind speed was so great that the windmills we could see had stopped rotating, automatically shutting down for safety. Countless tumbleweeds collected along the roadside fences.

Our detour to see all those windmills meant that we had to piece together a path along some back highways to get to Big Spring. Luckily, Sam had proven a bit more adept at the role of navigator than Nick ever had, so I didn't even have to threaten the dangerous maneuver of pulling out my own iPhone to check the map while driving. The wind made the hour-long drive to **BIG JOHN'S FEED LOT**, in Big Spring, feel especially lengthy and we were practically starving by the time we arrived. We waited for our order at a table underneath a window painted with the likeness of Big John. He carried a cleaver in one hand and a steer over

his shoulder, presumably on his way to butcher and smoke it. When the food arrived at our table, it painted a prettier picture: a pile of smoked meat rested on the blue enamel plate. The red-checked tablecloth on which the plate rested completed the homey picture of Americana. It was almost too pretty to eat, but we managed. Pull-apart-tender, the brisket was not. While a bit chewy from being undercooked, the thick bark and deep, rosy smoke ring held plenty of mesquite essence. When I asked the pitmaster about the brisket's doneness, which I deemed a bit lacking, he noted that it was deliberate. In the tall cabinet-like cooker in the back where the ribs, brisket, and pork loins all lay on metal grates directly above mesquite coals, the brisket will fall apart too easily at 190 degrees (according to him), so he keeps it at 180. The higher temperature is the normal target for a finished brisket to ensure tenderness. Whether it was done to my taste or not, I appreciated the deliberate decision. I also appreciated the generously thick ribs kissed with a sweet sauce. They too needed a little extra chewing, but they were worth the work. The dry, flavorless pork loin was another story, but the excellent German-style jalapeño sausage was gone before I knew it. The sausage came from Jackson Brothers Meat, in Post. I learned that the secret to the sausage's juiciness lay in a five-gallon vat of brisket drippings held in the smoker. Big John's "marinated" the links in the vat for thirty minutes before finishing them off on the cooking grate.

As we made our way out of town, we stopped at **HOG HEAVEN B-B-Q** on Business Route 20, just before it joined back up with the interstate. It looked like they were smoking the meat with indirect heat in a huge steel pit. By that point I knew it was likely that it would be mesquite fueling the pit, but I wanted to be certain. Normally when I visit an independently run small-town joint, I have the pleasure and the privilege to talk to the proprietor or pitmaster while I order, but that was not to be at Hog Heaven. The two staff members on duty were pretty much clueless about both the cooking method or the wood used. In response to my questions they gave me a look that suggested they were pondering for the first time that wood had actually been burned to create this meal. At least the kid cutting the meat knew the sausage came from the Sysco truck.

As the various meats were being sliced, I was encouraged to help myself to a vat of bacon-wrapped jalapeños called Armadillo Eggs. As I lifted the lid of the Crock-Pot, I got a nostril full of what can only be described as wet-ashtray smell. I waited to try one at the table so as not to blatantly offend. As it reached my nose the same natural reflex that would keep you from ingesting a lit cigar went to work. I took a bite anyway. How they managed to pack so much oily creosote into one bite is beyond my comprehension. My first reaction was to spit it out, and the second was to tell Sam and Nick that they had to try it. They refused, and instead munched away on baby backs so sweet they may as well have been dipped in simple syrup. The Sysco jalapeño sausage was a salt log studded with Velveeta bombs, so it was a wonder that the brisket was mostly right. I requested both a slice from the flat and a fatty end cut. Both were well smoked, without a hint of ashtray flavor. The well-rendered fat was woven between the crisp, dark edges of the fatty brisket. A bit more salt and seasoning would have elevated it from good to great. The lean brisket was a little tougher, but they had built a good foundation with some decent beef. Hopefully they'll get rid of the Armadillo Eggs.

With Big Spring behind us, we made a shallow ascent up the Caprock Escarpment as we climbed onto the vast mesa of the Llano Estacado, the sheer flatness of which had lulled me to sleep back in the Texas Panhandle. Midland—the halfway mark on our journey west—sits at the northern edge of the Llano Estacado and in the middle of the oil-rich Permian Basin. Originally named Midway Station due to its position at the midpoint between Fort Worth and El Paso on the Texas & Pacific railway line, Midland's identity was forever changed by the discovery of oil there in the 1920s. The epitome of a boom-bust town, Midland has stared down the barrel of its demise numerous times during its history as both oil production and oil prices have soared then plummeted.

The whole state is currently enjoying a boom in natural gas and oil exploration, but the skyscrapers that shot up in downtown Midland in the early eighties still stand mostly vacant, as oil company executives can happily monitor their wells remotely from Houston. One thing they won't be able to get through those fiber optic lines, though, is some home-made sausage from Sam's Bar-B-Que. And that's a pity.

I've experienced two crowning achievements in my life related to barbecue. The first came when I identified that a barbecue joint was using direct heat for its ribs and indirect smoking for its briskets, and the pitmaster confirmed I was right. The second happened the day Nick could identify the difference. He was a relative newcomer to the barbecue game

when I roped him into riding shotgun with me, camera in tow, but in just a few short months of concentrated carnivorous consumption he had gained knowledge that had taken me years to hone. When we stepped out of the car at **SAM'S BAR-B-QUE**, he just said, "Mmm. Smells like direct heat." He was right.

Sam's was empty as we came through the front door, which was less a reflection of its popularity than it was the time of day. It was five o'clock—too early for dinner and too late for lunch. The scant business meant that the pitmaster, James, aka Stinky, had the time to give us a guided tour. Stinky had started out as an apprentice to Sam's owner, Lee Hammond, when he was just ten years old. Before he was out of high school, he started working the pits for real. When we mentioned we were on a barbecue road trip he insisted that we try the Odessa location the following day, and we promised to tell "Mama" hello for him.

Because there's only one large steel barrel pit at Sam's, and two rounds of brisket come out of the pit every day, they do their cooking in stages. The direct heat from the mesquite coals results in brick-red St. Louis ribs with a good inch of meat tinted pink by the smoke. It took a little effort for my teeth to remove the meat from the bone, but the fat was well rendered, which helped the meat remain moist. The brisket had some chew to it as well, but it was well seasoned. The mesquite flavor kissed the white meat chicken as well, but its flaccid skin wasn't worth the calories. The only home-made sausage we would encounter in West Texas was at Sam's (and again the next morning at the original Sam's, in Odessa), and it wasn't a typical Texas-style link. The casing hadn't crisped and still had some elasticity. The beef-and-pork mixture was ground coarsely, so it tumbled out of the casing when squeezed. A spice mixture reminiscent of Chicago links included plenty of salt and sage like you might expect in a breakfast link, but Jimmy Dean isn't usually rendered over mesquite coals. There's a reason Sam's has weathered the lean years in Midland, and they should be in good hands with Stinky making that sausage and manning the pits.

We sampled a few other barbecue options in Midland, but none served up smoky goodness equal to the quality of the meat we got from Stinky. While **JOHNNY'S BARBECUE** didn't wow us in the smoked-meat department, they did make up for it with their nostalgic interior decorations and their hospitality. Out front, pig statues and plenty of neon graced the exterior of the fifties' era building; out back a couple guys manned an all-oak-fired Oyler rotisserie pit. The Oyler is the only commercial rotisserie pit that doesn't heat with gas, and Johnny's may be the only joint within a hundred miles of Midland using oak in their smoker. Inside, the walls were painted with murals depicting pigs in any number of activities, including chomping on ribs (owner Roy Gillean puts to rest concerns of cannibalism by insisting that the pigs are holding beef ribs). We'd seen so many signs by that point that depicted pigs cooking, serving, or eating barbecue, that it barely fazed us. Bright-red heat lamps so blinding that they obscured the meat almost completely echoed the neon outside. Although I could see the meat being carved, it was hard to know what I would get until I—and my plate—reached the register. What I got were overcooked and oversalted spareribs that were shy on meat. A brittle crust from too much time under the lamps made for an unpleasant, chewy texture. Tough brisket with plenty of thick, chewy fat on each slice didn't help anything, and an overly fatty sausage link hadn't taken on much of the oak smoke. On the south side of town, a stop at the sprawling bar and barbecue joint known as **KD'S BAR-B-Q** proved even less impressive. Hopefully the neighboring city of Odessa would have more to offer.

Jerry and Lee Anne Caddel, the parents of close friends, were not only gracious enough to put us up for the night but also to guide us to their favorite barbecue joint in Odessa, as well. **ROCKIN' Q SMOKEHOUSE** is their Friday-night hangout spot, so they showed some real barbecue dedication by taking us there on a Thursday. The joint seemed ripe for chain expansion. Cute teenaged girls took our order at the counter. In fast-casual style, we were given a number and found a table while we waited for our order to be called. Nothing we received was poor quality or

bad exactly, but it was certainly crowd-pleaser barbecue—in other words, barbecue aimed at the lowest common denominator. The ribs were tender, with a sweet and peppery glaze; the jalapeño sausage contained a hint of spice and a mound of salt; and the brisket had only enough smokiness— barely any, in other words—to let you know it wasn't baked. The moist, tender, all-white-meat pulled chicken mixed with a sweet sauce would be a perfect kid's meal, but it all lacked that unique touch of a pitmaster's hand and the honest smoke of great barbecue. It had been a long day of barbecuing, so we headed back to the Caddels' for some home-made brownies and warm beds. Tomorrow's forecast didn't sound too good.

Thankfully, the wipers took care of the sleet on the windshield the next morning. I hadn't set out on the trip prepared with a windshield scraper—hell, I hadn't even brought a jacket. Leaving the cul-de-sac on the east side of Odessa, we entered a working-class neighborhood of postwar single-family homes. A windswept, treeless landscape conspired with endless chain-link fencing to produce a visual cacophony of trash composed mostly of plastic grocery bags held tight to the fence lines by the chilly, relentless breeze. On the south side of downtown, we finally located **SAM'S BAR-B-QUE** on Dixie Boulevard—it was one of the only barbecue joints in our quest that did not show up on Google Maps. The original Sam's location occupied the back half of an old convenience store. The menu had a few more soul food items on offer than the Midland location, but the barbecue was largely the same. The skin of the chicken leg was a bit crisper, but a couple of spareribs were dry and tasted like yesterday's meat. The soul food seemed more promising, and the smell of fried chicken was hard to resist on such a cold day. I had to have some. The steaming-hot meat covered in crunchy skin was tender but needed a sprinkle of salt. So did the simple okra and cabbage, which injected some much-needed nutrients into our vitamin-starved diet.

The cold drizzle continued, so we opted for takeout from the drive-through window at **JACK JORDAN'S BAR-B-QUE**. The aged menu's prices had been revised a few times via duct tape and Sharpie. I went for the standard two-meat plate of brisket and ribs. I'd tried their cheap commercial sausage before when a good friend from Odessa had come to visit me in Dallas. Lindsay Caddel (the daughter of our previous night's hosts) knew about my love of smoked meat, so a few years earlier she had brought a fresh order of Jack Jordan's barbecue as a carry-on on a flight to Dallas. It was still warm when it hit my kitchen counter. Maybe the kind gesture has clouded my memory, but it was better then, even after the long voyage. On the day we were in Odessa the ribs had a dried and cracked exterior covered in a sweet sauce that provided much needed moisture. The brisket showed little evidence of the mesquite smoke in which it had been smoked, and the meat was chewy to boot. We quickly moved to the next destination in East Odessa.

THE ROSE BAR-B-QUE was little more than a shack clad in particleboard. A number of women offering up varying degrees of hospitality were running the place, taking orders at both indoor and outdoor windows. With the chill in the air, we made our way inside for a quick bite of mesquite-smoked meats. Because we would be eating nonstop throughout the day, the three of us split a single plate of food. When our waitress delivered our order to the table, she became confused and thought she owed us two more of the same order. We waved off her generous offer, but she still insisted on bringing out a few catfish filets and a bowl of Frito pie. After working through the pile of meat and a large bowl of German potato salad that consisted of what seemed like all the ingredients in a loaded baked potato whipped together, we came to a consensus that the fries and banana pudding were great. In fact, the crisp potatoes dipped into the cream pudding would be enough to bring us back for another visit, but the brisket, ribs, and sausage were all forgettable.

At this point we'd been wading through city streets for far too long. We yearned for small towns and the open road. A few miles outside of Odessa we came down off the Llano Estacado and into the vast openness

of the Trans-Pecos, which lies within the Chihuahuan Desert and is the most mountainous and arid part of the state. This sparsely populated region of Texas encompasses an area roughly the size of South Carolina but contains less than a fifth of its population. If we needed any reminder that we were in the desert (other than the in-your-face isolation), there were also a few sand dunes for the climbing. In the bitter cold, with my hands in my pockets, I ran up one for the first time in my life. I had tried to do it once before, at Great Sand Dunes National Park, in Colorado, but my young daughter accidentally threw sand into her eyes about ninety seconds in. Uncontrollable crying ensued, and we doused her face with water and left. As I crested that West Texas dune, I could feel every heartbeat in my wind-chilled, reddened, and quickly numbing ears. After emptying our shoes of sand, we set out to warm ourselves with smoked meat.

Monahans is one of many dying towns that we passed along Interstate 20. Closed and collapsing motels lined the old and little-used business route through town. Back down toward the interstate, a red metal building that resembled a barn housed **PAPPY'S BAR-B-Q**. At the counter the knife man hoisted a whole brisket out of a warming drawer below the counter. As it hit the cutting board, it shuddered slightly then recoiled back into shape, betraying its lack of doneness. A tender brisket will collapse on a cutting board as if it had just exhaled, so I knew I was in for some chewy beef. Its lack of seasoning and smoke only amplified its poor texture. Thick ribs were also tough, overly salty, and missing even a hint of mesquite smoke. When I asked for a recommendation between the original sausage and the hot link, I received the helpful input that I should get the hot link if I liked hot things. The hot link turned out to be little more than a soggy, mildly spicy wiener. Hopefully, Pecos would provide something to warm our souls.

Israel "Pody" Campos had a steady job as a police academy instructor in Austin until cutbacks eliminated his position. With few prospects in the capital, he moved back home to Pecos, bought an old Laundromat, and transformed it into a barbecue joint with the help of a few friends handy with a welder. **PODY'S BBQ** hit their stride in just six short months of business. Out back, two traditional offset smokers burning cherry wood and pecan handled most of the meat while a cylindrical behemoth with a

bottom-mounted firebox and a lazy Susan–style rotisserie inside was dedicated to briskets. As with most all the West Texas barbecue joints we visited, the briskets were smoked with mesquite, but Campos also threw in a little oak for sweetness. That made Campos the first pitmaster I'd found in the state who used four different kinds of wood to smoke just three kinds of meat.

When we ate at around 3:30, the brisket had been steaming in its constrictive foil wrapping for a few hours, so the meat tended toward spongy and soggy, but the black crust held an intoxicating smokiness. Even better were the tender and sweet strips of fat lining each slice. Show me a piece of smoky beef fat that melts on the tongue, and I'll show you a good brisket. A subtle sweetness on the jet-black spareribs didn't mask their smokiness. Usually a barbecue joint's attempt at a spicy sauce involves adding some cayenne or pepper sauce to their original recipe, but this one came with visible warning signs. Chunks of habanero the size of BBs floated in the thin sauce. A refill on iced tea was in order before I dove in, and before long my nose was running. The only cure was some thick and cheesy hominy, whose diced green chiles offered a cooling effect compared to the sauce.

The tingle on my tongue remained as we ventured further into the board-flat landscape. After listening to Charlie Robison's song "Loving County" on repeat for a good part of the trip, we were obliged to take a side jaunt up to the Loving County seat of Mentone. A cigarette-puffing clerk at the gas station, the only functioning business in town, was not impressed by my Loving County T-shirt, which I'd acquired at a Charlie Robison concert a few months earlier. Sitting outside the squat brick Loving County courthouse, we pondered the fact that in the late 1860s, more people came through Mentone on the Goodnight-Loving Cattle Trail than the scant nineteen people who inhabit it today. And Mentone is the most populous spot in Loving County, which is the least-populous county in the United States. If you're looking for isolation, this is the place to be: 677 square miles and 82 residents.

The Davis Mountains began to rise from the horizon as we left the desolate plains behind in the rearview. Our next barbecue stop was a few hundred miles away, well beyond that night's destination of Fort Davis. As nightfall approached, our anticipation grew keener for the star party we'd be attending at nearby McDonald Observatory. Sitting smack dab in the middle of nowhere, the observatory is known for the spectacularly dark sky—untainted by light pollution—arching above it, allowing for glorious star gazing. It was just our luck that the night was so completely overcast that we couldn't even see the full moon. Drinks were in order.

Fort Davis rolls up the sidewalks around eight, so we drove the twenty miles to Marfa. I didn't really expect to see the mysterious Marfa Lights—the floating "ghost" lights the land east of town is famous for—so I took advantage of another phenomenon unique to the place: total darkness. Halfway between Fort Davis and Marfa, on a dead-straight road, I turned off the headlights. Even though I knew what was about to happen, the moment I hit the lights, my heart pounded in those few seconds of the most complete darkness I had ever experienced. Even more enjoyable were the gasps of my unassuming passengers, who were scared shitless. Let's just say the fear helped us catch our second wind, which carried us to the neon beacon of the **LOST HORSE SALOON**, which simply read Beer. The dim light barely illuminated the painted letters below: B-B-Q.

Pool balls cracked the silence. A figure stood behind the bar, but I hesitated to order as I took in his features. Ty Mitchell was tall and lean. A long scar led from his eye patch to his bushy mustache, all of which were cast in shadow by the brim of his cowboy hat. A plaid shirt with pearl snaps was tucked into well-worn Wranglers. When he asked for my order, I half expected him to say, "Draw!" A couple of Lone Stars into our stay at the Lost Horse, the stereo began blasting Toby Keith's Christmas album (it was March). Ty rushed to switch his iPod to a different song, only to have a twangy version of "Winter Wonderland" invade the bar just three minutes later. Given the comic relief, I gathered the courage to ask him about the barbecue. Because the demand in Marfa for smoked meat is anything but steady, he usually waited until enough locals were clamoring for it before firing up the smoker. He had to know he would sell out, given the slim profit margins—which further suffered from Ty's insistence on using seasoned post oak trucked in from parts east. (Mr. Mitchell has a fondness for the famous Kreuz Market, in Lockhart, where he once lived. They use post oak. Attesting to the fact that barbecue preferences are hard to reengineer, he sees no reason to use anything else.)

The next morning found Sam, Nick, and me scurrying down a small mountain to the old site of Fort Davis. We had only an hour to dedicate to the well-preserved pre–Civil War fort before our date with Donald Judd. In addition to being a barbecue fanatic, I'm also an architect. Even during my schooling in Louisiana I'd been programmed to lust after an art-filled communion with Marfa, Texas. Back in 1971 Judd—the renowned minimalist artist—moved from New York City to Marfa. He bought a decommissioned fort, which he used for large-scale art installations—his own and others'. Since his death in 1994, the Chianti Foundation has maintained the site, which is home to a fantastic collection of modern art. We spent several hours exploring the grounds, as the bleak and overcast morning gave way to hints of sunshine. When the group broke for lunch the clouds literally parted overhead as we waited in line for Marfalafels at the **FOOD SHARK**, a food truck that's been ballyhooed by *Bon Appetit*, CNN, and the *New York Times*. Jaime Madrid, a Marfa local and Chianti guide, joined us for lunch and ordered two Marfalafels for himself. The Marfalafel shouldn't have worked, but it did. Impeccably crisp orbs of fried chickpeas rested in a giant tortilla. Crunchy buttermilk slaw and spicy home-made barbecue sauce topped off the falafel balls, and the whole

vegetarian mishmash was then fittingly tainted with two thick slices of bacon. Bursting with what should have been conflicting flavors but was instead a harmonious mix of savory textures, the Marfalafel was certainly filling, memorable, and delicious—but decidedly not barbecue.

With lifted spirits and rapidly thawing bodies, we completed our art tour in the sunshine. Winter in Texas was over, but our trek west was not yet complete. A brief stop at the Prada Marfa installation just outside Valentine was followed by a long drive past an oddly placed pecan grove that stretched for miles across the desert. When we hit the town of Van Horn, we swung west on Interstate 10, heading for Sierra Blanca, just a half hour down the interstate but on the other side of a time zone. **CURLY'S BBQ** sat along Sierra Blanca's main drag. A tiny yapping dog and a surly, chain-smoking woman named Teresa—who turned out to be the owner—were the only other occupants inside the humble adobe structure. "Watchya doin'?" she asked us condescendingly between puffs. "Taking photos" was my curt response. "Well, no shit."

After the warm welcome, Teresa took our order then proceeded to hover over the table while we ate, a smug look on her face as she awaited what she assumed would be positive feedback. A three-meat combo featured some dry pork shoulder, barely respectable sliced brisket, and sad slices of commercial sausage. Teresa was especially inquisitive about the sausage, which I said I didn't care for. I guessed correctly that it was Hillshire Farms brand and she confirmed, noting her love for the fatty, salty, and thoroughly homogeneous links. A plate called the Curly's Special proved to be a pleasing mound of roasted poblanos, juicy and smoky chopped beef, and melted mozzarella cheese. It was almost as good as the superb onion rings and the hand-battered fried okra. When I mentioned that beef ribs at Cattleman's Steakhouse were in our near future, Teresa insisted we try her treasured beef ribs, which were, in her opinion, better than anything we could get in the region. The ding of the microwave clued us in on the nature of the treat we were about

to receive. The beef ribs she brought out were pitifully overcooked. The meat fell off in a heap as I lifted the bone. A strange medicinal aftertaste followed the overtly smoky flavor. Surely Cattleman's could do better.

Although **CATTLEMAN'S STEAKHOUSE** is widely reputed to be the best steakhouse in El Paso (if not all of Texas), nary a glimpse of the city lights can be seen from its actual location in the countryside just beyond

Fabens, Texas. Just when we began to think we must have missed it, a collection of buildings appeared on top of a hill. Just driving up and around the grounds to get to the parking lot seemed like an adventure. Once inside the palace of meat, I quickly realized just how enormous it was. Just to get to the host's stand it seemed like we must have passed a hundred or so folks waiting patiently for a table. While Cattleman's functions mainly as a steakhouse, there are a few mesquite-smoked meats on the menu. A large combo plate of beef ribs and sliced brisket was available, as were barbecue beef cubes. The cubes are essentially burnt ends of brisket. The smoky, crusty bits of lusciously fatty beef went down with ease, even after a full day of eating. In true West Texas style, roasted chiles were served alongside the meat, providing a nice counterpoint to the beef. The large beef back ribs needed more time on the smoker if they had any hope of getting tender, and the thick, bland slices of brisket were missing the moisture and flavor of the barbecue beef cubes. Either way, they were leagues better than the Curly's beef ribs.

The sun had set by the time we reached El Paso, our westernmost destination for the trip, and we weren't sure if any of the barbecue joints on our itinerary would still be open. To my surprise, unlike most other cities in Texas, El Paso was a late-night barbecue town. Nine o'clock was the earliest closing time of the joints on the list. From the online reviews, Chris's Brisket seemed the most promising, but they were closed on weekends. That left **SMITTY'S PIT BAR-B-Q** as our first Saturday-night destination. Ominously, the "Pit Bar-B-Q" portion of the neon sign appeared to be burned out. Our three meats à la carte order came quickly, and I ferried it outside for a car-trunk picnic. The neon glow of the strip mall that houses Smitty's overwhelmed any visual cues as to the quality of the meat. Even eating blind, it took only a few bites to know that we'd be moving along soon. Both the beef and pork ribs were shoe-leather chewy, while the brisket was so horribly overcooked that it amounted to barely more than a salty mass, with the mouthfeel of a wet towel. Not a trace of mesquite smoke was evident. My throat wouldn't let me swallow. I took a glance at Sam and Nick, who quickly rebuffed any need to try it for posterity, and spit it back into the container from whence it had come.

Any hopes we sought to renew at **SMOKEY'S PIT STOP** were quickly dashed. I could practically feel the chewy, unrendered fat getting stuck in my teeth as I watched them slice off a few pitiful morsels of undercooked brisket, while the oversalted beef and pork ribs hovered just above edible, resulting in a quick stroll to the nearest Dumpster. Ever a group of smoked-meat masochists, we made a third stop, at **RIB HUT**. The striking A-frame structure towered above the street, but an advertisement for a twelve-inch cod hoagie special did little to boost our morale. Yet again, we placed another order at the bar, and ate another car-trunk meal, but at least the ribs proved to be respectable. El Paso was now three-for-three in joints that stayed open past nine, served beer and beef ribs, and smoked with mesquite, but as the closest option for New Mexicans to get their Texas barbecue fix, El Paso was a big barbecue disappointment.

I awoke the next morning filled with trepidation. My friend's parents were putting the three of us up for the night, and we had stumbled in long after dark. The father, Ron, had a military background, and I wasn't sure how he felt about our shenanigans. I greeted him with the warmest good morning my weary body could muster. When he asked about our plans for the day I couldn't help but think about the 450 miles between us and our next bed, in San Angelo. During a quick breakfast at Good Coffee (Note: they do not have good coffee), Ron and Catharine mentioned that we might want to check out Border Monument No. 1, which marks the westernmost point of the Texas-Mexico border (as well as the border between Texas and New Mexico). The monument was just west of town, at a site they described as difficult—maybe impossible—to access, which intrigued us. As soon as we polished off our huevos rancheros, we piled into the Audi, following Ron and Catharine's car out of town and up a dirt-and-gravel road that hugged the mountainside.

The first of three Border Patrol trucks on the road waved us on while radioing the next two guys to back off the road and let us pass. Up ahead, a white masonry obelisk about twelve feet tall rose above a concrete pad. A metal strip bisected the length of the obelisk's base. On

one side was the United States, and on the other was Mexico. We all
posed for the obligatory one-foot-in-each-country photo op in between
admiring the looming green sign which read Boundary of the United
States of America. A Mexican flag swayed in the breeze just beyond it.
For more than twelve hundred miles to the east, the Rio Grande forms
the border between Mexico and the United States, but from this point
west, the boundaries of the Gadsden Purchase—the 1853 acquisition
of almost thirty thousand square miles of land by the United States
from Mexico in order to build a southern route of the transcontinental
railroad—define the border.

The plaque on the monument reads: "This is Border Monument No. 1,
the first of 258 such obelisks that dot the desert borderlands all the way
to the Pacific, some 698 miles westward. Mexico lies to the south, about
three feet away, just beyond an improvised wall of rocks piled a few inches
high. The rest of Texas lies to the east, its most distant point farther away
from here than the last border monument, which sits outside San Diego,
California."

We were closer to San Diego than the eastern border of Texas? We
had a long return trip ahead.

From Border Monument No. 1, we drove up the Transmountain

Road, which cuts through the Franklin Mountains outside of El Paso and provides spectacular views of the sprawling city below. As the road crested the peaks, a vista of stark and endless desert spread before us. Waving good-bye to our gracious hosts, I pointed the car toward the Guadalupe Mountains and the highest point in Texas—Guadalupe Peak. A couple of days earlier, while we'd been enjoying some ribs and pozole at **CHUY'S**, in Pecos, Nick and Sam had convinced me that taking a route through the northern edge of the Trans-Pecos region would be more satisfying than driving back hundreds of miles on the interstate. I didn't take much convincing.

The only way to describe the absolute desolation and flatness of the road that stretched ahead is to say that we could see Guadalupe Peak from about fifty miles out. We played a game in which we'd sight slight elevations in the road ahead and guess how many miles it would take to crest them. Sometimes it took more than ten miles. There were only a few dots on the map between El Paso and Fort Stockton and I was desperate to find an active smokestack in one of them. Any sort of roadside barbecue out here would be a find—the quality hardly mattered.

Closing in on the striking edifice of El Capitan, also in the Guadalupe Mountains—and the signature peak of West Texas—we crossed the great Salt Basin. I'd been warned by Ron back in El Paso that the wind in the El Capitan mountain pass would be severe. The road was the only break in the limestone wall of the Guadalupe Mountains. Despite his warnings I still found myself chasing a tumbling ball cap when I left the car to take in the views at a small rest area. We hadn't found a scrap of smoked meat, and I was starting to get hungry. The road led back through Pecos and further south to Fort Stockton as we left the

mountains behind. I wondered aloud if it was the fact that we'd seen this topography before that was making it so monotonous, but Sam quipped that the desert can get pretty boring without mountains, which were now to our rear, as a backdrop. I think it was mostly due to my hunger.

The only barbecue joint in Fort Stockton, Rix Pit BBQ and Discount Warehouse, was closed on Sundays. I was still hoping for barbecue in our near future, so I decided to forgo a full meal and settled instead for a Blizzard and some onion rings at Fort Stockton's Dairy Queen. My barbecue hopes weren't encouraged, however, as we seemed to pass through only dead or dying towns along State Highway 67. Soon enough, though, we began to see windmill-topped mesas in the distance, a sure sign we were approaching civilization. As San Angelo grew nearer, we passed our first 70 mph speed-limit sign in days (they're 75 or 80 out toward El Paso). The scrub became bushes and the bushes became small trees. More and more cars joined us on the road and towns popped up every twenty miles or so instead of appearing at hour-long intervals. As it drew toward dark the lights of San Angelo became visible. We'd passed every remote possibility for smoked meat, and I sadly accepted that it wasn't to be.

That was the first and only day over the course of our barbecue adventures that we didn't eat any barbecue. Looking back, I'm no longer too surprised at our protein-starved fate. In the nearly five hundred miles that we traveled, we passed fewer vehicles than I pass on any given day during my ten-mile round-trip commute to the office in Dallas. If it hadn't been for **ZENTNER'S DAUGHTER STEAK HOUSE** in San Angleo, that Sunday would have been entirely meatless. A server took pity on us and let us in just fifteen minutes before closing, and we feasted on T-bones and a "bale" of hand-battered onion rings.

Our craving for barbecue was even keener the next morning. Reyna's

BBQ & Tortilla Factory on the north side of town seemed like a promising breakfast stop if in fact they served barbacoa, which I assumed they did, given the name. But our run of bad barbecue luck continued: Reyna's was closed on Mondays. The next joint didn't open until 11:00, so I proposed that we visit a custom boot maker to kill time. San Angelo seemed like the right kind of town for that sort of thing, and I suddenly felt the need to clad my feet in the hide of the animal that I had been consuming at an alarming rate.

The J. L. Mercer Boot Company in downtown San Angelo has been making custom boots since 1923. I went in to feel out the whole process and left an hour later with a design half-worked-out and instructions to call when I was ready to put down my deposit. (A custom pair of boots is in high demand there and takes months to complete, but the boots should be ready for the book tour.)

Boot maker Kyle Brock pointed us toward Highland Grocery, which he lovingly described as a dump that does good brisket two-thirds of the time. The owner of **HIGHLAND GROCERY** quipped that he's the only guy in Texas with a master's degree slinging hot links for a living. While their brisket had a good black crust and moist, tender meat, it lacked smoke and seasoning. A squirt of sauce and a cold white bun didn't really help to liven it up.

On the other side of town was **SMOKEHOUSE BAR-B-Q**. The current owners have been running the joint for the past twenty years, and they smoke everything in a home-made steel rotisserie fired with mesquite. As an older gentleman sliced a fresh brisket for my order, I asked him to leave on the fat. Despite the request—I think from habit—he kept slicing it away. His wife noticed what was happening and scolded him for cutting away all the good stuff, and he salvaged a nice fatty end piece for me. I liked her style. The beef that remained after all the trimming was a bit crisp around the edges from sitting in the warming pan in its own juices. The smokiness was certainly evident, as was a pleasant amount of salt. It was solid brisket that some moist fat would only have made better. The

ribs were coated in a thin layer of sauce over a black-pepper rub. They had a good, roast-pork flavor but were less smoky than the brisket. There was more awful commercial sausage that was fatty, watery, and limp. As we ate, we got caught up in a conversation with a fellow customer at the neighboring table. He was originally from El Paso, but now lived in San Angelo. We asked him if he thought San Angelo was in West Texas, but he wouldn't commit. Walking back to the car I noticed a painted sign that claimed the joint was West Texas's finest, so I guess that settled it. It sure felt like West Texas to us Dallasites.

At **BUBBA'S SMOKEHOUSE**, the sign featured yet another cannibalistic pig chowing down on a pork rib. A large steel smoker in a side smokehouse was burning all mesquite. We took our order to go. The heavily spiced ribs were reminiscent of the Bodacious-style ribs we'd encountered a couple months earlier around East Texas. The thin ribs were coated in a heavy rub of salt and black pepper and a glaze spiced with loads of cumin. They were well smoked, but needed a little more time to tenderize and for the fat to render. Still, they were better than your average ribs. A jalapeño hot link was missing any sort of jalapeño flavor—the heat felt more like it came from basic old cayenne pepper. The brisket was overseasoned and tasted like it had been injected with salt.

I hoped we'd meet with better luck at **PACKSADDLE BAR-B-Q**, on the shore of Lake Nasworthy. I should have known to lower my expectations when a write-up on the wall touted the many ingredients in the rub over the quality of the meat—but I ordered some of everything anyway. Mesquite was again the wood of choice, but Packsaddle used a gas-fired pit, which both the beef and pork ribs could have used more time in. They were underdone and chewy, with a strong, smoky aroma that didn't translate into smoky flavor. That intricate rub bordered on bland. The slices of brisket on the surf and turf plate, which included fried catfish, had a deep red smoke ring, but the beef tasted more like it was cured with stale smoke than rendered tender with high-quality smoke. The server recommended the turkey, which turned out to be the abomination that is smoked deli turkey. Adding a bit of salt to the hand-cut fries brought them up a notch from good to great, but the hand-battered onion rings were a miss—clots of uncooked flour pocked the batter.

The further we got from San Angelo, the more honest-to-god fields and trees we began to see. The desert was far behind us as we made our way into the Hill Country. Midway between San Angelo and Brady, a sign for **CHUY'S BBQ**, in Eden, caused me to give the brakes a quick tap. We suffered through bone-dry beef and steamed ribs while listening to the pitmaster and owner brag about Chuy's many cabrito championships in nearby Brady. There was no cabrito. Luckily he had brought in raw sausage from Pak Quality Foods in San Angelo, which he smoked to perfection with mesquite. The sausage, along with a home-made popover-like yeast roll and a remarkable potato salad with so much egg it tasted deviled, was worth a return trip in its own right. After that visit I made it a point to get myself into the judging at the Brady goat cook-off just to get a few bites of Chuy's cabrito.

It had been more than a thousand miles and several days since we'd had a bite of meat that wasn't mesquite-smoked, so it was a treat to see the pits at **MAC'S BAR-B-Q**, in Brady, belching out oak smoke. Mac's owner and pitmaster, Collette McBee, had divorced her husband and business partner several months earlier, but the joint appeared to be going strong. When I asked her if the barbecue was any better since the divorce, her immediate answer was "HELL YES!" I certainly couldn't agree more that it was some damn fine barbecue. Our late-afternoon arrival—it was 4:30 when we rolled up to Mac's—could have spelled dried-out lunch leftovers, but the meat was all good. The brisket had a good bark and a thick smoke ring, and the slices from the flat had a nice quarter-inch line of smoky fat clinging to the firm, flavorful meat. It didn't matter that we'd already been to five barbecue joints that day—no one at the table could resist the brisket. Thick spareribs with a deep red hue also had great smoke and deep flavor from the generous seasoning. The meat and fat could have used more time on the smoker to soften a bit, but the ribs were still commendable. After missing the joint on two previous visits to Brady, I was happy to have finally made it.

Somewhere on the road to San Saba my lead foot finally caught up with me. For the first and only time in nearly ten thousand miles of driving, I got a speeding ticket. The ticket put a bit of a damper on the day, which was made even worse when Gage BBQ, in San Saba, turned out to be closed for the day. I had enjoyed their smoked meats on

a previous visit and was hoping to catch them again. Schoepf's, in Belton, was supposed to be the final destination of the trip, but I realized it would be closed before we could reach it. It was time to tuck tail and get back to Dallas.

Seven days is a long time to eat any one kind of food, even when you love barbecue as much as I do. But though I was slightly weary of it, I had learned a lot from all that smoked meat. Before Nick and I set out on our quest, I'd consumed most of my barbeque in the Dallas–Fort Worth area or in Central Texas. I'd encountered so much oak, hickory, and pecan wood in those parts of the state that I had dismissed the notion that mesquite is the ubiquitous wood of Texas barbecue. But it was undeniable that points west of San Angelo use this scourge of a tree almost exclusively. I had unlearned a different cliché, however: the idea that cowboy-style barbecue—direct-heat cooking over wood coals—was the emblematic barbecue of West Texas. The method turned out to be so sparse in the region that I think I'll lead a campaign to rename cowboy-style barbecue Hill Country–style, which is where it really seems to live. Painful as it may be to admit, the West Texas desert was also a desert for good Texas barbecue. Sure, there were a few quality joints out there, but for the most part we were served sad briskets and tough ribs—and no one besides ourselves seemed to notice or care. Maybe they just don't know what they're missing out there. After all, it's a long way from El Paso to Brady.

7 Days, 1,782 Miles, 30 BBQ Joints

CHAPTER SEVEN

EATING WITH OUR HANDS IN CENTRAL TEXAS

How did a guy from Ohio become so obsessed with Texas barbecue? I was living in ignorant barbecue bliss in Dallas. It was ALL good. I hadn't met a barbecue joint I didn't like, and couldn't figure out why so many of my favorites received so few accolades. *Texas Monthly* magazine puts out a list of the top fifty barbecue joints in Texas every five years. The 2003 issue raised my interest, but why would I bother traveling around the state when there was so much barbecue in Dallas? I began searching for new barbecue joints in Dallas and stumbled upon a blog called *DallasFood.org* that provided detailed reviews on a number of barbecue joints. The blogger's name was Scott, and he had made a few trips to Central Texas. To my eyes, his comparisons of Central Texas and Dallas barbecue were smug and elitist . . . snobbish, if you will. His poor assessments of Dallas barbecue weren't emotional diatribes, but clinical takedowns. His travels to Taylor, Lockhart, and Luling were chronicled in rapturous blog posts illustrated with multiple photos of smoked meat close-ups. The stuff looked unfamiliar and, despite my resentment, I wanted to learn more. My friend Sam Watkins and I decided to find out for ourselves and set off for Central Texas. I didn't know what to expect, but I definitely thought I'd return to Dallas happy to keep on eating its barbecue. Hell, I half expected to return with an irrefutable rebuttal to *Texas Monthly* and Scott *DallasFood.org*'s specious arguments. But over the next three days Sam and I ate at sixteen of the best barbecue joints in the state, most of them east of Austin in Central Texas. Crow had never tasted so good.

By the time I began planning Nick's and my adventures, eight years had passed, but in an ironic twist, I was sort of right back where I had started. I had spent almost a decade eating barbecue mostly in the Hill Country and Central Texas and throughout Dallas–Fort Worth. Just as I had fervently believed Dallas barbecue was great and *Texas Monthly* and Scott were wrong, I now believed the best barbecue in the state was located in the Hill Country and Central Texas. I believed we weren't likely to encounter much great barbecue outside those safe zones, so in a selfishly pragmatic move, I planned a jaunt through Central Texas as our last trip, guaranteeing a satisfying grand finale. I wanted to be sure that we'd enjoy the hell out of our last leg of this crazy journey.

The trip began like the rest, in Dallas. Nick was in the backseat,

I was driving, and my friend Rob Borkowski—who did double duty as navigator and deejay—was riding shotgun. A couple of years earlier I had conducted a scorched-earth campaign on Rob's idea of good barbecue by taking him on an early-morning jaunt through Lockhart. He couldn't hide his giddiness as he ate burnt ends of brisket at Black's, and I was both pleased and a little smug about having converted another disciple. I was even more pleased to discover that that trip had warped Rob sufficiently that he now wanted to tag along on our Central Texas trip, even after seeing the itinerary. The proposed level of gluttony would have made a priest laugh, no confession required.

Yet again, I couldn't just drive past the exit for West. This time we weren't stopping for kolache, however, although we were tempted. West is also home to one of the oldest meat markets in the state: Nemecek Brothers Meat Market, which opened in 1896. Much to our dismay, it turned out that after 115 years, the taxman had finally caught up with Nemecek's. An IRS sticker announcing a United States government seizure was affixed to the glass door at its entry. The interior was empty. **NORS SAUSAGE AND BURGER HOUSE** was just a few blocks down Main Street. Although the building that houses Nors was built in 1892, Nors itself is practically brand-new in comparison—it opened in 2009. The interior reflected that combination of the old and the new; the high ceilings were a great example of Gilded

Age architecture, but the reclaimed wood floor was made of old truck flatbeds.

Our server, Raylene, was a tornado of talk and top-notch hospitality. Her suggestions proved spot-on. I hadn't considered ordering the sausage burger, but she persuaded me. The savory, juicy patty, which was topped with pepper jack cheese and sandwiched in a toasted jalapeño bun, was better than most beef burgers I've had. But the real draw at Nors is the house-made smoked sausage. Both the regular and the jalapeño links were all-pork with plenty of spice. The casing crinkled just right and had a pleasing snap. The ground pork filling was cohesive and didn't crumble when I broke the link apart, but the texture wasn't homogenous like a hot dog, either. The original link contained visible bits of red and black pepper, and the jalapeño-and-cheese link just brought some oomph to the original link. I'd eaten Nors's sausages before, but I remembered them as smokier and spicier. I asked Raylene if Nors had changed the recipe or the smoking process to be more crowd-pleasing, and she confirmed that it was the smoking method that had changed. A few months before our visit, Nors's owner, Matt Nors, had purchased a defunct meat market down the street. That market had an industrial-sized smoker, so they were doing all their smoking there now. They were still using a mix of mesquite and oak, but had to tweak the smoke level as they got used to the industrial-sized smoker. Matt assured us that their goal was a smoky link and they were just trying to get there. Either way, they were some of the best links I've had in the state.

I've eaten barbecue all over Waco with mixed results, but before we could put the town to the test on this newest go-round, I had to pay a visit to an old flame. In a previous life I was a Dr Pepper fiend. My mom put a twenty-four-pack of the stuff under the Christmas tree for me every year and it was usually gone by New Year's. Well, Waco is home to the Dr Pepper Museum, where, no entry fee required, you can amble up to the antique soda fountain counter and get a Dr Pepper mixed in the old-fashioned way, with soda and syrup served with a scoop of vanilla ice cream. I still drink plenty of the stuff on the barbecue trail, but that glass was special to me as it was straight from the source. As we were leaving, we ran into the museum's executive director, Jack McKinney, on the porch and he filled us in on a bit of the company's history. We hadn't had time to peruse the museum, but we learned from Jack that Dr Pepper was created right here in Waco in 1885, and that fifty years later another well-known Texas soda was developed in Waco: Big Red, which the Dr Pepper company now distributes. No wonder they both go so well with Texas barbecue.

For our first taste of Waco barbecue, we actually had to leave the city. **RUSTY STAR BBQ** is just outside the city limits, on the northwest side of town. It might be better known for its customers than its smoked meats: a

few years earlier, the unlikely duo of Anthony Bourdain and Ted Nugent shared a meal of Texas barbecue and Shiner Bock at the Rusty Star, putting it on the map. I had never heard of it before then, and I hadn't been able to visit— the joint's only open Monday through Friday. At Rusty Star, they smoke their meat in a gas-fired Southern Pride rotisserie fueled by pecan. The brisket was really good. A nice, dark crust surrounded tender and flavorful meat that had silky fat running throughout it. The pulled pork had the same good smoke, but the meat was a bit dry. The big pork spareribs just weren't very good, though. Their dominant flavor came from a rub that tasted like sweet poultry seasoning. They had no bark to speak of, and the meat was tough to get off the bone. As for the sides, I had to try the pea salad, a classic Texas mixture of cold peas, onions, cheese, bacon (sometimes), and a mayo-based dressing. At its worst, pea salad can be a pile of mush made with canned peas, but the version at the Rusty Star, made with thawed frozen peas, was excellent. The pop when each pea exploded between my teeth was a pleasing one. A mashed jalapeño-potato salad was also good but didn't make the same impression. Midway through our meal, the owners informed us that we had just missed Ted Nugent by three minutes. It seemed he actually was a regular. We quickly polished off the rest of our food, rushing out on the off chance that we could contrive a run-in with Nugent at the local farm-supply store. His huge, black truck was no longer in the parking lot. We considered driving toward his ranch, but after noting the stupidity of hunting for a man known for shooting anything that moves, we canned that plan.

The huge, black smoker sitting out front of **HOBBS QUE**, on the south side of Waco, was almost as big as the metal building in which they served the food. Owner and pitmaster Sylvester Hobbs greeted us at the ordering window. He was wearing a crisp, black T-shirt offset by the white apron tied around his waist. His sly smile was the perfect complement to the white chef's hat

set jauntily on his head. He had spent most of his life on the rough side of Fort Worth around Lake Como, then lived in Mexia for a while. Less than six months before our visit he had moved to Waco and opened Hobbs Que. He learned to barbecue using mesquite and still prefers if for the kick he says it provides, which he doesn't think you can get from oak. The popular pulled pork was gone for the day, so we opted for brisket, pork ribs, and chicken. It all came covered in sauce, but the sweet, light home-made mixture worked quite well with the sharply smoky meat.

The brisket was too tender, verging on overcooked, but still flavorful. A slightly dry bark on the ribs gave them a pleasing chewiness that was a great counterpoint to the tender meat juicy with the rendered fat coursing through it. The sauce worked especially well with the ribs' smokiness. The chicken, which had flabby skin and dry meat, didn't seem to be prepared with the same love as had the brisket and ribs. Even with his current big pit, Sylvester was on the lookout for a Dallas-made Bewley pit, which would increase his smoking capacity. If he finds it, we might just be able to get some of that pulled pork on the next visit.

Hobbs Que shared its parking lot with a shaved-ice stand. The stand's sign advertised pickle juice–flavored shaved ice, and I was intrigued. The concoction was better than you might think. The juice had been watered down to take away some of its salty punch, and the chill from the shaved ice made it almost . . . refreshing. Still, it wasn't going to unseat Dr Pepper in my hierarchy of the best barbecue thirst quenchers.

Rosebud, thirty miles south of Waco, is such a friendly place that they've posted a sign warning motorists to be aware of the speed trap on the way into town. That hospitality was in full effect at the **HIWAY 77 CAFE**. I had planned to stop there just for dessert, but when we arrived a sign out front said they were now serving honey mesquite–smoked barbecue Thursdays through Saturdays. Sue Sturrock, Hiway 77's owner, told us that she and her husband had been smoking for just a few months, and that they only used honey mesquite. This was a confusing distinction given that most all of the mesquite in Texas is honey mesquite, but most folks just refer to it as mesquite. They had moved back to Rosebud— Sue's hometown—from San Antonio with the express purpose of buying Hiway 77, which was abandoned at the time, and starting up their own café. Why they decided to try their hands at barbecue I'm not sure, but I'm glad they did.

We ordered sausage, baby back ribs, and brisket. The sausage was a local specialty, garlic links made by the Parcus family. The Parcus Grocery & Market—the empty storefront of which was just down Main Street—was no longer in business, but Mr. Parcus's son, Tom, was still making the sausage from the old family recipe and selling it at Tonn's Grocery just down the highway. Sue bought the garlic links raw and smoked them at the restaurant. The sausage tasted unmistakably like garlic, along with plenty of salt and black pepper. The casing was taut and dark from the smoke, which made for a boldly flavored link worth seeking out. A darkened crust encased some of the best baby back ribs I've had anywhere. They were simply incredible, for a beginner or not. The rosy meat came cleanly away from the bone but didn't fall off. The seasoning made its presence known, but wasn't overwhelming. The same was true of the smoke, which can sometimes get out of hand with mesquite wood. A decent brisket showed

they still had some work to do, but they were well on their way to providing top-notch barbecue across the board.

If the barbecue was solid, the sides were astounding. The batter was so crispy on the freshly fried onion rings that it shattered. As we ate, Sue came over with a bowl of home-made ranch dressing and a bottle of hot sauce and mixed up some of her favorite dipping sauce for us. We'd been eating all day, but after one dip of the fried squash slices into that sauce, we were fighting over the rest of the basket. The unique slaw was dressed with a hot vinegar mix that wilted the shaved cabbage. The bite of vinegar went well with the sweetness in the slaw, although I did miss the expected crunch. Dessert did us in: a light banana pudding into which whipped cream had been folded and a rich peach cobbler heavy on the cinnamon were a fitting end to an excellent meal. We licked our bowls clean.

After we ate, Sue showed us around. They did all of their smoking in a vertical cabinet smoker about the size of an armoire, which sat out back. There were still hot coals sitting at the bottom of the cooker. The cooking racks sat about four feet above the coals, keeping the meat from receiving much if any direct heat. True to her German roots, Sue was hoping to add a beer garden to the café out on the side lawn, but Hiway 77 Cafe was great as it was. For my money, Sue needed to provide little else, if anything, to keep me coming back.

We grabbed a to-go order from another family-run joint in town, **LIL' JOE'S BAR-B-QUE**—a tiny shack decorated with Dallas Cowboys memorabilia. The owner's niece filled our order. The sausage was about the only good thing in it. The brisket slices were overcooked and dry. They were almost flavorless, aside from the smoky crust. The ribs had a heavy rub with too much sugar in it, and they'd been overcooked far beyond tender. The bones came right out of the ribs, and their heavy creosote aftertaste lingered for a number of belches afterward.

JAKE 'N' BOO'S BACKDOOR BAR & GRILL wasn't much better. Three things struck me about the joint. There were barbecue competition trophies on display everywhere, the owner was ridiculously friendly, and the bad barbecue made me wish the other two weren't true. Across the state, I've found that pitmasters who meet with success on the competition circuit rarely put out exemplary smoked meats in their restaurants. I'm not sure exactly what accounts for this phenomenon, but I think some of it has to do with the vastly different requirements of the two contexts. At a barbecue competition, you have to cook one or two perfect briskets, which you serve immediately, whereas at a restaurant, you have to smoke a dozen briskets at a time and hold them all day long.

When our plate arrived, all of the meat on it was the same dark brown—there was no rosy smokiness to be found. Add to that that the meat looked soaked, as if it had been sitting in a vat of liquid. It was so salty, I assumed that yes, it had been sitting around in a vat of liquid, and that the liquid was some sort of broth—or that it had been braised after smoking. Either way, it all had far too much salt and sugar and no hint of smoke from the oak-fired pits. For folks so particular about their wood (at Jake's they prefer oak grown in sandy soil) I don't know how they could have thought this was exemplary barbecue.

Full from eating several meals in quick succession, we were moving slowly. The drive took on a more leisurely pace. We admired the rural landscape and stopped at a historical marker in the town of Buckholts, which led us to a white octagonal building with a bright silver pitched roof. The building was home to SPJST No. 15. SPJST stands for Slovanska Podporujici Jednota Statu Texas (Slavonic Benevolent Order of the State of Texas). It's a Czech fraternal society that promotes the preservation of Czech cultural heritage, functions as a social club, and, most important, provides life insurance benefits for members. The SPJST started as a sort of insurance co-op in 1897, and its outposts spread across the state. The

building in front of us had been erected in 1936, but the first SPJST building was designed by Josep Slovacek (yes, just like the sausages we had back in West). Like most of the SPJST buildings that have been preserved in the state, there was a barbecue pit outdoors, alongside the building. Designed for direct heat cooking, it would have been perfect for warming a couple of those garlicky Czech sausages so common to the area, but the fire box was cold today.

The rest of the drive to our hotel in Hutto was fruitless. The meat market in Thorndale had just closed for the evening and there was no barbecue to be found in the town. A notable joint in Rockdale was long gone. We were going to hit Louie Mueller in Taylor as part of the next morning's itinerary. The only thing left to do was stuff our pie holes, literally. The Texan Cafe, in Hutto, has some of the best pies in the state. My tablemates went with some fancy concoctions, but I opted for a simple rhubarb slice that was perfectly balanced between tart and sweet, and had a flaky, buttery crust. After dessert we happened upon an angry couple engaged in a rapidly escalating argument outside the Downtown Hall of Fame, a bar next door to the Texan Cafe. There was a liberal amount of cursing and threats to call the cops. We felt compelled to stick around for the show, so we grabbed a pitcher and three stools inside the bar. Police would come and arrests would ensue, but we left unscathed.

Confused about their hours, we arrived too early at **LOUIE MUELLER BARBECUE** in Taylor, so we plunked down on the concrete steps waiting for their eleven o'clock opening, which was still a half hour away. After about fifteen minutes they showed pity on us. Pitman Tony White came out front and asked if we wanted a tour of the back, an offer we eagerly took him up on. We walked past stacks of split post oak as we entered the joint through the back door. Owner Wayne Mueller was busy stuffing beef sausage made from his dad's old recipe. They do three varieties—the original, one with jalapeños, and an even spicier link with chipotle peppers. Wayne opened one of the smokers to reveal a bevy of briskets nearing the end of their cooking cycle. Vats of salt-flecked black pepper sat waiting to be rubbed

onto raw meat. Wayne was already sweating from the humidity, but he cursed it more for how it was affecting the meat than him. The joint—which under normal circumstances has a line out the door—was quiet in a way that I'd never seen it. I could almost hear the beef ribs contracting in the brick smokers. It was like visiting a cathedral between services.

Louie Mueller Barbecue was the pivotal spot in the maturation of my barbecue palate. On that virgin megatour of Central Texas back in 2006, Louie Mueller had been our very first stop. Sam and I had arrived early, our anticipation growing as we waited in line. When we got our plates, we carried them reverentially out back, where we sat on either side of a picnic table and took simultaneous bites of the brisket. We just stared at each other in wonder, both smiling and nodding emphatically. We knew it was gonna be great, but it transcended our expectations. On that morning, there wasn't time for words as long as there was meat left on the butcher paper. We knew instantly that it was barbecue on a different level than we'd ever enjoyed, and we needed a few minutes before we could comfortably stand up.

Louie Mueller first opened his grocery store in 1946. Three years later he was serving barbecue, but it was a decision he'd made based on business considerations rather than out of a love for the pits. As his son Bobby noted in a 2007 interview with Southern Foodways Alliance, "My father never struck a match in [there]." It was Canadian-born pitmaster Fred Fountaine who brought in the barbecue accolades. When Louie retired in 1974, Bobby who'd been working as a butcher in the store, took over and began working with Fred to learn how to master a pit. When Fred retired in

1987, Bobby ran the whole shop and manned the pits on his own. While Bobby gleaned plenty of pit knowledge from Fred, the sausage recipe was all his, which is why his son Wayne Mueller wouldn't think to change it. Wayne's been running the joint since his father's untimely death at age sixty-nine in 2008, and his respect for the tradition and history of the family business is one of the reasons it's still so great.

Nick and Rob walked around the joint to take in its atmosphere—time's patina varnished every surface. Smoke has tinted the hand-written butcher paper menus tacked to the walls. Next to them hangs the James Beard Award Louie Mueller's received in 2006, when Bobby was still tending the pits. I was stationed up front to place our order. The counter man offered up the Louie Mueller standard amuse-bouche of a piece of chunked brisket, just like six years earlier, when Bobby himself had handed it to me. I savored the hot, fatty beef knowing there'd be plenty more. A heap of fatty and lean brisket slices were soon piled next to a jalapeño sausage link, a mound of pork spareribs, and baby back ribs. A mammoth beef rib that weighed in at over a pound and a half anchored the other end of the tray.

The heft with which the layer of black pepper was applied to the brisket and beef ribs seemed to mock those who might prefer subtler flavors. After just a few bites there was pepper on my face, under my nails, and in my iced tea. It was like hair glitter in a sorority house—it might be annoyingly pervasive, but those lingering souvenirs are a reminder of a great time when you notice them several miles—or days—later. The fatty brisket was lusciously tender, and every bit of the fat was edible. Well-smoked fat is good fat, and good fat means good meat. The slices from the lean end, where a thick line of fat cap holds tight to the meat, were dense and stable. Where the fatty end of the brisket melted in my mouth, the lean end provided a pleasant level of chew. The jalapeño sausage was pleasing for its snap and the noticeable bits of jalapeño. The link actually tasted like the chile rather than just heat. The fat ran clear, untainted by paprika or other distracting spices, and the gray filling confirmed the sausage was fresh and preservative-free.

You can always take a giant bite out of a whole beef short rib if you dare, but balancing a pound of meat precariously on the bone can be dangerous. The cut is better enjoyed by pulling mouthfuls of meat from the whole with your hands. No other cut of beef contains such generous levels of intramuscular fat and collagen. The collagen takes many hours to break down, but once it has, the meat will shred effortlessly like it did that day. With only four bones per rack, half of every rack is an end rib with lots of crusty goodness from the heavy rub on the edges. Be sure to save some of those intensely flavored crusty edges for your last bite.

Wayne Mueller came to sit with us and check on how our meal was

··· BEEF RIBS ··············

Beef ribs come in two categories: beef back ribs and short ribs. If you've ever seen a whole standing rib roast with the bones attached, then you've seen a rack of beef back ribs. When the bones are removed, you're left with a prime roast in one hand, and the intact rack of beef back ribs in the other. A butcher who separates the two before putting them into the case will leave very little meat on the bones in order to cut as heavy a prime rib roast (or boneless rib eyes if the whole prime rib is sliced) as possible, since the prime rib is such an expensive cut. The resulting rack is mostly bone and full of shiners (exposed bones without a meaty cover), with meat only between the bones. Beef back ribs is the only common cut of smoked beef that doesn't come from the front of the animal (as do brisket, shoulder clod, and short ribs).

Short ribs, on the other hand, have a thick layer of well-marbled meat over top-wide bones from the front of the animal. Also known as *serratus ventralis*, these four rib bones must be removed from the brisket during the butchering process. (In the old days you can find references to "boneless briskets," suggesting that it was once common to leave the short ribs attached to the whole brisket.) What remains is one of the most collagen-rich cuts of beef. They require long cooking times, but the payoff of silky, rich meat is unparalleled.

going. The table gushed about the brisket. It was on today, and Wayne knew it would be. He described the jiggle test he uses to determine when a brisket is perfectly cooked: he pokes the brisket, and if the surface quivers back and forth, it's ready. He said that the briskets had been quivering all morning, which was one of the few things that could still make the kitchen staff giddy after so many thousands of pounds of meat.

We still had the pork ribs to consume. The huge spareribs were seasoned simply with salt and pepper. The crust on the ribs had a ruddy, brown hue, unlike the midnight-black brisket. The smoke was evident and the meat was nicely layered with ribbons of juicy melted fat. The baby backs were a new addition to the menu. They called them southern-style baby backs, and their reasoning for including them on the menu was the exact reason I didn't like them. I don't look at barbecue from a businessman's standpoint, but more as a connoisseur and a historian. These ribs had been added as a crowd pleaser for out-of-towners unfamiliar with Texas barbecue. A sweet baby back rib was something they could relate to and were comfortable ordering and eating. But in my opinion, experiencing new things and getting a little uncomfortable is what travel and cultural exploration should be all about. The last thing I want in Memphis is brisket, and the last thing I want in one of the temples of Texas barbecue is a sweet and spicy Mississippi pork rib. If they don't like the incredibly smoked traditional Texas options, send them to Chili's.

As if Taylor didn't offer enough in the way of smoked meats with Louie Mueller, the town is also the location of one of the oldest barbecue joints in the state, helmed by the godfather of all Texas pitmasters. Vencil Mares has been running **TAYLOR CAFE** for as long as my mother's been alive. He bought the joint for $2,200 in 1948, after he got out of the army. He's added a few walls around the pit area and removed the ones that once separated the "White" and "Colored" sides of the bar, but otherwise, little in the building has changed since then. The only air-conditioning in the joint comes from a small window unit in Vencil's tiny office in the back. A memento to his longevity sits behind the bar in the form of a Lifetime Achievement Award from Foodways Texas, the organization that preserves, promotes, and celebrates the diverse food cultures of Texas.

As most folks describe it, Louie Mueller is a barbecue joint that serves beer and Taylor Café is a beer joint that serves barbecue—the ladies running the bar will let you borrow a koozie for your beer while you wait for the barbecue. Just remember to bring cash, because credit's not an option. After I handed over some cold, hard cash for our food, a foil-lined paper plate arrived at our table, piled with saucy meat. Neither the brisket nor the ribs had a deep smokiness or an exemplary black crust, but it was still respectable barbecue. A home-made turkey sausage was a cut above the other menu offerings. The one-hundred-percent ground turkey link, seasoned with a secret blend of spices, was stuffed into a natural hog casing and cooked until the oak smoke had colored it a deep brown. It wasn't a juicy sausage, but it wasn't too dry, either. Its flavor was reminiscent of breakfast sausage. A home-made beef sausage had a complex flavor I thought might be from star anise, but I got an odd look from pitmaster Scott Morales when I proposed that possibility.

On any given visit to Taylor Cafe, you're likely to find Vencil holding court at the end of the bar, wearing his trademark red apron over a starched white shirt with a Vencil name patch sewed on the chest. These days Scott Morales does most of the cooking, though. While Vencil chatted with another group of guests, Scott showed us around the pits. The briskets, which are rubbed with salt, pepper, garlic powder, and chili powder, are smoked in a brick behemoth then, when they're almost finished, wrapped in butcher paper and stacked tightly into a huge igloo cooler. The heat trapped in the cooler finishes cooking them overnight and they're still hot in the morning when it's time to serve them.

After our tour of the pits, I sat down with Vencil at the bar. I had tried to talk to Vencil at a few events in the past, but had rarely gotten past hello. On this trip he was feeling talkative, though, as well as a bit cantankerous. I tried to follow his side of the conversation the best I could, but his office would have been a better venue for talking, as it was away from the whine of the electric knife and the rumble of the train outside the screen doors. After covering his time as a medic in Normandy we got into more lascivious stories from his twenties, when he closed down the dance halls waiting for the increasing dimness to improve the looks of the lonely older ladies looking for companionship. While he may be physically feeble, Vince is certainly a man with plenty of spunk left in him. Any true Texas barbecue fan needs to make a pilgrimage to Taylor Cafe just to shake hands with this legend while he's still around to give them out.

On the other side of the tracks and down a ways off the main road was **DAVIS GROCERY & BAR-B-Q**, owned and operated by the Reverend James Davis. There were actual dry good groceries lining the wall, but it was the fruits of the mesquite smoke coming from the back that lured us in. I'd had some exemplary smoked meat there in the past, so I was surprised at the rather flat and chewy brisket. Some fatty mutton ribs—ribs from sheep that are more than a year old—were much better (technically, only meat from sheep less than a year old can be called lamb). I prefer to peel away the chewy, salty top layer of fat on mutton ribs and enjoy just a hint of gaminess. Feel free to bite right through those multiple layers of thick fat, but no matter how well rendered it may be, brace yourself for some serious twang on the tongue. It's the fat that holds most of the signature gamy flavor that folks shy away from. You could call me a general advocate of ingesting well-smoked fat, but one of the few times I suggest setting it aside is when eating mutton ribs. According to Jennifer McLagan, author of the cookbook *Fat*, it would be difficult or even impossible to tell lamb from beef if all the meat's fat were removed. The meat structures of both are similar and the meat itself provides little flavor. Davis Grocery also had a few sausages on offer. Though none of them were home-made, a local pork sausage from O'Brien Meats was excellent. It was made even better with a swipe through Davis's barbecue sauce. He calls the thin, dark, and sweet mix his "come back juice" and it's one of the better sauces I've had anywhere.

Vencil's place may have been around a while, but just twenty minutes away in Elgin there's a joint that calls itself the oldest in Texas. **SOUTHSIDE MARKET** first opened its doors in 1886. It's so old that Vencil Mares actually learned how to barbecue there, though not in its current building. Ownership of the joint has changed hands many times, but the Bracewell family has been running it since 1968. "Hot guts" are what made Southside Market and the town famous—they're the reason the Texas State Legislature named the town the Sausage Capital of Texas. Hot guts is the regional name given to these spicy, naturally cased links, but soon after the Bracewell family took over, they yanked out the heat. The wimpy palates of the day demanded blandly spiced meat, and those who'd grown accustomed to the heat had to doctor their links with a splash or two of the hot sauce provided on the tables. To be honest, I prefer it that way. I like being able to drown the sausage in the vinegar-rich sauce and sop up the remnants with crackers. It's a simple meal, and a link is cheaper than you think and won't leave you hungry. If you still need to top things off, just don't bother with the brisket. This is the rare occasion

where I recommend the chicken. Crispy skin covered half a bird that was intensely juicy and full of sweet smoke flavor. The mutton ribs at Southside were great, too, though they were actually lamb breast— Southside calls it mutton just to keep the old-timers happy. The meat between the layers of fat on the lamb ribs was still intensely flavorful (there is always some intramuscular fat in there) and well seasoned by the post oak smoke. Dousing it with a little of the hot sauce made it even more irresistible.

Across town was the relative adolescent of Elgin's barbecue joints. Though they may have been making sausage since the forties, **MEYER'S ELGIN SMOKEHOUSE** didn't open a restaurant until 1989, when they started serving cooked sausage. Nowadays they have a full barbecue menu (most all of it overly salty on a couple of previous visits), but we were just there for the sausage. When our order arrived, a squat and stubby garlic pork sausage sat next to a thin and lengthy beef sausage on the stark white butcher paper. After a relentless schedule of meat eating (this was our fifth stop of the day and it was still early afternoon) our brains were clouded, we'd hit a level of deliriousness ripe for sausage-related penis jokes, and the meal quickly deteriorated into an uncontrolled laughing fit. We preferred the beef sausage over at Southside, but the taut and juicy pork sausage was a thing of garlicky beauty. How we'd be able to eat the couple of barbecue dinners ahead of us was hard to fathom.

All you can see of the little town of Coupland from State Highway 95 is the city limits sign. Take a turn to the east at the sign, drive over the hill, and you'll find the **OLD COUPLAND INN AND DANCEHALL** right on the main drag. The bed-and-breakfast wasn't open, or we might have taken a nap before our early dinner. It didn't take long for a plate of barbecue to show up at our booth. Fatty brisket slices were a bit underdone, but the smoke in the crust was phenomenal. Dark-crusted St. Louis–style ribs were exemplary. The ribs' well-formed crust made a pleasing textural contrast to the moist meat beneath, which had just the right amount of smoke and ample seasoning. It needed only a tug to get it off the bone. A peppery sausage link was also good and sides of surprisingly spicy slaw and mashed potato salad were further evidence of the care taken on the food preparation here. A tub of peach cobbler was far more than we could finish by that point, but we gave it our best shot.

I asked our waiter what kind of wood they used in the pit and a moment later, the Coupland's owner, Tim Worthy, came out to tell us. The answer wasn't as simple as we expected. Some years back, Tim had hired the town drunk to watch the fire in the pit overnight. He gave him strict instructions to stoke the fire from a pile of oak. The adjacent pile of mesquite was just for the fireplace inside. The next morning the barbecue was exceptional, but didn't taste the way Tim expected it to. When Tim asked what wood he had used, the drunk pointed cross-eyed to the pile of mesquite. From that point forward Coupland's has used the oak for the fireplace. The old drunk has since gone to prison, so now all the cooking duties fall to Tim. His wife, Barb, runs the hospitality department and does it well. When she learned about our quest to eat our way through Texas barbecue, she quickly disappeared into the kitchen and returned with an off-menu item they were testing out. Finding a use for leftover brisket is always helpful if you're committed to serving only the fresh stuff (as everyone should be) and damn, they had found a use for it. They were stuffing halved jalapeños with shredded brisket and chicken-frying the neat little package. A deep fryer has never seen a better-stuffed jalapeño. Coupland is a bit off the beaten path, so you can only eat and dance at the Old Coupland Inn and Dancehall on Friday and Saturday nights, but it's worth the drive from Austin or even Dallas. Even if those stuffed jalapeños haven't made it on the menu, be sure to ask for them and enjoy a few with a cold Shiner.

About eleven miles southwest of Coupland is the even more remote town of Cele. It ain't on the way to anywhere and if you drive through it too fast you might just miss the delightfully decrepit **CELE STORE**. The store opened as a saloon in 1891, the same year that it got its last coat of paint. We entered through a set of double screen doors and walked into a world of taxidermied animals, old photos, horseshoes, and neon beer signs. A green Cele City Limits sign hanging on the back wall listed a population of ninety-two. Generous. Every table had a white piece of paper on it, with a name and reservation time written on it. Yes, you must have a reservation for one of the few tables in this joint. We sat at a table right next to a makeshift stage, and just as the food came out, a duo struck up some old country covers. There was only one way to order and that was family-style. Baby back ribs, sliced sausage, and pieces of brisket that were oddly cubed rather than sliced came out on white butcher paper alongside dill pickle spears, jalapeños, sliced white onions, and batonettes of cheddar cheese. I can't say we were hungry in any way, but I tried to be an honest judge of the food. Even chunked up, the brisket was still chewy and lacked smoke. The ribs had a caramelized crust and good smokiness, but the meat was harder to liberate from the bone than necessary. The smoky slices of the peppery sausage were passable but not particularly memorable.

I exhausted every option trying to find accommodations for the evening closer to Lexington, where we'd be eating our breakfast. I was soon resigned to the fact that we'd be rolling our bloated selves back into the beds at the Holiday Inn in Hutto. We just couldn't get enough of the concrete hippos—the town mascot—that dotted every local business, house, and parking lot, as they were apt reminders of the way our distended bellies felt.

Saturday breakfast in Lexington, Texas, has become a rite of passage for the Texas barbecue aficionado. **SNOW'S BBQ** broke onto the scene when *Texas Monthly* named it the best barbecue joint in the state back in the summer of 2008. What was once a tiny joint that served a few hundred pounds of smoked meat to the surrounding community was transformed overnight into a darling of the entire state. More than an hour away in Austin, it was common to hear folks bragging around the lunch table that they'd had Snow's brisket for breakfast a few hours earlier. Owner Kerry Bexley and pitmaster Tootsie Tomanetz tripled, then quadrupled, their output to meet the demand. Lexington locals grew angry as their lunch option disappeared, since more than a thousand pounds of meat barely lasted two hours after opening time at 8:00 A.M. Four years later, nothing's changed. If you want Snow's, you have to get up early, and it has to be on a Saturday morning.

The highways in this sparsely populated section of Central Texas are pretty empty around sunrise on a Saturday morning. There were probably more people in line at Snow's than we'd passed during the hour-long drive from Hutto, and we were all here to get some brisket for breakfast.

About a month earlier I'd been contacted by Steve Dean. He's a Texas dance hall fanatic first and barbecue fiend second. Steve is the cofounder of Texas Dance Hall Preservation, Inc., which promotes the use and preservation of historic dance halls around the state. In his travels he also passes plenty of hidden and unknown barbecue joints. He agreed to meet our group at Snow's and share some smoked-meat leads with us. He was just finishing up his meal at one of the outdoor picnic tables when we walked outside with our steaming tray of meat.

Most of the meats at Snow's are cooked over oak coals using direct heat—except for the brisket. The briskets have a dedicated pit and are smoked indirectly with post oak. Kerry prefers to buy smaller briskets and wraps them in foil about two-thirds of the way through smoking. This method steams the meat, which limits the integrity of the crust that remains but does nothing to

diminish the flavor in this case. At Snow's, they cut the briskets with an electric knife, which gives the slices a shaggy look that makes them seem more dry than they are. The meat that morning was moist, tender, and kissed with sweet smoke. Like at Louie Mueller's, Snow's seasons their meat with a simple combination of salt and pepper, but the flavor of the briskets at the two joints hardly resembled each other. The crust had a rusty-red hue, and the meat had a deep pink smoke ring that covered more than half of each slice from the lean end. If Kerry is being honest about the simple seasoning and the simple methods, then that brisket was a testament to how much barbecue can differ in the hands of different pitmasters. The beef at Snow's was sweeter than at Louie Mueller's, with a grilled flavor I would expect from direct heat, but not from indirect heat. If smell accounts for half of taste, then my only explanation is that the direct-heat smoke swirling around us at the picnic table must have affected my palate.

The meat they do cook over coals includes simple spareribs, sausage, and a thick pork steak, sliced from the shoulder and heavily seasoned. On other visits the pork steak had been transcendent, but that day it was merely good, with too much poorly rendered fat in the meat. According to Kerry, spareribs have always been a challenge to him, but they were perfect. The exterior of the ribs was crisp and chewy, and the meat was eminently moist and luscious, with liquid fat coursing through it. They were the best ribs I'd had there in about a half-dozen visits. The sausage was also a hit. I was on a jalapeño sausage kick, so I continued the trend. The sausage meat was coarsely ground and packed into a well-wrinkled casing. The heat wasn't muted, but certainly wasn't anything that would burn you.

Steve Dean and his friend Deborah Fleming joined us about midway through our meal. Now even though I always appreciate other folks' tips about barbecue places I should visit, more often than not they end up being fairly well known joints—at least to me. But it only took a few e-mail exchanges with Steve for me to realize he was a gold mine of back-road barbecue leads. After beating our own path for thousands of miles across the state, we handed the reins over to Steve and Deborah. I was happy to let my newfound barbecue oracle guide us to the next place.

Deanville is not along any route I would take to get anywhere. Just a half hour east of Lexington is the **DEANVILLE SONS OF HERMANN HALL**. The Sons of Hermann is a fraternal order that promotes German cultural and social events as well as provides life insurance for its members. At Lodge No. 301 in Deanville, there was the requisite dance hall and an adjacent barbecue pit. Unlike the pits at every other dance hall we'd visit over the course of the trip, the Sons of Hermann's was smokin'. Just like Snow's, it is only open on Saturday mornings, but instead of encountering long lines, we were the first visitors of the day—they were just opening when we arrived at 10:00 A.M. An older Czech man was tending the pit, and he eyed our group with suspicion until we started ordering with abandon. There was no brisket on the menu, but there were pork steaks, ribs, sausage, and chicken, all cooked directly over oak coals.

We took our haul into the lodge and sat down next to a couple of older gentlemen playing dominoes. I went for the beef and pork sausage first. It was light in color and had just a hint of smoke and reminded me—in both texture and flavor—of the Alsatian sausage we had eaten in Castroville. The finely ground meat was cohesive but hadn't reached frankfurter territory. The chicken was nothing special. The pitmaster's skills were best suited to the pork. The hefty pork steak we had ordered weighed in at a couple of pounds. It had a nice, dark outer layer from the coals that contrasted with the meat within, which was white with a rosy outline. The juicy meat had a nice chew and plenty of well-rendered fat throughout. I thought that stunning cut would provide the best bite of pork—until I grabbed a rib. A simple salt-and-pepper rub was the perfect complement to the thick, but tender, meat. There was a bold flavor from the searing coals. The meat could be pulled from the bone with ease, and the fatty knuckles of the rib ends provided a few extra heavenly bites. Given its remote locale, lack of reputation, and generally cool setting, the Sons of Hermann Lodge No. 301 would prove to be the most memorable stop on the best leg of our Texas tour. If the barbecue is that good on any old Saturday, I can't imagine what it's like when they really put their mind to it for their giant Fourth of July celebration. No fireworks necessary.

Our final destination was a long ways away, in Shiner, so our next few stops were a bit spread out. After some soulless highway driving, we came up against the heavy traffic and relentless stoplights of Manor, where we were headed for **TEXAS TRADITIONAL BAR-B-Q**. I felt bad that they had to follow our visits

to Lexington and Deanville, and though they put up a decent fight, they didn't stand a chance. The ribs were thin and had too little meat for all the rub applied to them. The salt-to-smoke ratio was skewed way too far toward salt. The sliced brisket was respectable. The meat was tender enough and had good smoke, but it had been sitting in its own juice in a warming pan and one of the edges was too salty to enjoy. The sausage was odd. We had a new crew member—Rob's fiancée, Alli, met us in Manor— and she thought the sausage tasted like Old Bay Seasoning. I have to admit I was thinking about crawfish boils after just a few bites. The best thing there was easily the pork steak. The thin cut looked kind of sad sitting on the tray, but the meat flaked away nicely like a good piece of fish. Still moist with good smoke and a heavy, black-pepper rub, it was a good chunk of meat, and easily the best of their arsenal.

The drive down to Creedmoor on the new Tollway 130—also known as the Pickle Parkway, after US Congressman J. J. "Jake" Pickle—took no time at all. We were on the lookout for a Valero gas station that was also home to **WILHITE'S BARBEQUE**. I'd never been there, but I'd read so many glowing reviews of the place it was a must stop. I would not be disappointed. Where else can you find a mayor who's also a hell of a pitmaster? Robert Wilhite's dad opened the joint in 1962, and Robert carries the torch today. He replaced the old pits with pits of his own design, which a metalworking buddy in

Colorado fabricated for him. The twin steel pits are encased in stone and fed with post oak. The racks on the inside of it are circular and rotate like a lazy Susan. Most of the time Robert only needs one of the smokers, but he'll get both going on a heavy weekend.

After showing us the pits, Robert showed us the goods. He hoisted a midnight-black brisket onto the cutting board, and I knew it was gonna be good as he sliced through it with ease. I could hardly stand the wait as he piled it up on the brown butcher paper, but I was a good guest and didn't touch a bite until I got to the table. The meat was superbly tender and plenty moist. The smokiness permeated the silky fat cap that remained, and a rub heavier in salt than pepper woke the meat up. The ribs weren't as dark, but they were just as smoky. The meat came away from the bone without falling off, and every bit of the nicely rendered fat was edible. An all-beef sausage came from Meyer's in Elgin, and I laughed about how much better it was at Wilhite's than it had been at Meyer's. The difference was that Robert started with fresh raw sausage from Meyer's, which he then smoked himself. Robert joked that even the Meyer's delivery driver came inside his place to buy smoked sausage. Across the board, it was outstanding barbecue, and Robert had done right by the Texas trinity.

There's no such thing as a direct route from Creedmoor to Shiner, but we had Steve to direct the meandering for us. After a scouting trip through Lockhart, we resisted the urge to stop since we'd be back here tomorrow, and kept driving. It was too late for R&G Bar-B-Que in McMahan, but we drove by anyway on the off chance anyone was stirring. The whole town was shut down, so we kept moving east, toward Cistern, where Steve knew of a good bar with a decent smoked-pork sandwich. I was ready to stop anywhere to relieve myself. Everyone else seemed to feel the same way—we all raced toward the single restroom in the **CISTERN COUNTRY STORE**.

In my single-mindedness to get to the john, I barely

noticed the V&V Sausage factory across the street. Nick and I had eaten so many V&V sausages, it was odd to find its factory out here in tiny Cistern of all places. Back inside the store, they didn't offer sausage. My meal consisted of a Shiner Bock and a smoked-pork sandwich on cheap white bread dressed with pickles, onions, and sauce. It's hard to explain how the humble pork sandwich can be so good, even when made with meat of dubious quality, but the smoky sliced pork at the Cistern Country Store was downright good. Hunger hadn't crept into my mind for several days, but I still managed to finish the whole thing.

A few miles back, in Jeddo, we had blown past the B & B Charcoal factory with full bladders. You can find bags of B & B in nearly any grocery store in Texas. Instead of briquettes, B & B bags hardwood lump charcoal that's popular with backyard barbecuers and weekend pitmasters. We had to get back and see the operation. It was Saturday, so there was little hope that we'd be able to look around, but it was worth a shot. On the way back to Jeddo, Steve directed us to an abandoned dance hall outside Cistern at the corner of Rosanky and Jeddo Roads. Weeds grew all around the once-handsome structure, hiding it from the main road. It had a solid roof, but was otherwise in severe disrepair. As a barbecue fanatic, it hits a nerve when a hallowed joint closes its doors, but I'm always comforted by the fact that there are new legends in the making. The new that "out with the old" can lead to is often great, and a continuation of barbecue traditions. That cycle doesn't exist for historic dance halls. They're not lucrative to repair or run, and changing cultural entertainments have rendered most of them obsolete. I could see the pain on Steve's face as he stood there taking stock of the damage. If the old place wasn't saved soon, it would be gone forever. There wouldn't be a replacement. That's when I realized how important Steve's mission is. His passion is only matched by the utter helplessness of just watching these priceless pieces of history crumble when the building's owner has no interest in maintaining them.

A group of men were working out in the yard of B & B Charcoal. Men with hammers surrounded a pile of oversized chunks of hardwood charcoal. They were busy breaking down the pieces that were too large to bag up, their faces covered in soot like a coal miner's. I asked them about the charcoal-making process, but none of them spoke English. Steel and concrete relics that had once burned the wood to coals stood in a row. They were so charred and warped it was as if we could almost see the countless fires burned inside them. Endless cords of wood were stacked all over the property awaiting their fate. A breeze picked up while I was standing next to a massive cord of chopped oak. The smell on the breeze was unmistakable—bourbon. It made sense, considering that my favorite brown liquor is aged in oak barrels, but somehow I'd never grasped before how significant a connection there is between the flavor of bourbon and the barrels it's aged in. Now I was thirsty.

Steve was still in the lead on our way to Shiner. He stopped just north of town in a grassy clearing, where an old barbecue pit stood next to a building with Sulphur Park Swimming Pool painted on the front. The old pool, built in 1930, was still there, surrounded by weeds. It was empty but had once been fed by a natural spring. It was a poignant sight. The pool, which had once been such a popular hangout back in the thirties and forties, was now just a forgotten and neglected landmark along State Highway 95.

Our first stop in Shiner was for dinner. The owner of **SHINER RESTAURANT AND BAR**, Randy Rouse, actually lives in San Antonio and commutes to Shiner to run the kitchen and fortify the bar with great beer. I had met him once before at JMueller BBQ in Austin, and he insisted I come by and check out his place. I had mentioned this particular Saturday, so it came as no surprise to me that the nightly special was smoked prime rib. I am powerless to turn down nearly any smoked item on a menu, and in this case I had to assume Randy had it on the menu for me. While the rest of the group ate salads and various fried foods, I dug into yet another slab of beef, just to be polite to Randy. Even after a full day of eating meat, that chunk of medium-rare beef was incredible. I'm usually not a fan of smoked prime rib, but this one wasn't overcooked or too smoky. The outer crust was heavily seasoned with a powerful punch of black pepper and smoke, but the interior was still red and incredibly tender. It was a great slab of beef.

After dinner, Steve and Deborah went back to Austin, but the rest of the crew, along with Randy Rouse, headed to a gas station on the other side of town. Howard's not only sells gas and convenience items, they also have multiple types of Shiner on draft for $1.75 per pint and live music on the patio out back. It made for a relaxing night in tiny Shiner. After the others headed for the motel, Randy and I went back to his restaurant. The bar staff were shutting things down, but he had the keys to the kingdom. We drank like kings that night and on into the morning. I can't tell you when I made it to bed, but I can tell you that when my 11:00 wake-up call rolled around the next morning, it felt mighty early. Good thing there would be plenty of barbecue to fortify me in Lockhart.

Driving more than an hour in the rain with a hangover made me question how wise it had been to stay in Shiner for the night. Alli and Rob had driven on ahead, and Nick and I were doing our best to catch up. By the time we pulled into the gravel lot just outside the back door of **SMITTY'S MARKET** in Lockhart it was 12:30 and the line was out the door. Most days the line snakes right out into the lot outside of the back door that's held open more often than it's shut. Most joints in Texas would be hollering to keep the door shut and the cold air in, but there's a good chance that even on the hottest summer day in Texas it'll be hotter just inside the door. You see, there's a big, roaring fire right there on the floor next to one of the pits. While in line, you'll be blasted by its heat. Standing directly across from it *might* be comfortable on the coldest January day. The fire says plenty about the attitude of this place. It burns quite literally on the floor right in front of you—there is no barrier around it. If you've

got a curious toddler, this is a good place to test out that new leash. With this fire, Smitty's is telling their customers and visitors that the ownership respects their intelligence enough to continue providing this spectacle from another era for their enjoyment. They assume that you won't step into the fire because, well, because it's fire. Once you order and are safely inside the dining room you can also ask for barbecue sauce. It's provided under the same conditions as the spectacle of the embers. They offer it because they expect anyone with a lick of brains won't bother to use it. Then if you do spray the sauce all over your meat, everyone else around you will quickly see that you're an idiot.

Smitty's is a temple of Texas barbecue that many folks ardently claim is their favorite in Texas. I won't deny them that right, but I also won't deny that I've had some pretty spotty visits at Smitty's in the past. On my last visit, I had arrived early in the morning, before a line had formed. Early morning is often the most special time at a barbecue joint since you can chat it up with the pitmaster and get a read on the best offerings of the day. But on my last visit, I had been treated as if I were little more than an inconvenient interruption during a smoke break. Today was different. A group of cookers, cutters, and cashiers worked in well-oiled unison to keep the line moving. They were going through meat so fast there was no way it wasn't going to be fresh off the pit. At that point I began to understand the sour attitude on that earlier visit. Smitty's is a joint built for high-volume barbecue. The folks working here seem most comfortable at the frenetic-yet-efficient pace that dominates the several hours of their lunchtime rush. They give it their all during those hours, even offering a few smiles, and there just isn't any left to go around in those unfamiliar moments of rest.

There were mutual smiles when my butcher paper–wrapped meat was passed over the counter. The four of us took spots on either side of a long communal table in the dining room. Unwrapping the meat exposed what I could tell might be the best sampling of barbecue I'd had at Smitty's. Slices of brisket from the lean end and thick slices of hot beef clod were a contrast in textures. The long fibers of the clod pulled apart easily and the cut was cooked to a pleasing level of tenderness. The brisket was the best I've had there, even if they don't value smokiness as much as other joints. At Smitty's, they cook the meat quickly with a much higher heat than is normal in an indirect smoker. Temperatures reaching 500 degrees don't make for low-and-slow. The meat has a dry chewiness because of it, which I'd chalk up to poor pit management at most joints, but at Smitty's I really think it's their target. I wish that they'd aim elsewhere, but the meat was still very good.

Beef clod is a cut you don't see much anymore, but it used to be extremely popular in barbecue joints across the state. For most of the century that meat has been smoked in Smitty's building, brisket was not considered a good cut for barbecue. The tough muscle was more likely to end up in ground beef. On the other hand, the beef shoulder holds a huge cut that requires little trimming and is laced with fat. This cut, referred to as the clod, wasn't much good for steaks and became a stalwart in the barbecue pits. Its high fat content makes it less temperamental than brisket when exposed to the fluctuating and sometimes searing heat in the pits at Smitty's. With Black's superior brisket just down the street, I'd much rather partake in Smitty's clod anyway, if given the option.

Pork is also a strong suit of Smitty's, where they smoke whole racks of pork and cut chops from them to order. The end cut is the best for good char and great smoke, so be sure to ask for it specifically. The fat, salt, and tender meat all coalesce at the edges of the rack of pork. The interior muscle of a rack can get a bit dry, but the bones are worth cleaning off by hand. The meat on some thin pork spareribs come easily from the bone. You might expect an old-time joint like this was to eschew seasonings beyond salt and pepper, but an unexpected sweetness enters the palate from the glaze applied just before the racks come off the pit. The crust on the ribs was slightly chewy, in pleasing contrast to the perfectly moist meat and the hot liquid fat coursing through the whole rib. Speaking of fat, no meal at Smitty's is complete without a ring of their signature beef sausage. When they're hot, you can see the fat bubbling beneath the translucent casing. Bite into the end, and you'll risk a first-degree burn from the fat trail on your chin. The best way to enjoy them is to lay a place mat of saltines on the butcher paper, tear the sausage in half at the apex of the horseshoe-shaped link, and let the fat run out onto the crackers. These will now make great buns for tiny sausage sandwiches—but first, take a big bite out of the freshly drained link and roll the coarsely ground meat in your mouth. This is Lockhart sausage.

When the meal was complete, what I had feared came to fruition. Rob's meat fatigue met head-on with a fiancée who was yearning to take him back home, and he was out. Grand promises of sticking with us to the

···SAUSAGE·················

It is a bit ironic that Smitty's, a temple to the old German-style meat market, cooks its sausage incorrectly. It may be the style all across Central Texas, but those crumbly links with rendered-out fat gushing onto the paper beneath are cooked too hastily. To get a sausage to set and hold together when sliced, you have to let it form a binding gel at the beginning of the cooking process. A factory will use ingredients like casein or whey protein to "set" a sausage, but traditionally a sausage is set by bringing it to a temp around 130 degrees, then slowly bringing it up to the final temp of 160 degrees. Heating the meat and fat slowly keeps the fat from rendering out of the fatty tissue and creating a greasy sausage. The high-heat smoking of Central Texas renders the fat out into a liquid before the meat batter can set or "gel," and the result is a crumbly, greasy sausage. None of this makes me like them any less, but I used to think the crumbly texture was just from a coarsely ground filling.

end were traded for the sure comfort of his own bed in the near future. I told him that I had been contemplating the title to this chapter. One was the simple "Central Texas Barbecue" and the other was "Rob Borkowski Is a Pussy." The choice was his. In the end, I was the one without enough cojones to follow through with the threat, and he was riding shotgun with someone a lot prettier than either one of the balding duo that remained. Just as we said good-bye the skies opened up and released sheets of rain. I spent the next hour waiting out the storm and scrolling through my Twitter account, which I'd ignored the entire day previous. The irony of doing so while stationed at an ancient stool on the far end of a historic dining room wasn't lost on me.

Smitty's sits a block off the main square of Lockhart. The impressive and imposing Caldwell County Courthouse occupies one side of the square. North Main Street leads away from the side opposite, and just a few blocks down North Main is **BLACK'S BARBECUE**. The line was out the door, and despite my full belly, I hadn't completely kicked my hangover. It was time to give in to the oldest and most reliable remedy, so we walked into Lilly's Bar to wait out the line at Black's that we expected to thin out by midafternoon. The interior of the tiny bar was covered in tin foil and elephant figurines. A refrigerator had neatly stacked Jell-O shots organized by color on every rack. We just needed a couple of Budweiser longnecks, and we were back in business.

Black's sometimes gets a bad name from barbecue purists who shudder at the generous offering of vegetables, salads, and desserts just inside the door. You have to pass by the display before entering the chamber of meat, and it makes a decidedly bad impression. I'm able to see past it, but for many on the barbecue trail it's an image as

hard to shake as the open fire pits back at Smitty's. I don't think I've ever picked up a plate for the veggies or a scoop of beans at Black's, though. I just head straight back to the ordering counter, where all the rewarding meaty transactions are made. A man with a knife carries hunks of meat to a cutting board within easy view and clear earshot. Another person helms the register so the knife man can stay focused. Every order at Black's can be a custom one if you so choose, and I always do. The satisfaction of pointing to a specific portion of a specific cut of meat and seeing it land on your tray after a few quick swipes of the blade is hard to match. That is how all barbecue should be ordered.

On that day my proximity to the cutting board also clued me in that the meat was getting to be on the dry side—it was already late in the afternoon. We retired with our tray o' meat to one of the picnic tables on the side of the building. Fatty and lean brisket, baby back and spareribs, a ring of sausage, and some turkey made for an imposing sight, but we tackled each cut with precision. As I suspected, the peppery and smoky slices of lean brisket were beyond dry. Even the nice fat cap left on the meat had begun to crinkle. The fatty brisket wasn't much better. A sparerib had frayed and dried edges, and the baby backs weren't quite tender enough. One of my favorite joints was letting me down a bit. That was until I dove into the smoked turkey breast. Some places opt for salt-injected and precooked deli turkey, but Black's turkey starts out as a raw breast that's generously rubbed with salt and cracked black pepper. The turkey breast had remained lusciously moist, and the meat was tender and flavorful. The fatty beef sausage rings were just as good. In flavor and texture they were very similar to Smitty's, but Black's links might have been even better. The big chunks of black pepper were unapologetic. A mix of 85 percent beef and 15 percent pork was ground coarsely along with plenty of fat in the mix. Low-fat links these were not, and thank the sausage gods.

Letting the meat settle a bit, we whiled away a bit of the remaining

afternoon chatting with folks at adjacent picnic tables. After checking into the hotel in town, it was time for dinner. If your carnivorous ways make you shy away from the veggies at Black's, then a visit to **CHISHOLM TRAIL BAR-B-Q** might be too much to take. Their buffet line was stacked solid with green-colored items, and they even sold a veggie plate. This deep into a meat-filled trip, Nick and I enjoyed the novelty and were happy to munch on some broccoli, cabbage, and a salad. We ordered some meat too, of course—ribs, brisket, and sausage—and I was a bit surprised when it was sliced and then thumped down right on top of my three veggies, one of which was a ranch dressing–covered green salad. The beef gods must not be big on green salads. Either way, the three meats and three veggies rang in at just under nine dollars, so it's little wonder that locals prefer this place to either Smitty's, Black's, or Kreuz Market. Lockhart might be the designated Barbecue Capital of Texas because of the other three joints in town, but locals voted the Chisholm Trail best barbecue joint in 2011 in the *Lockhart Post Register* poll. The lack of a line out the door probably doesn't hurt its standing with the local folks, either.

After I wiped off the ranch dressing from the rib, it was beyond just passable barbecue. A rich, red hue covered the outside of a large sparerib, and the rosy interior had plenty of good smoke. The brisket may have

been the best of the day—it had a black crust that almost crackled under my teeth. The generous fat left on the slices was nicely rendered, and there was just enough seasoning to be noticed. A beef sausage similar to the rest in town had consistently been a favorite of mine, and that day was no different.

Chisholm Trail, which opened in 1978, is the young guy on the block in Lockhart. Kreuz and Smitty's, which are owned by the same extended family, share a history that dates back to 1900 and Black's has been operating since 1932. On Chisholm's website, owner Floyd Wilhelm is quoted as saying that opening a barbecue joint on the hallowed grounds of Lockhart, Texas, was like "putting a ballpark across from Yankee Stadium." The rest of the family is equally humble, and even late on a Sunday night, Floyd Jr. was happy to show us around. Huge piles of post oak were stacked behind the building, ready to feed all three of the smokers on the property. The ribs and chicken are prepared in a couple of squat, rectangular steel smokers with heavy steel lids. A rotisserie smoker dedicated to briskets was a bit more modern, but still used only wood for heat. A clock radio in the pit room was covered in a thick layer of smoke and melted a bit from the intense heat, a reminder of what a pitmaster's lungs have to endure as an occupational hazard.

After three packed days, it was nice to have a light day where we ate at only three joints, all in the same town. Our bellies needed the break, and the greens at Chisholm Trail did wonders for the digestive system. We'd need all the sleep and energy we could get to tackle a couple of very aggressive days ahead.

Lockhart is a small, quiet town whose notoriety for great barbecue draws a great many tourists on the weekends. The town seems to slow down to a more unhurried pace by the time Monday rolls around. To take full advantage of that, we opted for an early-Monday-morning visit to **KREUZ MARKET**. The enormous redbrick building sits in the center of an equally large parking lot, in which ours was the only car at 10:20. The building lacks the historic qualities of Smitty's building, where Kreuz Market used to operate. These newer digs were built back in 1999 after a disagreement led to the closing of the original location. Rick Schmidt and his brother, Don, bought the business from their father, Edgar, in 1984, but not the building. Their sister, Nina Sells, then inherited the building from their father when he died in 1990. His sister becoming his landlord wasn't a big deal until it was time to renew the lease in 1998, and they just couldn't agree on terms. If you talk to Rick, there was no feud, and while he wasn't happy about moving at the time, he now sees how the new building has really allowed the business to expand in a way that wasn't possible before.

When Rick moved Kreuz Market to its new location, he took a wheelbarrow of hot coals from the original Kreuz smokers to start the fires anew. More important, he also brought along Kreuz's pitmaster Roy Perez. Roy had fallen into the job when Kreuz's previous pitmaster was killed in a car accident. Up until then, Roy had been a housepainter, a job he enjoyed for its solitude and the luxury of working at his own pace, but then Rick Schmidt asked him to come work at Kreuz because he was shorthanded. The biggest hurdle Roy had to overcome at Kreuz was all the people. He was a shy guy who didn't enjoy being on display, and when you're the man with the meat and the knife at Kreuz, you are part of the show. After a while he grew comfortable in the role and started to enjoy being part of the entertainment. At the end of our meal, he showed his meticulous side. For the last twenty-five years Roy has kept a smoked-meat journal. He charts the amount cooked and sold for each different meat on every day that Kreuz Market is open. This provides him with some historical context when he has to determine how much meat to cook for a special occasion, like Cinco de Mayo weekend. At our request he brought the journals out for us to look at with a mix of nonchalance and curiosity as to why we'd find them interesting.

Roy is something of a barbecue celebrity. With his stocky stature, serious muttonchops, and skin that seems tanned from the years of smoke, he is an imposing figure. If he's not wielding a large knife, then he's carrying a sharply pointed stainless steel rod a little longer than a pencil, which he uses to poke the meat and check for doneness. These implements, along with his meat-stained apron, only add to the allure that has drawn countless photographers to snap his portrait. His face has shown up in many magazine stories and more than a couple of books on barbecue. Roy is the public face of Kreuz Market. If you arrive at Kreuz just as they open on a weekday morning, it's his face you'll see on the other side of the glass as he turns the Closed sign around and unlocks the door. This could be the job of anyone on their large staff, but it's Roy who says when Kreuz opens for business.

Keith Schmidt, Rick's son, started running the place in 2011. Keith quickly understood that Roy was the face of the smoked-meat side of the business and made him the restaurant's manager. Rick Schmidt, while no longer on the payroll and happily retired, is still pleased to stop in and offer his management tips as well. On the morning of our visit he was there to eat, decked out in his signature cowboy hat and Kreuz Market–issued work shirt.

As a rule I do not announce myself before I go to a barbecue joint, and I don't ask for favors while I'm there. Neither was possible that Monday morning when Roy greeted us as the first customers of the day—I've talked to Roy a number of times on previous visits, and we know each other on Twitter. Unlike his perceived persona, Roy is at once shy, accommodating, generous, and most of all humble. On a previous trip, a few friends and I took some photos of Roy slicing a shoulder clod on the thick cutting boards behind the registers. I asked him if we could get a photo. He nodded his head and went to grab my camera. I kid you not that Roy thought I was asking him to take a photo of my friends and me. After a laugh, I got my photo taken with Roy while holding his knife. Like I said, humble. On our Monday morning visit he showed his generosity again. After gathering that we wanted a taste of the full menu, he loaded up some butcher paper with the beef course. He wouldn't accept payment, so I put a couple of twenties in the tip jar when he wasn't looking. The pork wasn't ready yet, so we took our clod, brisket, prime rib, and beef sausage to the empty dining room. We could have any table, and of course the photographer chose the one next to the window. The camera needed little assistance to make this stuff look good, and my stomach ached in anticipation as I waited patiently for Nick to finish photographing the meat.

Back on my first real barbecue voyage Kreuz was, of course, one of the required stops. Sam and I had been eating with our hands at most of the joints leading up to our stop at Kreuz, but it was there that we really embraced it. Their no-forks policy makes this a given, but I remember diving into the meat with abandon. With barbecue, the sense of touch is just as important as taste and smell in determining the quality of smoked meats. Gauging the amount of pressure required to pull apart a slice of brisket and feeling the resistance—or lack thereof—on a well-smoked fat cap tells you something about your impending level of enjoyment before you even taste it. Handling the meat adds to the anticipation in a way that mindlessly slicing and chewing can't provide.

We dug right into the prime rib since it dries out the quickest. Even in the hands of the best pitmaster, I just can't get on board with smoked prime rib. I've never had a slice of it that was better than a medium-rare roasted version. The brisket was some of the best I've had at Kreuz. It was smoky and tender, and a triangular cut from the brisket end was lusciously fatty. I think getting it fresh in the morning right off the pit makes a big difference. The cooking method at Kreuz is not low-and-slow. A large brisket may smoke for only six hours at temperatures as high as 800 degrees. Shoulder clods are put on the pit for just four hours. Because shoulder clod is thicker than a brisket the smoke doesn't penetrate as much of each slice. This allows the beefy flavor to shine through. The link of sausage was hot and bubbling with fat. The coarsely ground beef and pork mix had great flavor and black-pepper bite. The casing was snappy and not at all chewy. At that point we tried to pace ourselves for the impending pork course.

Roy brought out a few ribs and two slices of pork chop. Roy smokes the whole rack of chops at once, instead of smoking individual chops, and we got one from the middle and a nice bronzed end cut. You will not find a finer pork chop than what Kreuz puts out daily. The end cut had a tea-colored exterior and lots of seasoning. The meat was ridiculously juicy and there was no need to cut around the fat as it just melted in the mouth. We had to hold off on the ribs, since Roy felt they needed ten more minutes on the smoker, but they were worth the wait. When I caught the first glance of the ribs after unwrapping the butcher paper, I knew I was in for a treat. They were glistening with fat and juice was dripping out of the middle. A heavy, black-pepper crust wasn't as salty as I remembered, and that was a good thing. The meat was hot, with crisp edges akin to bacon and a porky interior that just dripped with meat juices. I felt sorry for the rest of the places we'd visit that day. If there was a finer meal in store for us it would be a miracle, but I was ready to go find out.

Some of my favorite barbecue memories were formed in Luling, Texas. Several years back I drove from Helotes, west of San Antonio, to Luling for breakfast at **CITY MARKET**, only to drive straight back to meet with friends uninterested in the leftovers and puzzled as to why I would have made the trip. A year later, these same friends would discover the beauty of City Market barbecue after we braved the hellacious lines that form during Watermelon Thump weekend in late June. The Thump is a huge festival that celebrates the watermelon harvest, and we were fresh from the Spitway, where we'd tried our skills at spitting watermelon seeds for distance. After sending a seed further than thirty feet, I felt I deserved some brisket.

This Monday morning was a little slower than those others, but there was still a line snaking away from the pits. The restaurant is set up so that you order sides, drinks, and sauce at a counter in the dining room in the front of the restaurant. For meat, you head straight to

the back, through a set of doors, and into the pit room. Only the Texas trinity of brisket, pork ribs, and sausage is available. All three were quickly cut, weighed, and assembled on some reddish butcher paper for our dining pleasure. We needed none of the standard side items, but I did have to grab some cheddar cheese and some of their famous sauce before finding a table.

The brisket was sliced on the bias, creating long, thin slices. The black crust and exemplary deep red smoke ring only wanted for more fat, since most of it had been trimmed off. The meat was dense like you'd expect from a hot-and-fast cook and not as tender as I remembered. The pork ribs were trimmed close to the bone, so there wasn't much fat on them, either. That worked out fine, though, since the meat was naturally moist. The texture was perfect on the ribs, which were coated with seasoning and a sweet glaze. The layers of seasoning and glaze formed a crust that had a little chew to it, and the meat below was perfectly tender. It was easy to get those bones clean. The rings of beef sausage were similar to the Lockhart-style links; the filling was coarsely ground and seasoned with lots of black pepper. The filling hadn't gelled, and the meat fell apart as I removed the casing. Just about every table appeared to be using the same method for sausage consumption: spoon a pool of orange-colored sauce on the butcher paper and commence dipping the link before every bite. The sauce had a vinegar kick from the mustard that tempered its sweetness. As someone who's not a huge advocate of sauce, I couldn't leave the City Market sauce alone.

Out front you'll see a Bar-E above the sign for City Market. This is the name of the ranch run by the owners, the Ellis family. The joint used to source their beef from the ranch, but the pile of

IBP boxes in the back room are evidence of our country's more modern beef production methods. IBP stands for Iowa Beef Processors, the company now owned by Tyson Foods, which accounts for 25 percent of the US market share for cattle processing. Back in 1967, IBP introduced boxed, vacuum-packed, prebutchered cuts of beef and pork to the market—before that most meat reached consumers via butcher shops, which broke down half beefs into custom cuts. These days, it's hard to keep from tripping over an IBP box in a pit room. Their enormous processing facility in Amarillo probably does as much for their ubiquity around the state's barbecue joints as their name recognition, but there's no doubt that they are everywhere. I can count on one hand the joints I know of who bother to seek out another source for their beef.

Out back, a stack of split post oak awaited the pits. I was stunned to see a Southern Pride smoker in the corner of the pit room, but Joe Capello, the pitmaster, promised that it was only used on peak weekends. Even if it was barely used, I still didn't expect such a hallowed Texas barbecue joint to value quantity over quality, even if only for a few weekends a year. The real workhorse of the room was a huge brick pit with large metal lids. Joe had on his signature yellow hard hat when he opened the pit to show us the meat. The briskets had already been pulled for the day, and the pork ribs were finishing up. He poked a few with a pointed steel rod (just like Roy Perez's) to check for doneness and closed the lid. He gave us directions to the old Ellis Ranch northeast of town, but we were headed south.

"Deep in the Heart of Texas" is a song familiar to many Texans and non-Texans alike. Its most well-known line is about the stars at night being big and bright, but it's a rather long song and you rarely hear anyone sing the second half of Gene Autry's version in which, following an instrumental, he sings, "The oil wells are full of smells. . . ." I'm reminded of this line every time I take a stroll around Luling, where the smell of oil (or money, depending on who you're talking to) is so thick in the air you wonder how anyone gets used to it. The song played in my head as we walked the two blocks from City Market over to a completely different world at **LULING BAR-B-Q**. The differences between the two were noticeable as soon as we walked in. First, there wasn't a line. You place your order at the counter, not in the pit room. Instead of a concise menu of three meats and a few sides, Luling Bar-B-Q wows customers with no less than half a dozen meats and sides like broccoli salad and macaroni and cheese. The parallels between this joint and Chisholm Trail, in Lockhart, were undeniable. The word on the street is that the locals prefer the barbecue here rather than at the touristy-but-more-revered City Market. Owner Lee Chambers is unfazed by his famous neighbor. "They don't hurt our business here," he said of City Market. "We hold our own."

They do indeed, with better-quality barbecue than you'll find in most towns around the state. The home-made sausage links had a more rustic look, but tasted just as good, if not even a bit smokier than the sausage at City Market. I enjoyed the simple seasoning and smoke of the brisket at City Market, but Luling's was better cooked. Slices from the lean end had a great line of rendered fat along the top and were moist with melted fat. The meat was perfectly tender. It was some fine brisket. The overseasoned ribs weren't as successful. The meat was gray instead of the rosy color that denotes good smoke. They were also a little tenderer than I like. A squeeze of the City Market knockoff sauce helped them out. For a joint that runs a gas smoker every day, they were putting out some pretty good mesquite-and-post-oak-smoked meats.

Luling Bar-B-Q may have nearly cracked the code to the secret of City Market's barbecue sauce, but just down the road at the Bone Shack, the sauce relies on a secret ingredient no one will be able to duplicate: the pitmaster's blood. It's a serious health code

violation, but then again, you can only visit the Bone Shack if you happen to find yourself transported to the fictional world of *Planet Terror*, the zombie apocalypse film directed by Austinite Robert Rodriguez. The historic Zedler Mill served as the site of the fictitious Bone Shack. The mill, which was built in 1888, stands on the banks of the San Marcos River, which was dammed at the site of the mill to supply power to it. The family of the mill's founder, German immigrant Fritz Zedler, ran the mill until the fifties, when new technology rendered it obsolete. The city of Luling restored the mill and its adjacent buildings in 2002, including Fritz Zedler's old home, and the whole complex is now a public park and historical center—but the most popular attraction on the grounds seemed to be an old tree with a long limb overhanging the deep river. Kids were lining up for the climb and eventual jump into the river below.

State Highway 80 out of Luling heads right for Belmont, Texas, where I'd heard there was an old, run-down joint worth checking out. The tiny town consisted of little more than a church, a seasonal pecan shop, and the Belmont Social Club, home of the barbecue we were seeking out. The social club was closed on Mondays, though. We were surprised, given that a banner hanging out front said they were open every day around this time. We waited around a while in hopes that the owner had just stepped away for a bit. Losing patience, and with some time on our hands, we decided to drive further south than originally planned, to the area around Panna Maria, the oldest Polish settlement in the United States, in hopes of finding some good kielbasa.

We passed Chambers Bar-B-Que in Nixon, which was closed for good. The Market in Karnes City was open for lunch on Friday and Saturday only. By the time we found **POLAK'S SAWSAGE FARM**, we were hungry and happy to find this joint open on the outskirts of town. The curious spelling continued on their menu, which included the following: pickels, smotherd chicken, and a ruben sandwich. A combo plate of the sawsage and "bar-b-q beef" came out quickly. Sides of German potato salad and kraut were a nice change of pace, as was the slice of home-made white bread. The brisket was an abomination to the good name of barbecue. A thick slice had been warmed on the flattop in the kitchen. It was a uniform brown as a result, with a sad-looking sheen from the intense heat. The edges were so dried out they had the texture of pork rinds. I cringed in anticipation before taking the required bite, and it was actually worse than it looked. Luckily, I'd saved the sausage for last. While not the familiar kielbasa consistency, it was good home-made sausage. The beef and pork mix was coarsely ground and heavily seasoned. The texture of the casing was probably a result of boiling rather than smoking, but it had great flavor. If I hadn't eaten some of the worst brisket of my life there, I might have come away with a positive opinion.

We had enjoyed Pollok's sausage from Oakville to Hondo in our South Texas tour, so when we passed the storefront of **POLLOK'S GROCERY & MARKET** up the road in Falls City, we had to stop. There was nothing at the meat counter that was hot and ready to eat except for some rings of dried sausage. I was tempted to buy a few raw links, but I knew I wouldn't have an appetite for them at the end of the day. Even the purchase of some dried sausage was more for show than sustenance. Our next planned stop, Seguin, was still an hour away, and it was getting close to dinnertime.

On the south side of Seguin we passed a place I'd never heard of called **JOHNNY'S BAR-B-QUE**. The scent of mesquite smoke rolled in our open windows, so we pulled over and I went in to order. I could see them loading the to-go box as the lady waiting on me explained that her sister had recently purchased a new gas-fired smoker because doing it the old way was just too hard. I wished I could take my order back. The pork ribs were overseasoned, overrubbed, and oversmoked. The rack of spices coating the ribs almost masked the creosote aftertaste. The brisket was little more than underdone pot roast. The fat was still chewy, and the meat had a density you might get from steaming the meat. To add insult to injury, the pie wasn't even all that good. On to our intended Seguin destination: the original location of **DAVILA'S BAR-B-Q**.

Normally, when a joint opens a second location, they do their best to make it clear where to find the original place while marketing the new spot. Even if the food is equally good at both locations, it's hard for most people to shake the feeling that the original joint serves superior barbecue—a fact that the owners of barbecue joints know all too well. So I found it odd that Davila's Bar-B-Q's web presence was almost entirely dedicated to its new location out on the bypass. Austin blogger R. L. Reeves Jr. had written about the beauty of the beef links at the original, so I actually had to get in touch with him for the address. The Davila family first started a meat market in Luling back in the fifties, then moved the business to Lockhart and started selling smoked meats. When Seguin began to expand in the middle of the twentieth century, they decided to leave Lockhart and its stagnant economy behind. In

1959 they opened Davila's Bar-B-Q in Seguin, and the family still runs the business today. Of course, the irony is,

if they had stayed in Lockhart—the Barbecue Capital of Texas—they would probably be better known today.

Edward Davila Sr. runs things at the original location and he was on hand to show us around. Davila's smokes with all mesquite and eschews gas cookers for circular rotisseries of their own design. I like their cooking methods for sure, but their method of holding meat is suspect. The red heat lamps blasting the piles of brisket made for some dried-out meat for sure, and we didn't do them any favors by showing up thirty minutes before closing, so I was especially looking forward to trying their home-made sausage. There's plenty of handmade sausage to be had in Lockhart and Luling, but it's still the exception in most of the state. Most joints order their links already smoked. A few might use the local meat market to get fresh sausage, but making sausage from scratch is a dying art in most Texas barbecue joints.

During the tour the kitchen staff put together an impressive sampler plate for us. Adrian Davila, Edward's son, manages their second location but dropped by during our tour. It's rare that a barbecue joint wants truly honest feedback, but Adrian really sought it out. That alone made it less uncomfortable for him to be sitting there while we ate. I started with the good. Once you worked around the fat in the lamb ribs, what was left was excellent smoked meat with a nice crunchy texture to the outside edges. The sausage links were superior to most I've had in the state. The casing on the all-beef links snapped easily under the teeth. They were aggressively seasoned and much spicier than most other sausages we'd tried to that point. The links alone were reason enough to return. The outside crust of the pork rib came away cleanly from the meat like a slice of bacon, but that was just a result of being very dry. The slices of fatty brisket had opaque fat running throughout them, which made them chewy and unappetizing. I requested some additional slices from the end to see if the quality would improve, and it did. The fatty nuggets were surrounded in a smoky, black crust with outstanding flavor. I quickly had images of a burnt-end-and-sausage sandwich, but I would have to wait until next time.

Poor planning took us back to Austin for the evening, but our guide from a few days earlier, Steve Dean, was happy to grab a drink with us at the Continental Club on South Congress. He agreed to join us the next morning at 8:00 A.M. for a drive to Smithville. **ZIMMERHANZEL'S BAR-B-QUE** opens early like so many other barbecue joints in Central Texas, so we ambled through the glass door at 9:15. We had the place to ourselves. Nick and Steve took a seat at one of the empty tables while I went to the front to order. The brisket wouldn't be ready for another twenty minutes, so I got us some pork ribs, sausage links, smoked chicken, and a slice of buttermilk pie—it was breakfast, after all.

The large, thick spareribs were sturdy, flecked in pepper, and deep brown in color. The meat was juicy and toothsome like a good pork chop, and the crust was bathed heavily in post oak smoke. The chicken had a similar smokiness that reached deep into the meat. Even the breast was still moist, and the skin was seriously crispy to boot. Just five ingredients went into their sausage link, which was a lesson in the pleasures of simplicity. Beef, salt, black pepper, and red pepper were stuffed into a hog casing. They didn't go easy on the seasoning, which really woke up our tired taste buds. They were some seriously good links, and ramped up our anticipation for the brisket.

I watched as Zimmerhanzel's coowner, Dee Dee Bunte, readied a fresh whole brisket. She cut several slices from the corner, and when it looked as if she might not include the edges on our plate, I quickly intervened. With a mix of fatty and lean slices, we had quite a good-looking plate of brisket. It didn't matter from which side we ate. The lean brisket was still moist, with a beautiful, translucent quarter-inch line of fat running along the top. The slices from the point had luscious fat running through every inch and a natural sweetness from the concentrated flavors on the darkened edges. All of it was eminently smoky and divinely tender. It was brisket worth waiting for.

The staff was busy getting things ready for the day, so I was hesitant to ask for a tour. I asked if we could see the pit room, and we were granted access with a quick nod. There's a certain romance in the general lack of cleanliness to be found at the usual barbecue joint. A failing health department score can be seen as a rite of passage, but Zimmerhanzel's was different. The steel pit was right there in the kitchen, and every inch of the tile walls and concrete floors around the pit were spotless. It may have been the cleanest pit room I've seen. I tried to catch up to the pitmaster, Bert Bunte, who was running back and forth between the kitchen and the back door, but it was obvious he was scrambling to finish things up. I got in a few questions as he walked toward the building next door with a large blue tub in hand. His voice trailed off as he walked through the double doors, and he held the door for a second in a halfhearted invitation to follow. I took it.

Inside the building, I found Bert stationed at a stainless steel table, where he was stuffing sausages and rhythmically twisting them into links. I watched, mesmerized at the swiftness with which he filled that big blue tub with raw sausage links ready for the smoker. Another door off the room opened. I looked through it as the person inside stepped out. The room beyond was a cooler and inside of it hung dozens of half beefs hanging tightly together. "Is this a slaughterhouse?" I asked Bert. Without a word Bert motioned his head to an open doorway into another room behind me that I hadn't noticed when I walked in. I turned just in time to see a man carve a hoof off a freshly skinned steer. Its detached head looked on at the process from the floor. When the butcher was through with cracking the hoof off the leg, he heaved it toward a blue trash can, where it landed with a hollow, reverberating thud. The butcher then made quick work of dismantling a cow head at the other end of the room, before it too made a larger thud in the same blue trash can.

This isn't where I preach about the fact that you must be able to watch a butcher at work in order to have the right to eat beef. It's gruesome stuff that I happen to have the stomach for. I wouldn't personally feel comfortable consuming so much beef if I couldn't at least witness cattle being butchered. I will admit that seeing a few more head of cattle staring through the fence outside just on the other side of the chute that led into the butchering room was startling and made me keenly aware of how quickly they went from steer to beef. I was also amazed at how much more powerful and uncomfortable the image of a skinned cow with four legs jutting into the air was than the comparatively benign image of a half beef hanging in a cooler. It was a quick lesson in how the processing of beef rapidly erases the image of a slaughtered animal. By the time it's a single brisket in Cryovac, it's easy to forget it was ever a cow.

After the unexpected run-in at the slaughterhouse, I was pleased with my still-raging appetite. Just forty-five minutes northeast of Smithville, we hit up **CITY MEAT MARKET** in Giddings, right at the intersection of US Highways 290 and 77. The pace slowed dramatically when we walked through the front doors into the meat market. A meat case just inside the door looked pretty sad—more like an homage to butchering days gone by than a display of top-notch beef. We walked on back to the pit room through a blue door labeled

In, where the market actually sells the smoked meats and where pitmaster Gerald Birkelbach does his magic.

Post oak burned hot at the edge of a steel smoker lined with white tile. I ordered up some beef and a half brisket was taken from a vat of hot liquid by the meat cutter. It dried visibly after being sliced. She added a link of wrinkled sausage to the tray along with some slices off of a pork steak. The ribs were not yet ready. A few bites of the brisket were pleasing enough on the palate, but the meat was as dry as it looked. The beef links had a nice coarse grind and plenty of good seasoning. The casing was wrinkled and a tad chewy, but it was still a fine sausage. The pork steak had a pleasant chew in all the good bark that had been left on, and the fat was perfectly rendered throughout the juicy meat. It might have been my favorite cut here if we hadn't had any ribs, which were finally ready just as I was finishing up the pork. Two stupendous-looking spareribs arrived at our table. They each had a ruddy exterior covered in a generous sprinkling of coarsely ground black pepper.

The juicy meat glistened in the sunlight coming through an open door. They were the smokiest meats there and easily the best. The meat came away from the bone without falling off, and its flavor, rich in salt and pepper with a hint of cayenne, was phenomenal. It only made it clearer to me that if you see something, anything, coming straight off the pit when you're visiting a barbecue joint, order it. There's a high probability that the cut, fresh out of the fire, will be at its peak, and those ribs drove the point home. Steve and Nick remembered to pace themselves, so I finished the meat that they had left on the bone of their rib, as well as finishing the one I started with.

Those ribs were much different than the bone-dry ones I'd eaten on my last visit about a year prior. What further amazed me was that Gerald remembered my last visit. He noted that my last review had complained of dry ribs. Instead of the rebuke I thought I might get at this point, he just said that he remembered the day well. He had overslept and cranked up the fire in the pit to get things finished more quickly. He knew it might affect the quality, but he was in over his head at that point. His detailed memory was staggering to me, but I guess like any competitor, he remembers the bad ones more than the good ones.

Our next stop was in the small and picturesque town of La Grange, which sits below a prominent bluff on the Colorado River. The town feels transported whole cloth from an earlier time. The ruins of the Kreische Brewery, one of Texas's first commercial breweries, sit on the bluff overlooking the town. On the east side of town is the site where the famed Chicken Ranch once serviced many country gentlemen. Right in the middle of the town square is a beautifully restored courthouse. Just across the street is the **PRAUSE MEAT MARKET**, which opened in the 1890s, a historic spot that has bucked the trend of most great smoked-meat purveyors in this part of the state. So many of the famous barbecue joints in Central Texas have a story that goes something like this: Back in 18XX a German/Czech/Polish immigrant opened a meat market. They started smoking the cuts of meat that didn't sell so well or were going bad. Soon the barbecue became as popular as the raw meat. Sometime in 19XX they ditched the meat market business and started selling barbecue exclusively.

Prause Meat Market did eventually start selling barbecue, but they have never relinquished their core business as a meat market. You could even say their sideline in barbecue is a backdoor business. Regulars park alongside the building and enter the pit room through a small back door. There you'll find Monroe Schubert shuffling between the pit and the counter up front in the market proper. Monroe has been around a while. The owners here joke that he learned how to cook on the *Titanic*—he's been tending the post oak fires at Prause since 1965. If you walk in the front door looking for barbecue you'll be met with a glass meat case that wraps around the cavernous front room, full of freshly cut steaks, chops, and sausages. You might even think you're in the wrong place— that maybe you missed the barbecue joint next door—but keep walking toward the back counter and you'll find smoked meat sliced and sold by the pound. A sign by the counter states unequivocally "We do not make sandwiches!"

A meat cutter stands at a butcher block awaiting your order to determine how much smoked meat you're looking for and from what end you want it cut. An end cut from the pork chop was otherworldly good. The bronzed exterior gave way to a rosy interior with lines of translucent fat dripping all over the slices. "Juicy" doesn't do the meat justice. As I cleaned the meat off a bone while standing at the counter I was happy that Prause Meat Market didn't frown upon eating with your hands. I was also happy to have perfected the inside-the-jeans-pocket-wipe. It had become my trusty hidden napkin. I waited until we got to one of the long red Formica tables before tearing into the rest of it. The brisket here can be a tough code to crack. From a few past visits I knew that if I ordered brisket before 10:00 A.M. it might be from the previous day. Order at 11:00 and there might be no brisket at all—yesterday's will be gone and today's won't be ready. Fresh ones were coming off the pit when we arrived. Thick slices came off the whole brisket with ease under little knife pressure. A crust was well formed, but the flavor was less smoky than I remembered. A rub heavy in salt had deeply flavored the fat surrounding the slices and the nub of an end cut that we'd requested. A waterfall of fat enveloped my chin as I bit into a peppery link of house-made sausage. Steve was undeterred by the spray of sausage grease that hit him as he chewed on some brisket. The casing's snap was audible and the fat just kept coming, as if I'd activated the widget in a can of Guinness. The boneless pork roll made from the shoulder was dry and didn't come close to matching the ethereal pork chop.

I'd heard a rumor that the business was up for sale, and the Prause family members present confirmed it. For four generations the Prause Family Name had been running the joint, but no one in the fifth generation was interested in filling the job titles as listed on the market's Facebook page, most of which are held by family members:

> Monroe—Pit Master
> Dennis—Meat Prep
> Kathy—Head Heifer/Only Mad Cow You'll Find/Books
> Brian—Cow Slayer/Butcher
> Gary—King of the Saw

Mark—Jerky Extraordinaire
Scott—Meat Prep

I was sad to leave knowing that that this could be my last visit. Without a family connection, a new owner or investor would be unlikely to maintain the quality of the barbecue. Places like Prause die after enough family members do the same. You hear about them all the time, but it felt different to witness the beginning of that slow death, which was acknowledged by every head turning away quietly at the mention of the market's uncertain future. If I could talk to the Prause children I'd explain what a treasure they're throwing away and plead with them to trade their well-paying jobs with predictable hours for a life of cutting and smoking meat for my enjoyment. I'd be asking them to do something that I'm not willing to do, but that's just selfish human nature.

If you've never been to Central Texas then it may seem mysterious why there are so many German and Czech meat markets in this part of the state. The reason is fairly straightforward. In the nineteenth century, the ports of Galveston and Indianola were major points of entry for German, Polish, and Czech immigrants. The two cities simply couldn't contain them all, so they made their way up to Fayetteville, La Grange, Industry, Schulenberg, Panna Maria, and Praha (the Czech pronunciation of the old capital, Prague). Our next stop was in one of those German-founded towns—the name of which is no mystery when you see it written, but which you may not recognize if you only hear it spoken. Here in Texas, Weimar sounds a little more like Why-mer than Vy-mahr.

Down a Weimar street named Old Sausage Avenue, we found the aged storefront of **KASPER'S MEAT MARKET**. Since 1917, Kasper's has been cutting meats and making sausages. Very little in the store has changed since then. I nodded in agreement with a hand-painted sign hanging on the back wall that declared "7 days without beef makes one weak." The only ready-to-eat item from the counter was an excellent chewy beef jerky

with loads of pepper hanging precariously from its dried surface. As
I munched on a stick I checked out their meat menu. Along with the
standard chops and steaks, there was a whole cow head—with tongue—for
just fifteen dollars. My cooler wasn't big enough.

Steve had heard some rumors that a new joint just south of
Schulenberg was putting out some good meat. **DOC'S BBQ** had the look
down pat, sure. Peeling paint flaked from the sides of the tiny sloped-roof
building. A Texas flag blew in the breeze. But the rumors were unfounded.
It was some sad barbecue and it probably hadn't been any better the day
before, either—when it was cooked. The only decent item on the plate
was a commercial sausage and it was only passable. The beef was dry
and tasteless and the crunchy ribs tasted of nothing—definitely not the
mesquite and post oak that they were supposed to have been cooked over.
It was a disappointing visit for sure, but you can't be too picky about where
you stop when you're trying to find the next hidden gem.

Skipping right through Flatonia we headed toward Waelder. Over the
last year I had heard some very good reports about Waelder Grocery and I
was anxious to try it, so I was crestfallen to see a sign reading **BALDERAS
GROCERY & BAR-B-QUE** freshly painted on the brick facade. A man
working the register in front grunted toward the back room, where we

placed our orders from the pit. We stood at the counter waiting for anyone with a knife to show up and weigh some meat. I was hoping for the best, but expecting the worst. Bricks had fallen away from the pit, revealing the steel liner. A fire extinguisher so covered in soot that the tag could not be read made me laugh. When someone finally showed up he seemed put out by our presence. We ordered brisket, ribs, and sausage. Steve, Nick, and I had been riding together long enough by then that when we opened the foil and saw the withered ribs, we all gave each other a wordless glance that pretty much said "You first."

No one bothered to check on us after we found a table to share. A couple of slices of brisket wouldn't have passed for good roast beef, even with a side of mashed potatoes and a ladle of gravy. The overcooked sausage crumbled when I cut into the casing and its flavor was more Chicago sage and red pepper than it was Texas black pepper. Instead of clearing the table into the nearby trash can, we left the food on the table as a silent protest against the quality of the meat they were trying to pass off as Central Texas barbecue. Then we sulked away.

For Steve it was just the last stop on a daylong barbecue journey. But for me and Nick, it was the culmination of many months' worth of travel, during which we had consumed more smoked meat and discovered more about this great state than we ever imagined possible. We had been on a search for the ultimate in smoked meats from Beaumont to El Paso and Dalhart to Brownsville and I had engineered this final leg to be the best—or so I had thought. In my hopes for a poetic conclusion to our travels, I imagined we would herald Waelder Grocery as one of the finest in the state, which had gone undiscovered by most. Instead we met with bad service and even worse food. Back in the car we both tried to think of another stop to end the trip right, but we knew the search could just as easily be in vain. Barbecue is a harsh and unpredictable mistress and in any case, we had already enjoyed an embarrassment of barbecue riches on the trip, some just as recently as that morning.

That childish yearning for the appropriate ending was a reminder of what a selfish endeavor the whole experience had been. We had temporarily abandoned our wives and children for personal gain. We took substandard barbecue as a personal affront on many occasions. We scoffed at "lazy" pitmasters who used tools that made their barbecue more consistent and increased their general quality of life. We proudly held fast to our dogmatic faith that the kind of barbecue for which we evangelized could only be achieved by toiling with fire through the night, every night to the detriment of the pitmaster's health and well-being. We expected their children to do the same so we could keep enjoying their timeless smoked offerings. We were unabashed culinary Luddites, seeking the destruction of the modern machines of barbecue cookery that have infested kitchens across the state and helped cheapen the quality of good smoked meat. Damn all gas ovens!

But the thing is, while this craft seems timeless, it's always changing. Today's traditions were just yesterday's innovations. The changes might come about to keep up with the times or just because of a simple changing of the guard. As much as we want these places to remain the same in order for us to relive our fond experiences, it's inevitable that some will falter and others will fall by the wayside. That leaves it up to the innovators to shape their own traditions. Keeping Texas barbecue culture alive and nurturing it with adequate reverence falls onto their shoulders, and in my own selfish way, I hope they can still smoke a damn fine brisket.

6 Days,
1,331 Miles,
33 BBQ Joints

THE

TEXAS
TRIANGLE

· ·

Seven hundred ten miles of interstate form the border of the Texas
Triangle. It's a region within the state of Texas where Dallas–Fort
Worth, Austin, San Antonio, and Houston are connected by the
soulless interstates of I-35, I-10, and I-45. Two-thirds of the state's
population lives within twenty miles of these interstates. With such
a high percentage of possible pitmasters, you'd think the cities along
this corridor would be rich with great barbecue, but that's hardly the
case. It may sound folksy, but the truth is that Texas's best barbecue
is a rural creation. Small towns are bound to have better barbecue
per capita than any big city. People usually cite strict city health
codes as the reason for the disparity, but there are county health
inspectors out in the country, too. I suspect the difference has more
to do with the lower expectations of an urban population when it
comes to the quality of smoked meats. When chains like Dickey's and
Sonny Bryan's—which are both mediocre on a good day—flourish
in places like Houston and Dallas, then you know that too many
city folks have a skewed view of what constitutes good brisket. A
few months after what was supposed to be our last barbecue road

trip, Nick and I decided to set out one more time. There were still a few stories we needed to gather and some missing photos to capture, and, to be honest, we actually kind of missed being stuck in a car together as we ate our way around the state. So why not see if we could mine some jewels in some of Texas's major cities?

To fortify body and soul for the 710 miles of monotonous interstate ahead of us, we started with lunch at a familiar venue. Since **PECAN LODGE** opened in the Dallas Farmer's Market in 2009, it has served some of the most consistently great barbecue in the state and gained a loyal following. Justin and Diane Fourton initially conceived of Pecan Lodge as a southern food restaurant that happened to serve barbecue. But it didn't take long for folks to discover the Lodge's mesquite-smoked brisket and pork ribs and to hail the restaurant as Dallas's best barbecue joint. After the restaurant made an appearance on the Food Network, its lines have steadily grown. Nick and I dutifully queued up and settled in for the wait, eager for our date with one of their newest menu items—a giant beef short rib.

Despite the restaurant's name, pecan is not the wood of choice in the pits, nor are the nuts featured on the menu. Nope, the restaurant was named after a Fourton family ranch back in Abilene, where Justin learned to smoke meat using mesquite, which is native to the area. Justin kept the mesquite tradition going when he set up shop in Dallas, where he smokes meat all night long without tainting it with harsh creosote flavor. It's hard to show restraint when ordering at Pecan Lodge, so I usually end up with a five-meat plate of brisket, pork ribs, sausage, pulled pork, and a beef rib. All are coated heavily with a secret rub that favors salt in proportion to pepper and has a bit of a cayenne kick. Of all his skills, Justin's most finely honed is the seemingly simple task of knowing when a cut is done, and, more important, not done. The brisket was perfectly tender and moist with a smoky wallop. A crisp natural hog casing enveloped a liberally seasoned pork filling in the excellent house-made sausage links, and the

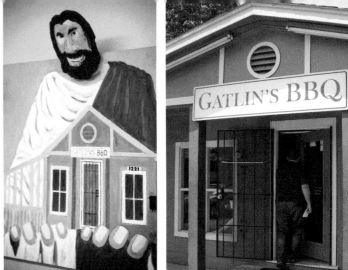

Welcome to Gatlins!
"Where Love is the secret ingredient"

Family Favorites
♡ Peach Cobbler
♡ BREAD PUDDING
♡ BANANA Pudding

Today's Special
FRIES x BBQ SAUCE .50 + TAX
LOADED FRIES $8.25/
BEEF / PORK SLIDERS 7.95

luscious pulled pork was served with (gasp) a vinegar sauce—on the side, mind you. The pork ribs were fine, but it was the beef rib that took our breath away. Because the beef ribs weighed in at a pound and a half each, we opted to split one. The collagen and fat laced heavily throughout the meat was so well rendered that it barely took a tug to come away with a handful of glistening beef. The flavor of the rub was heavy on the surface, like a salty punch in the mouth, but a large bite of the deeply smoky meat was enough to mellow it out, and large bites are mandatory. A side of sturdy mac-and-cheese laced with bacon and green chiles, and a dessert of what might be Texas's finest banana pudding further fortified us for the long ride to Houston.

Unlike our previous trips, where stops along the FM roads at random historical markers or an unexpected site were frequent, the drive from Dallas to Houston was all business. We had the hammer down as we hit the three lanes of concrete interstate to make it to H-town for an early afternoon snack. Sure, we'd already been to **GATLIN'S BBQ** on a previous trip, but it was so good that another visit was in order. Our old pals and Houston residents Chris Reid and Michael Fulmer (whom you might remember from the East Texas trip) joined Nick and me, and the follow-up visit didn't disappoint. Between bites of the beautiful brisket slices, we made a game plan for our next few hours in Houston.

The only open pit left in Houston is at **PIZZITOLA'S**, where they will never refurbish the tiny kitchen for fear of how a new permit would affect the status of their beloved brick pit—which only exists thanks to a grandfather clause from the city of Houston. I'd eaten there before and gotten the full tour, but I brought new curiosity and high hopes to this outing. Pitmasters are usually old dogs unwilling to

even try new tricks let alone learn them, so it was especially newsworthy when Jerry Pizzitola and Tim Taylor, Pizzitola's coowners, announced they had changed the way they smoked their briskets. The change was inspired by a trip to Snow's BBQ in Lexington. Jerry and Tim returned to Houston angry that Snow's brisket was so much better than theirs, and they vowed to improve. The afternoon we were there, however, the brisket in front of us showed little difference from the brisket of my previous visits. Fatty "slices" were more a moist mound of meat devoid of crust and smoke. A request for lean brisket produced a couple of slices just clinging to their last bit of moisture, but with considerable smoke flavor from the oak- and hickory-fired pit. At least the old reliable pork ribs were there to munch on. The rub on the ribs was generous with black pepper, but it was finely ground as opposed to the coarse stuff you'll find in Central Texas, which created a pleasant heat in every bite. After a few slices of the well-smoked V&V-brand pork and beef sausage, we threw in our napkins to save room for the next few stops in Houston.

Adrian Handsborough opened **VIRGIE'S BAR-B-QUE** in 2005 in the same building in northwest Houston where his parents once ran a grocery store. A fire closed Virgie's down in 2011, but Adrian is back and his juicy pork spare ribs are better than ever. A quarter-

inch-thick smoke ring and a darkened crust clued us in that the ribs might be smoky, but the first bite let us know that the pecan and oak smoke went all the way to the bone. I think Fulmer ate three by himself. The brisket was also stunning—once we put it in our mouths. It truthfully wasn't much to look at compared to the ribs. In fact, the slices looked a little gray and their surface was dry, but after the third slice all I could taste was incredible beef that was plenty moist after all.

By all accounts, we were on a solid run of barbecue. I had heavily curated the list up to this point to ensure maximum gastronomic satisfaction, but the next few stops in Houston were a series of wild cards, although wild cards from the same deck. You see, Roy Burns Sr. was the original owner, pitmaster, and barbecue patriarch of Burns BBQ on De Priest in northwest Houston. Several months after he passed away in 2009, the ramshackle joint was temporarily shut down for health code violations and then closed permanently. In 2011 Roy's daughter, Kathy Braden, opened a

new **BURNS BBQ** location on North Shepherd Drive. A few months later, Roy's son Gary Burns opened **BURNS OLD FASHIONED PIT BAR-B-Q** a few miles away on Antoine Drive. Finally, a year later Steve Burns—another of Roy's sons—reopened the original location on De Priest as **BURNS ORIGINAL BBQ**. A city that had been without a single Burns BBQ for several years now had three. Chris had written about the Burns family history a bit, so it was good to get his insider info as we drove from joint to joint, especially when he warned us off bringing up the other family members at each joint.

    BURNS OLD FASHIONED PIT BAR-B-Q (Gary's place) was the first of our three stops. As soon as we entered the joint we were hit by the powerful and unrelenting smell of post oak. The smoke was so thick in the pit room that our eyes watered during the tour Gary gave us. Gary

himself was wearing a professional painter's mask to keep things bearable. All of that made me expect more than the incredibly dry brisket we were served. It had very little flavor, let alone good smoke. The pork spareribs were just as dry. As Fulmer pointed out, the topmost layer of meat came away from the rib easily and its crispiness was such that we could have mistaken the rib meat for bacon if our eyes had been closed. A few slices of moist pork shoulder were much more enjoyable, but a pair of home-made sausages was by far the best part of the meal. The hot links had a deep red hue courtesy of a heavy dose of spices that delivered serious heat. We needed a chaser of plain sausage, which relied on a tamer black pepper kick, just to cool things down. Both types of sausages were moist, smoky, and had casings with the perfect snap.

The next stop was **BURNS ORIGINAL BBQ** (Steve's place). During a 2002 visit to the original Burns BBQ—which now houses Steve's incarnation of the joint—Anthony Bourdain noted that it looked like "a decent sneeze would level this place." (The three-minute segment from *A Cook's Tour* is played on a loop with full audio on the only big screen inside the joint; in a long line it gets old fast.) The renovations haven't done much to change that. I took a container of brisket and homemade links out to the picnic table where my crew of barbecue hounds was waiting. We cleaned up every last slice of the excellent links, but most of the brisket waited longingly for a taker. We all knew just by looking that the gray cardboard-like slices weren't going to be any good. I confirmed as much with a few obligatory bites, and we were off to the final Burns of the day.

BURNS BBQ (Kathy's place) on Shepherd was just a mile away. It was noticeably less crowded there. That late in the day, they were mercifully out of brisket. Chris explained after we sat down that many of the black-owned joints in town don't see sliced brisket as the highest form of barbecue. Unlike in Central Texas, where a naked slice of beef is the ultimate in smoked meat, at joints like the Burnses', which specialize in a

more East Texas style,
they'd sooner see the brisket chopped and mixed with sauce and then piled into a generously stuffed sandwich. The meat needs little moisture, flavor, or smoke when the liquid-smoke-infused barbecue sauce can provide all of that. Brisket or not, we were still going to eat, and the homemade links once again impressed and the tender pork ribs were the best of the multiple Burns locations.

We rubbed the meat sweat from our brow and called it a day. The insatiable Chris and Fulmer most likely had a night of food and drink still ahead of them in Houston, but Nick and I hit the pavement once again for a few more hours on the interstate. Heading due west, our next stop was not in one of Texas's big cities. When you're driving anywhere near Lockhart, the barbecue capital of Texas, you must stop there. No exceptions allowed. We had enjoyed a drink at Lilly's in midafternoon on a previous trip and thought it would be a good meat-free option for the evening. At night Lilly's was a different place. It was packed wall to wall with locals waiting to hear their song on a jukebox that featured nothing but Tejano music. If you weren't in a seat, you

were on the dance floor. There
weren't any seats available, so
Nick and I offered up just enough
shimmies to look respectable, but
not enough to look like a couple.
We downed our beers and left
to turn in for the night. While
we were making a quick stop for
gas, three police cars came flying
through the middle of Lockhart,
lights and sirens blazing. They
went straight to Lilly's and we went straight to bed.

SMITTY'S MARKET in Lockhart officially opens at 7:00 A.M., which
might seem a little early for barbecue. They don't actually have their full
menu ready until 10, but since we'd already stopped there on our last trip
through town we weren't too concerned about missing out. At 7:00 they
had only the sausage ready. Two links and a chunk of longhorn cheese
sounded like the perfect start to our day. A bottle of Big Red would have to
substitute for coffee. They weren't quite ready for customers who were
dining in, so we took a couple of chairs down from a tabletop and devoured

our sausage in

silence. It's a rare occasion when you can experience Smitty's dining room in peace and quiet, and we soaked it up.

Just down the road in Luling is another joint that's terminally crowded. **CITY MARKET** didn't live up to its well earned reputation on our last visit, but since then it had been named one of the "101 Best Places to Eat Around the World" by *Newsweek*. Brisket toughened from too quick of a cook and ribs still tough from not enough cooking didn't help our rapidly diminishing opinion of the joint, but one bite of their juicy beef sausage dipped in that golden sauce had me leaving City Market with a smile. We headed out of Luling at 9:00 A.M. in time to hit a few joints for a second breakfast in San Antonio, just an hour away.

We were the first customers of the day at **TWO BROS. BBQ MARKET**, and pitmaster Emilio Soliz was pulling a few briskets out of the smoker when we showed up. He gave us a quick tour of the smoky pit room before we followed him and his brisket back inside the dining room. The knife man cut the corner off the brisket and set it on an empty tray in front of us. The bite was intensely smoky from a well-formed bark that coated all but one surface of the triangle of meat. We ordered a little lean and a little fatty brisket, some cherry-glazed ribs, and then some of the pitmaster-recommended pork loin and the bacon-wrapped smoked jalapeños.

Cherry-glazed baby back ribs aren't what I expect to see on a Texas barbecue menu, but this joint is owned by a chef, Jason Dady, who also owns several popular and well-respected San Antonio restaurants. Jason's chef training probably had more than something to do with the trio of barbecue sauces and the array of pickle varieties lining the condiment bar. Fruity or not, alongside the thick fatty beef, pork, and jalapeños they made for a beautiful sight against the backdrop of the stark-white butcher paper. I immediately ate the slice of lean beef. Nick rebuked my impatience then took a few photos of the fatty brisket slices. We didn't realize at the time how powerful the shot was until Nick reviewed it at home and decided it was worthy of the cover. We were more interested in eating at that point, and Nick was lucky that I had lasted that long. It had been almost two hours since we last ate. The slices of pork were ridiculously moist, especially for a cut that dries out so easily. There's no doubt they were helped by the early hour, but the meat was smoky and the ring of fat around the slice melted in my mouth. The jalapeños had some heat, but it was restrained. What was most noticeable was how perfectly crisp the bacon was on an item where the bacon can easily turn out flabby and undercooked. One bite of the fatty brisket was all it took to know how thoroughly well smoked it was. The meat and fat easily commingled on my tongue and the smoke enveloped all

of it. It was great brisket that was going to be hard to match in our next few stops.

Brisket is a hard meat to smoke consistently. Even the same batch of beef coming out of a single smoker can vary widely in quality, which we witnessed at **CONGER'S SMOKE SHACK**. It's located in a trailer parked underneath an old gas station canopy along I-10 in San Antonio. When I ordered at the window with my I Love BBQ T-shirt on, I didn't expect to receive some sorry scraps from the end of a brisket, but there they were alongside some tantalizing pork ribs. We dug into the ribs first, which were generously seasoned and topped with a sweet glaze. The meat's tenderness was exemplary—it was perfectly cooked. It made the dry brisket taste even worse by comparison. Our swift meal was wrapping up when the owner came by our picnic table. There was a twinkle of recognition in his eye as we chatted, and he asked for an honest assessment. I was honest. He quickly tucked back into the trailer and returned in a flash with several slices of appetizing fatty brisket and a small portion of pulled pork. Both were very good, and the whole experience was a great example of what can happen

when a barbecue critic is recognized. It's true that a barbecue joint can do little to improve the overall quality of their meat for a food critic. They can only work with what is already smoked, but there are choice cuts that can be presented—or those choice cuts can be held back, which might reveal even more about a joint than one serving of bad brisket.

On our way out of town we made a couple more stops in search of a hidden gem. Both **BARBECUE STATION** and **THE BIG BIB** provided respectable smoked meat. Considering how great the barbecue was that we had sampled up to this point, they would have needed to be truly special to make an impression, but nothing at either place stood out as a prime example of great barbecue. Next stop, Austin.

I've been singing the praises of **JMUELLER BBQ** since it opened in 2011. The mercurial personality of pitmaster John Mueller (brother of Wayne Mueller, who runs Louie Mueller Barbecue, their father's old place in Taylor) has been well documented. Few would disagree that he is one of the state's most talented in the smoked-meat arts, but his past is littered with disappointments and squandered promise. Given that, many weren't sure how long JMueller BBQ would last, even though John was wowing barbecue hounds who traveled across the state for his huge peppery beef

short ribs, sweet-glazed pork ribs, home-made sausage, and powerful brisket with a hefty bark thicker than most trees'. His sauce was more like a hot onion soup meant for dipping. Even on the hottest days of summer I preferred to drink the steaming concoction right from the cup it was served in. This was a place where leftovers never materialized, and I was smiling through every bite of my beef rib no matter how full I'd become.

A few months later it all came crashing down unexpectedly. John was out. His own sister had taken control of the business and forced him to the curb, instead hiring John's "temporary" protégé and friend (I'm guessing *former*) John Lewis to man the pits. Within days the joint had reopened under the name La Barbecue and John Mueller was cooling his heels at home in Taylor. I have a strong feeling that he'll be back at it before this book goes to print, and I can't wait to include his new joint in the sequel.

We'd already enjoyed the barbecue at **STILES SWITCH BBQ & BREW**, but it was so good before that we felt like another stop was necessary. Once again they did not disappoint. The joint is solid.

Our last stop reeked of ulterior motives and preconceived notions. **RUDY'S COUNTRY STORE & BAR-B-Q** is a statewide chain with a loyal following. They generally put out better than average meat, but the quality can vary given that most locations are individually owned and operated. With the rise in popularity of joints like Franklin Barbecue and JMueller BBQ in Austin, it had become fashionable to bash them as mere darlings of the barbecue elite. A common theme was that Rudy's, seen as barbecue for the common man, was just as good, if not better. Most of my barbecue visits begin with a thoroughly open mind, but after eating some

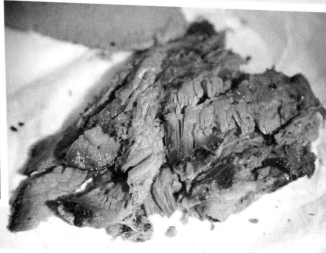

of the state's best brisket over the
previous two days, I wanted to see
how Rudy's brisket would compare.
Rudy's didn't stand a chance. We went to the location on the north side of
town along Highway 183, which is generally regarded as the best location
in town. I got in line to order and noticed a big screen above me labeled
"Cutter Cam." The screen displayed a live feed of the meat cutter rapidly
going through briskets to keep up with the constant stream of orders
coming from six different registers. How cute. When I approached the
counter I asked for a pound of lean and a pound of fatty brisket. "Do you
mean moist, sir?" Rudy's calls their fatty brisket "moist," I guess because
it makes your ass smaller that way. The question was uttered in the same
tone as the snooty response from a Starbucks employee when they pretend
they can't translate "large" into *venti*. "No, I mean fatty." Nick and I
shared one last car trunk picnic with the two pounds of brisket. I thought
ordering such a large quantity offered us a better chance of finding some
great morsels that might help the case of the Rudy's worshippers, but
there were no meaty jewels. It was all just a notch above average. Aaron
Franklin didn't have anything to worry about.

Our last journey was complete and we headed back to Dallas. Of
course, the journey is never *really* complete. I'm always searching for
the next great joint. This being a book about road trips, my home city of
Dallas hasn't gotten the attention it deserves. There are a number of joints

that I get to enjoy regularly without even needing to hit the road. Imported Kreuz sausage, smoked deviled eggs, and spreadable "rib jam" can be found in the Oak Cliff neighborhood of Dallas at **LOCKHART SMOKEHOUSE**. Their brisket and ribs can be up and down, but the upside is very high. For a guy who preaches about the sanctity of sliced brisket untainted by sauce, I do like to indulge in the guilty pleasure of a saucy chopped beef and sausage sandwich at **MAC'S BAR-B-QUE**. Sides of crispy fries and ranch beans are a must. My favorite sausages in North Texas are made by Tim Byres at **SMOKE** in Dallas where a trio of homemade links feature beef, pork, and rabbit. **MESHACK'S** is one of my ultimate barbecue finds. The meat was great on my first visit back when they were undiscovered, and they still have some of the best ribs in town—along with great brisket.

Across the Metroplex in Fort Worth you can find **SMOKEY'S BARBEQUE**, whose buttermilk pie was good enough to be served at Governor Rick Perry's last inauguration party. Their pork spareribs and tender brisket are pretty phenomenal, too. And I wouldn't want to leave out **OFF THE BONE B.B.Q.** in any discussion of ribs. Their deeply smoky baby backs alone are enough reason for a flight to DFW, but it's all just down the road for me. Ohioan by birth, but Texan by the grace of God.

**2 Days,
770 Miles,
17 BBQ Joints**

TOTAL

35 Days,
10,343 Miles,
186 BBQ Joints

PITMASTER ★★★ PROFILES

• •

AND IN A LEAP THAT WOULD GIVE A
LEXICOGRAPHER WHIPLASH, A VOCATION THAT
HAD BEEN BUILT LARGELY ON THE LABOR OF
ENSLAVED AFRICAN AMERICANS BEGAN REFERRING
TO ITS BEST PRACTITIONERS AS PITMASTERS.
—JOHN T. EDGE

The romanticized notion that barbecue can only be learned from scratch through thousands of repetitions is a falsehood. The trial and error method has some value, but there is enough written out there about proper smoking techniques that starting blind would be laughably inefficient. Some of the best pitmasters in the state are relatively new to the craft. It's not simple repetition that makes great barbecue, but a desire for excellence from a pitmaster and a reverence for the craft. In his lecture "Pitmaster: An Homage and Rumination," John T. Edge discusses the relative youth of the term as it's used to describe people who have mastered a barbecue pit. I hesitate to use the term at times when it's clear that the person acting in this role hasn't mastered much of anything. What follows is a series of profiles of men and women who exemplify the term, and about whom there is no doubt that pitmaster is the proper title.

The beauty of this collection of recipes is that these folks have offered their "secrets" in full. In a show of humility they give over all the ingredients necessary to replicate what they do every day, but it's a false humility. With these recipes, each pitmaster is telling you, "Here it is, no secrets, now good luck." The point is that the secrets of a pitmaster aren't in the ingredients of the rub or the sauce or the wood or the cooking time. The secret is their skill at knowing how to react to the meat and to the fire all the way through the cooking process. If the key to great barbecue was that thirteenth ingredient in the rub, then we might be inclined to call them pantry masters. We know their skills are harder to pass on than with a simple recipe, but this collection at least represents the starting line for anyone who one day would like to be called a pitmaster.

BUBBA BARNES

MUMPHORD'S PLACE : VICTORIA

Ricky Mumphord started this joint back in 2000. It's a family affair, so it's no wonder that his brother-in-law Bubba Barnes tends the pits. He shares this duty with Earnest and Carlos, but it was Bubba who gave us a full tour of Mumphord's where every pit has a different name, but all are made for direct heat cooking over wood coals. When I asked Ricky how they all learned to cook that way, he noted his family's long history in the area (down the road in Placedo, Texas they held their 108th family reunion in 2012) allowed him to learn to cook meat from his grandfather. His straightforward response to my question about using a more modern gas-fired smoker was "I don't know no other way. I think we're doing it the right way and we're not changing it."

• • • SMOKED TURKEY BREAST • • • • • • • • • • • • • •

MEAT: Whole muscle turkey breast from US Foods or Sysco. Four breasts come in a twenty-pound box.

RUB: An unspecified mix of salt, pepper, granulated garlic and white sugar

WOOD: Dry mesquite and oak, aged at least eight months, burnt down to coals in a separate pit. Pecan is too ashy, and live oak is preferred over other oaks if they can get it.

PIT: Rectangular steel pit with coals below and steel lid that opens from the top. They use the pit named "Chicken Cooker" for the turkey.

FIRE: Hot enough that the palm of our hand can only last a few seconds over it

TIME: An hour and a half

IT'S DONE WHEN: A fork glides in easily. They don't mind poking meat around here as it cooks.

REST: It can be served immediately, but they hold them in the "Lil' Bow-Wow" pit to keep them warm for serving.

PRO TIP: Don't turn your back on that turkey or it will dry up on you before you know it

Ricky doesn't know if the next generation will limit their obsessive interest in a myriad of sports long enough to consider working the pits, but as someone who learned to cook the old-fashioned way from previous generations, he sure hopes a few of them will be here to take things over. If they choose to use a formed and processed turkey breast that you'd find at your deli counter, I think Ricky and Bubba would be less than pleased.

BRYAN BRACEWELL

SOUTHSIDE MARKET: ELGIN

Bryan is the third generation of his family to own and operate Southside Market in Elgin. I first met Bryan at a meeting for Foodways Texas in College Station. After the meeting we went out for a few beers and I told him I had a website that rated barbecue and that his family's joint had ranked near the bottom. My honesty and his humorous reaction were both fueled by a few Dixie Chicken beer pitchers, but he took it with a laugh. He just made me promise to come back and give them another chance. I have returned more than once and was pleasantly surprised to find my favorite smoked lamb in Texas alongside their more famous hot gut sausage.

• • • MUTTON RIBS •

MEAT: Lamb breast, choice or higher from Superior Farms (USA lamb), 3 to 4 pounds on each rack (piece)

RUB: Southside Market Original Barbeque Seasoning, which contains, in descending order, salt, black pepper, cayenne, garlic powder, paprika, and other proprietary spices (but no MSG according to the nutrition label on the packaging)

WOOD: Texas-grown post oak

PIT: Texas-style BBQ pit with offset pit box

FIRE: 300 to 325 degrees

TIME: 45 minutes with bones up, breast toward the fire, then flip the rack bones down, breast toward fire for another 45 minutes to an hour

IT'S DONE WHEN: 175 degrees internal temperature or when the bones pull away from the meat cleanly

REST THE MEAT: In a covered pan on top of the pit (not the firebox) for 45 minutes

PRO TIP: Lamb breast is really fatty so don't be afraid to cook it hotter than most barbecue meats to render the fat and create a fatty/crunchy crust on the meaty side of the rack of ribs. The different layers of fat really protect the meat during cooking to keep it moist and tender even at the higher temps and quicker cooking times. Place the ribs on the pit as close to the firebox as possible.

• •

Bryan explains that while they no longer use mutton, they still have to use the term on the menu. "The old-timers still call it mutton, but we actually use lamb breast. They tell us that if we start calling it lamb, they won't buy it anymore! It's almost impossible to cut through a lamb breastbone, so you know they are cooked right if they come to pieces during cutting and are greasy as hell!"

TIM BYRES

SMOKE: DALLAS

"Chef" might be a more accurate title for Tim Byres than "pitmaster." His résumé reveals a fine dining past—Stephan Pyles and the Mansion on Turtle Creek in Dallas. In order to develop the menu at Smoke, where he is now chef and part-owner, Tim set a course for the rural American South. There, he found restaurants living by the mantras "local" and "sustainable," which are usually employed as PR buzzwords rather than strict philosophies of urban fine dining. He returned from that trip with a passion for smoking and for using raw ingredients from both the restaurant's garden and local suppliers. As part of their ethos of handcrafted local food, they grind and stuff their own sausages. Rabbit, beef, and pork are used in three distinct links which are all made using traditional natural casings, wood smoke, and the modern touch of a chef.

• • • VENISON SMOKED POLISH SAUSAGE • • • • • • • • • •

MEAT: 12 pounds of venison neck meat, 3 pounds pork shoulder

VEGGIES: 1 cup Gaujilo chili purée (dry chile toasted and rehydrated to paste), 1 cup Passilla chili purée, 3 garlic cloves

SEASONING: 3 cups dry milk powder, 7½ tablespoons kosher salt, 3 tablespoons dextrose (fine sausage sugar), 1½ tablespoons ground black pepper, 3 teaspoons pink salt, insta cure #1, 1½ teaspoons fresh chopped marjoram, 4 cups cold water

CASING: Natural pork casings (pig intestines)

PROCEDURE:

Rough-chop all vegetables and run through the food processor.

Grind meat through medium plate.

Combine water with dry ingredients, mix into meat.

Add seasoned ground meat to food processor and emulsify in food processor.

Refrigerate, then stuff into 1 pound links and hold.

SMOKING:

Remove bottom and middle racks to replace with sausage dowels and preheat pit.

Smoke with oak, pecan, and hickory at 130 degrees until the skin is dry, 45 minutes on bottom rack.

Once the skin is dry, raise the sausage dowels up a shelf to 165 degrees and smoke until the internal temperature is 150 degrees.

Remove to an ice bath to stop cooking and hang in walk-in to let meat set up for at least one day.

CESAR CORONADO SR.

CASA DE CORONADO: WEST DALLAS

Cesar Coronado Sr. grew up on a goat ranch outside San Luis Potosi. He came to the US a couple decades back and has worked construction all over Texas and Oklahoma since then. Back home in West Dallas he is known as the go-to barbacoa man for the neighborhood. If there is a local celebration, chances are his backyard pit will be fired up for the occasion. It's just not a party without some of Cesar's barbacoa.

• • • BARBACOA DE CABEZA • • • •

MEAT: Cabeza de vaca (cow head) with tongue

RUB: Nothing.

WOOD: Mesquite

PIT: 4-foot length of 3-foot-diameter concrete pipe into the ground. Topped with a metal lid and at least 6 inches of dirt to cover it.

FIRE: Burn plenty of wood down to coals until at least 12 inches deep. Remove any remaining wood that hasn't turned to coals. When the fire is ready, place a metal grate on the coals. Line the bottom and sides of the pit with maguey (agave) leaves and place the meat on the bed of maguey. Fold the leaves over the meat, then place the lid on the pit. Cover with dirt and wait. Don't forget to have a few Modelos on hand. There's plenty of waiting involved.

TIME: Cook overnight. 12 hours minimum, and up to 16 hours with a hot fire.

IT'S DONE WHEN: It better be done when you open the lid, because there's no going back.

REST: Eat it ASAP.

PRO TIP: Feel for hot spots on the earth covering the pit. Add more dirt until hot spot subsides.

• •

Just before the meat is ready, it's a good idea to have the table prepared with warm corn tortillas, guacamole, hot salsa, and the traditional garnishes of cilantro, chopped white onion, and lime wedges. You'll also find a salt shaker on the table. The meat hasn't been seasoned, so it's up to the eater to shake a few grains onto the meat in the midst of forming a taco. Repeat several times.

WILL FLEISCHMAN
LOCKHART SMOKEHOUSE: DALLAS

Will is a thinking man's pitmaster with a palate that's beyond refined and a curiosity for ingredients that is unmatched. His creativity couldn't be contained in just one recipe, and it just didn't seem right to harness him with choosing a traditional Texas cut given his comfort with experimentation. The next two recipes display both his prowess with a smoker and his uncommonly deep repertoire as a cook.

• • • RIB JAM •

MEAT: 5 pounds sparerib ends already smoked to completion and minced (a great use for leftover ribs)

OTHER INGREDIENTS: 8 medium red onions (fine dice), 8 cloves garlic (fine dice), 13 to 15 jalapeño peppers (fine dice), 6 cups brown sugar, 3 to 5 cups red wine vinegar, bacon fat, water (1 quart to start), 3 to 5 pounds seasonal fruit, and a bit of your favorite booze.

PROCESS: Remove all bones and cartilage from ribs. Combine all ingredients and reduce over low heat in a big ole pot. Add more water as the mixture reduces to maintain a moist consistency.

TIME: What you're looking for is a spreadable condiment. This can take a while . . . like 6 or more hours.

PRO TIP: Think about your fruit and booze pairings and find a combination that makes sense. Apples and whiskey work well.

Will shared this recipe with me some time ago. I routinely have a fridge full of uneaten smoked-meat leftovers after a crazy day or week of barbecue road-tripping. As one who hates to waste food, I find myself over the stockpot cooking down leftover ribs. I can attest that rib jam and some crackers work quite well for breakfast, lunch, dinner, and dessert. It's as versatile as Will's menu.

JUSTIN FOURTON

PECAN LODGE: DALLAS

Before they opened Pecan Lodge in 2009 the husband and wife team of Justin and Diane Fourton were in the corporate world. The daily grind was getting to them, so they decided to lighten their workload by doing some catering that included smoked meats. The workload never lightened, especially after they opened their permanent location in the Dallas Farmer's Market. One of the few smoking with mesquite in Dallas, Justin knows his way around a smoker and nothing highlights his skills more than the Pecan Lodge smoked brisket.

··· SMOKED WAGYU BRISKET ·····················

MEAT: Whole 8- to 10-pound locally raised Wagyu brisket from SalasSpur Meats (available at Local Yocal in McKinney, Texas)

RUB: Our brisket rub is a trade secret, but this is a good all-purpose rub that will get the job done: 6 parts paprika, 3 parts garlic powder, 3 parts onion powder, 2 parts salt, 1 part black pepper. Mix thoroughly in a bowl and apply liberally to all sides of the brisket. Apply an additional layer of butcher's-grind black pepper and kosher salt until it looks right.

WOOD: Seasoned Texas mesquite

PIT: ¼-inch-thick steel custom offset pit. Our firebox is offset to the rear of the pit. Most pits will have the firebox offset to the left or right. We get more even temperatures this way and it allows us to use more grate space than usual.

FIRE: 250 degrees

TIME: 10 to 12 hours

IT'S DONE WHEN: We rely on a thermometer to check the progress of the brisket, but the decision to pull it off the pit is based on feel. When it gets to 190 degrees we're close, but only experienced hands will know when it's time to call it.

REST THE MEAT: Not necessary, but if it finishes early, wrap it in foil and put it in a small ice chest until ready to serve.

PRO TIP: Pay attention to how the wood burns and watch the smoke coming out of your stack. We can tell how hot our fire is burning by smell alone. If it's too hot, the wood incinerates and burns without smoking.

· ·

Wagyu is a well-marbled beef with a hefty price tag. It's popular on the barbecue competition circuit, but the high cost keeps it off most every barbecue joint menu in the state. Pecan Lodge is the only one I've found that offers it, but come running when they tweet the special. It goes fast.

AARON FRANKLIN

FRANKLIN BARBECUE: AUSTIN

Barbecue legends usually grow with age, but Aaron Franklin has proven that young guns can smoke some mean protein as well. At just thirty-four years old, he has gained more accolades per year of age than any pitmaster in recent history. In true Texas form, his briskets are magically tender and smoky due to simple ingredients and simple methods. Neither special recipe rubs nor beef broth injections nor apple juice marinades have a place in this man's kitchen. In short, Aaron has no secrets.

• • • SMOKED BEEF BRISKET • • • • • • • • • • • • • • • • •

MEAT: Whole 10 to 12 pound all natural Angus brisket

RUB: 1:1 ratio of 16-mesh black pepper and kosher salt

WOOD: Texas-grown post oak

PIT: ¼-inch-thick steel barrel pit with offset firebox

FIRE: 225 to 275 degrees

TIME: 12ish hours

IT'S DONE WHEN: The fork will tell you

REST THE MEAT: 1 hour wrapped in butcher paper

PRO TIP: Keep a water pan in the smoker close to the firebox

The long smoking time at low temperatures brings this brisket to the point of falling apart. It doesn't have the structural integrity of the firmer briskets you'll find at Kreuz Market or Cooper's in Llano. The meat is smoked until it surrenders, and some may consider it a bit overcooked. With its buttery texture and lines of fat that melt on the tongue like cotton candy, I consider it the best in Texas, therefore the USA, therefore the world.

GREG GATLIN

GATLIN'S BBQ : HOUSTON

A smoker in the backyard has been a fixture in the Gatlin household in Houston since Greg can remember, but he never really thought he'd be making a living with one now. The Rice University graduate traded in his football cleats and opened this small joint up in the Heights neighborhood of Houston, and the accolades have been rolling in ever since.

• • • PULLED PORK • • • • • • • • • • • • • • • •

MEAT: A whole bone-in pork butt around six pounds

BRINE: Water, apple juice, salt, sugar, chopped onions and bell peppers and bay leaves (proportions not divulged). Brine at least four hours, but preferably overnight. Dry the meat once it's out of the brine

RUB: Mix yellow mustard, brown sugar, honey, salt, black pepper, garlic powder and a few other things. Rub it onto the meat thoroughly and liberally just before smoking

WOOD: Hickory

PIT: Offset smoker made of thick gauge steel

FIRE: 275

TIME: Smoke until it gets the right deep brown color (around 5 hours) then wrap in foil for final hour or so until tender

IT'S DONE WHEN: The bone pulls out cleanly from the meat

REST: None needed. It's ready to serve. Do not leave the meat wrapped while it's being held for service as it will continue to steam and get mushy.

PRO TIP: Physically pull the meat into chunks rather than slicing or chopping it and pour the juices collected in the foil wrapping over the pile of pulled pork before serving

Without taking into account the ubiquity of pork ribs in Texas barbecue joints, outsiders tend to think Texans can only smoke beef. Well, we can do a bit of mutton, poultry, and certainly pulled pork, but admittedly it shows up on few menus. More often than not it's well smoked, and here at Gatlin's it's a little better than just well smoked. The pieces of pulled meat have a nice variation in texture and size, the meat is incredibly moist, and they leave in all the good bark and fat for a bold and rich flavor. If more Texans tasted Greg's pork, they'd be demanding the same from their local pitmaster.

ADRIAN HANDSBOROUGH

VIRGIE'S BBQ : HOUSTON

Adrian Handsborough did the thing that any good son would do: He named a BBQ joint after his mother. Virgie used to run a small grocery store out of this building with her husband (and Adrian's father) Jessie. The guy next door sold wood, so they put a small pit beside the building and Virgie would sometimes smoke ribs and sell them in the store. When the store closed down Adrian quit his trucking job, took over the building, and opened this joint in 2005. With ribs being the family specialty, he admits that his first brisket was shoe leather, but he's got it down now. That brisket is now some of the best anywhere, and at eighty-three years old, Virgie still comes by to get some of her son's ribs.

• • • SPARE RIBS •

MEAT: 4½ pound (large) rack of spareribs. Use fresh ribs not those vacuum-packed in a salt solution. Pat dry before rubbing.

RUB: Make a paste with seasoned salt and Italian dressing and rub at least 8 hours before they go on the pit.

WOOD: Post oak seasoned at least six months

PIT: Offset barrel smoker made with thick gauge steel

FIRE: The pit temp varies from 250-275

TIME: Four and a half to five hours before checking the meat temp. Turn it every hour or so and mop the meat (mop recipe not divulged).

IT'S DONE WHEN: The internal temp of the thickest rib is 165 degrees

REST: For at least 30 minutes

PRO TIP: Cut off the brisket bone, or sternum (often sold as "regulars" in Houston) before smoking the rack and smoke it separately. After cooking remove the two small ribs on either end of the rack. Adrian saves these off cuts for special requests or for hungry folks in the neighborhood who need something cheap to eat.

• •

Most barbecue joints in Texas work with a smaller more manageable rack of ribs. St. Louis ribs or the more popular "three-and-a-half and down" spareribs (meaning the full rack weighs less than 3.5 lbs.). Adrian prefers a larger rack with more fat to keep them moist during a long cook. It's harder to get these ribs tender, but he doesn't mind taking the time to get them right.

CHARLES HUGGINS

HOG'S HEAVEN BBQ: WEATHERFORD

Charles learned to cook barbecue from his father. After a stint in the baseball minor leagues he opened up a barbecue joint in Huntsville, Alabama, with his brother. When his brother moved to Texas, Charles decided to follow and take his talents to the small town of Weatherford, Texas. The man knows his pork, and that is most evident in his ribs. In Charles's words, patience is the key to good barbecue. "If you don't have time to cook them slow, then don't cook 'em."

• • • ST. LOUIS PORK RIBS • • • • • • • • • • • • • • • •

MEAT: Pretrimmed St. Louis–style ribs in racks 2¾ pounds or less

RUB: 2 parts garlic powder; 1 part each seasoned salt, coarse black pepper, and garlic salt; ¼ part white sugar; red pepper flakes to taste. Apply to ribs one day before smoking.

WOOD: Kingsford charcoal and hickory logs

PIT: Cabinet-style steel pit with front loading doors. The grate is held 5 feet above the fire, which is directly below the meat.

FIRE: For a case of ribs (12 racks), start a 10-pound bag of charcoal until white coating appears. Add a hickory log 30 minutes before placing ribs in smoker. Add another log 2 hours later.

TIME: Smoke for 3½ to 4 hours

IT'S DONE WHEN: Look for the meat to retreat from the tips of the bones by about ¼ inch, then start testing them with a spatula inserted under the rack at the midpoint. If the rack bends nicely, it's done.

REST THE MEAT: Rest unwrapped in a warmer at 145 degrees for about 2 hours

PRO TIP: Spray a mop sauce on the ribs once an hour, as they tend to dry out over direct heat if left alone. For the mop sauce mix white vinegar, lemon juice, water, Worcestershire sauce, and a little rub.

• •

St. Louis ribs are common in Texas. They're nothing more than spareribs with the rib tip removed in order to get a more consistently sized rack. At Hog's Heaven they use a very uncommon smoking method that's a bit of a hybrid. In Memphis it's not hard to find joints using only charcoal, but here Charles adds in the smoke from hickory logs, too, and still gets the tenderness and smoke that you'd expect from an indirect smoker without a remote fire by placing the meat high above the heat source.

STEPHEN JOSEPH

RIVERPORT BAR-B-CUE: JEFFERSON

January 15, 2012, is a date that Stephen Joseph won't forget. He spent that morning cleaning up the burned-out remains of his restaurant. By July of the same year it was back with renewed purpose. Stephen knows he's one of just a few pitmasters in East Texas trying to buck the trend of lean and dry meats covered in sauce that so many in the region are used to.

• • • SMOKED PORK LOIN •

MEAT: A 6- to 8-pound boneless pork loin (I prefer IBP brand)

RUB: 8 parts kosher salt, 8 parts granulated sugar, 4 parts chili powder, 4 parts coarse black pepper, 2 parts granulated garlic, and cayenne pepper to your taste

WOOD: Seasoned white oak wood harvested locally in East Texas

PIT: A. N. Bewley Model 1100 with offset firebox

FIRE: 250 to 275 degrees

TIME: About 3 to 3½ hours

IT'S DONE WHEN: It is slightly firm to the touch

REST THE MEAT: Wrap the loin tightly in foil and let it rest for about 30 minutes

PRO TIP: Slice thin and serve on a bun with barbecue sauce, jalapeño, mustard, sliced onions, and dill pickles

When you eat a pork chop, you're eating a slice of pork loin with a baby back rib attached. When the rack of baby backs is kept intact and separated from the loin, what you're left with is a whole boneless pork loin. Smoke it too fast or too long and what you'll end up with is meat that's dry as a bone. Smoke it just right and you'll have juicy slices of lean meat with a nice ring of fat on the exterior.

SCOTT MORALES AND VERCIL MARES

TAYLOR CAFE: TAYLOR

The godfather of Texas pitmasters is Vencil Mares. He's been running his joint in Taylor since 1948 and is still a fixture there every day, but these days the heavy lifting back in the pits is done by Scott Morales. Scott came to work with Vencil a few years back after being laid off from his tech job in Austin. These days he couldn't imagine working anywhere else, even if he doesn't get the comfort of air-conditioning.

••• SMOKED BRISKET •••••••••••••••••••••••••••••

MEAT: IBP briskets at 8 to 10 pounds

RUB: Proprietary mix of salt, pepper, and a touch of garlic powder

WOOD: Texas post oak

PIT: Brick pit built in the 1970s

FIRE: 300 to 325 degrees

TIME: 6 to 8 hours

IT'S DONE WHEN: It has sat overnight in an Igloo cooler

REST THE MEAT: Yes. Several briskets are wrapped in butcher paper and stacked tightly in an Igloo cooler that sits overnight as the briskets finish cooking at low heat inside the insulated walls of the cooler.

PRO TIP: Leave the pit doors closed. Every time you open the doors you add 15 minutes to your cooking time.

While researching this book, I read an essay in *The Republic of Barbecue* where Vencil was quoted as saying, "I get asked, 'How you make this thing?' I never tell them the truth; they might try to take my business away." After reading that, I spent the rest of the day looking over this recipe to see where I was misled. I guess I'll only know if I try the recipe and taste it against Vencil's.

GAYLAN MARTH

BIG BOY'S BAR-B-QUE: SWEETWATER

The Texas Hill Country is full of barbecue joints that cook over direct-heat fires, while it's more common to find indirect smokers in the rest of the state. Out in Sweetwater, Texas, Gaylan Marth is an outlier. At least 150 miles from anything considered the Hill Country, he's still using the cooking method taught to him by his German grandfather. He cooks mesquite wood down to coals every morning to use in his homemade steel pits, and you'd better not call them smokers.

• • • MY RIBS (COUNTRY-STYLE PORK RIBS) • • • • • • •

MEAT: Whole pork butt deboned and sliced into 2-inch-thick steaks. Cut those steaks into 1½-inch strips.

RUB: A proprietary mix of seasoned salt, coarse black pepper, white pepper, garlic powder, paprika. Apply to meat 30 minutes to an hour before cooking.

WOOD: Local mesquite wood

PIT: Homemade rectangular pits made of 16-gauge steel. Coals are placed directly below the grates and meat is cooked over direct heat.

FIRE: Spread a thin layer of coals on the bottom of the pit. The target temperature is around 275 to 300 degrees, but Gaylan doesn't have a thermometer in them.

TIME: Cook for 2½ to 3 hours

IT'S DONE WHEN: A deep bronze color starts to develop and the meat starts to break apart under the pressure of the tongs. The meat should still stay together.

REST THE MEAT: No need

PRO TIP: Consistency is important, so measure your rub ingredients and keep track of those measurements until you find your preferred mix. Write that mix down and use it every time. If you've found what you like, there's no reason to wing it.

• •

Gaylan understands the desire of most customers for a traditional rib on the bone like the St. Louis ribs he has on the menu, but Gaylan would rather eat a country rib. These really aren't ribs at all, so there's no bone to contend with. They're called "My Ribs" on the menu to denote that Gaylan prefers to keep these for himself if he's cooking both styles of ribs at home. The St. Louis–style ribs are called "Your Ribs" on the menu.

JOHN MAYWALD

SISTERDALE SMOKEHOUSE: SISTERDALE

An accountant by day, John Maywald runs this joint with family and friends just two weekends per month. He learned his way around a pit in his own backyard and honed those skills on the competition circuit. When he couldn't unload a restaurant building he'd purchased with the intent to lease it out, he opened up a barbecue joint. He trucked a used Oyler pit back from a dealer in Dallas and spent the next few weeks seasoning the pit with oak since he said he could taste the pecan residue from the previous owner.

• • • SMOKED YARD BIRD • • • • • • • • • • • • • •

MEAT: Yard bird, 30 pounds of split chicken halves—fresh, not frozen

RUB: Proprietary blend of spices (salt, garlic powder, onion powder, lemon powder, thyme, sage, sugar, paprika, pepper), but you can use any number of commercial rubs. One in particular is Bolner's Fiesta Chicken Rub; this is an excellent over-the-counter rub.

Apply the dry rub liberally on both sides of the chicken half at least 12 hours prior to cooking. We apply our rub 72 hours prior to cooking.

WOOD: Seasoned Texas oak (live oak and post oak)

PIT: 1976 model well-seasoned Oyler pit (a commercial rotisserie pit that uses only wood for fuel)

FIRE: 275 to 300 degrees, indirect heat

TIME: 4 to 5 hours. Cook the halves with the skin side up. Do not turn them over.

IT'S DONE WHEN: The skin is a crispy golden brown and the internal temperature is 175 to 180 degrees. Keep in mind these are smoked chickens and the meat touching the bones may have a pink hue to it.

PRO TIP: Keep the door to the pit closed as much as possible—no peeking.

• •

The prolonged smoking time of a brisket or pork butt is to transform the meat's structure into something edible. Smoking chicken is more a problem of getting enough smoke into the meat in the short time required for poultry to cook before it begins to dry out. If I do order smoked chicken at a barbecue joint, what I most often get is either rubbery undercooked skin and moist meat beneath or crispy skin and dry meat. The worst of them have both the flabby skin and dry meat, but Maywald's was special because they got all the textures right on the same bird.

JIM MITCHELL
THE QUE SHACK: MARLIN

Local pitmaster Ben Jefferson was Jim Mitchell's mentor. Rumor is that he was just as happy smoking squirrels and armadillos as he was smoking ribs, so it's no wonder that Jim went against the grain with the beef selection at his now defunct barbecue joint (he's still available for catering). After a friend convinced him to start cooking this cut usually reserved for pits in California, he started selling it like crazy at an old gas station he used to run. After he brought his businesses to Marlin (Jim also runs a used-car lot, a bail-bond business, and a check-cashing outfit), the tri-tip followed.

• • • TRI-TIP •

MEAT: 3 pounds IBP choice tri-tip; fresh not frozen

RUB: 1:1:1 ratio of seasoning salt, cracked black pepper, garlic powder, with cayenne pepper to taste. Shake it on after you start the pit and let the meat rest at room temperature for 30 minutes.

WOOD: Kingsford charcoal. Add a mesquite log right at the end for some color and some twang.

PIT: Steel barrel pit with a door on one end and stack on the other end to provide some draw

FIRE: 370 degrees. Place charcoal on a third of pit, and do not spread. It takes about an hour to warm pit. Place meat on the other two-thirds.

TIME: 2ish hours

IT'S DONE WHEN: Thermometer should slide in easily and the target temperature is 165 degrees

REST THE MEAT: 4 hours unwrapped in an Igloo cooler to tenderize and steam

PRO TIP: Don't open the pit or the cooler when the meat's in it. It's cooking, not show-and-tell.

• •

Jim insists that what he does is not smoking—it's cooking. He uses mainly charcoal and his cooker does not have a separate firebox. Just like Ben Jefferson, the man who taught him about barbecue, Jim insists that those who use indirect smokers are amateurs who haven't figured out how to control their fire. Cooking directly over the coals takes more skill, he says. No matter your opinion about the method, Jim's results are hard to argue with.

LISANDRO MORENO

BRISKETS & BEER SMOKEHOUSE: LAREDO

After retiring from the Army National Guard, Lisandro Moreno thought he might take up the hobby of smoking meats. Having been the de facto caterer for many parties that required smoked meat he thought he'd perfected his brisket enough to go into business. That was in 2007. After a short time he realized that being in Laredo meant he needed to provide at least some Mexican food on the menu. Guisado and chalupas made an appearance but all the while he was toying with a recipe for smoked beef cheeks. This is the method he settled on.

• • • SMOKED CACHETE BARBACOA • • • • • • • • • • •

MEAT: 1 case beef cheeks (about 50 pounds)

RUB: Put into smoker unseasoned. Lightly apply equal parts ground cumin and garlic powder before slow cooking.

WOOD: Local mesquite

PIT: An old steel butane tank with a side firebox attached

FIRE: Maintain 400-degree heat in smoker and 250 degrees in the electric cooker

TIME: Smoke the cheeks for 30 to 40 minutes or until the surface has browned. Place in an electric cooker overnight or about 12 hours.

IT'S DONE WHEN: The meat falls apart easily

REST THE MEAT: No need

PRO TIP: Serve on a freshly made flour tortilla with chopped cilantro, onion, lime, and hot sauce.

• •

Unlike traditional barbacoa, where the whole head is cooked, Lisandro cooks only the cheeks and serves it every day instead of the norm of making it a weekend special. While using just cheeks is not out of the ordinary these days, it is very rare to find barbacoa that has been smoked and seasoned before it hits the table. This creates a flavor so unique it's like you're not even eating barbacoa, but there's not a better breakfast than this beef on one of Lisandro's home-made flour tortillas.

JOHN MUELLER

JOHN MUELLER MEAT CO.: AUSTIN

John has been cooking barbecue longer than most. As Bobby Mueller's son, he spent much of his childhood around the pits of Louie Mueller Barbecue in Taylor. He learned plenty from his dad, enough even to move to Austin, where he opened award-winning John Mueller's BBQ on Manor Road in 2001. Despite being named one of *Texas Monthly*'s Top 500 BBQ joints in 2003, the joint was gone three years later. John's triumphant return to Austin with his JMueller BBQ trailer was cut short by his unceremonious departure at the behest of his business partner and sister. He has since opened John Mueller Meat Co., but this time without any help from the family.

• • • PORK SPARE RIBS • • • • • • • • • • • • •

MEAT: Medium-weight rack of pork spare ribs from IBP, about 4½ pounds per rack, with the wide bone on the end removed.

RUB: 2 parts of coarse ground black pepper to 1 part kosher salt, measured by volume. Apply the rub just before the ribs go into the smoker.

GLAZE: 2 parts Italian dressing, 2 parts light corn syrup, and 1 part butter is applied to the meat side of the rack about 20 minutes before they're done and again just before removing from the smoker.

WOOD: A mix of primarily post oak along with live oak and red oak, all relatively young. John likes greener wood that burns longer.

PIT: A thick steel pit made from an old 1,000-gallon propane tank with a large offset firebox attached.

FIRE: 375 to 400 degrees in the middle of the smoking chamber.

TIME: About 2 ½ hours

IT'S DONE WHEN: The rib meat is soft to the touch and the meat surface breaks under the bend test.

REST THE MEAT: Wrap the meat and let it sit for at least 15 minutes before serving.

PRO TIP: Get ribs close to room temperature, then apply the rub just before cooking. Cold ribs don't take the rub as well and lower the temperature of the smoker. Rubbing the meat the night before allows the salt to draw out too much moisture.

• •

The ribs at Louie Mueller are seasoned with the simple salt and pepper rub, but John wanted to amp up the flavor for the Austin crowd. When the trailer first opened, the simpler seasoning was employed and the ribs came out a bit dry. John toyed with a remedy that led to the glaze in this recipe. They are now some of my favorite ribs in the state.

WAYNE MUELLER

LOUIE MUELLER BARBECUE: TAYLOR

After a couple of decades away from the family business that saw Wayne win a few championship rings in the sports consultancy business in Houston, he returned home in 2007 to help ease his father Bobby into retirement. After his father passed unexpectedly in 2008, the Central Texas legend of James Beard Award–winning Louie Mueller Barbecue was in his hands. Things were rough to begin with. One longtime pitman departed not so amicably and another, Tony White, came aboard. The going might not have been smooth, but after a few years the place is back into its groove. For those who still say this joint isn't what it used to be, I say they're living in falsely inflated memories. A finer beef rib cannot be found in Texas.

• • • BEEF SHORT RIBS • • • • • • • • • • • • • • • • • • •

MEAT: Angus short ribs, choice grade or better

RUB: 9:1 (by weight) ratio of coarse black pepper to salt. Apply rub the night before smoking.

WOOD: Texas post oak

PIT: Brick pit with offset firebox

FIRE: Heat pit to around 325 degrees, then lower to 250 midway through

TIME: Cook on high heat close to the fire with bone side down until the meat retreats off the bone ends and leaves about an inch of bone showing (about 4 hours). Reduce heat or move to a cooler part of the pit and smoke another 4 to 6 hours.

IT'S DONE WHEN: You can poke your finger easily into all four corners of the rack.

REST THE MEAT: Wrap in butcher paper and rest.

PRO TIP: Unlike briskets, beef ribs are even tempered. Keep the bones facing down toward the heat source to protect the meat, and it's hard to dry them out.

• •

Beef back ribs might be more common in Texas, but they're also damn cheap. It's a treat when you find the meatier short ribs with a few solid inches of meat covering the bone. They sit right next to the brisket on the carcass and share the generous marbling. They aren't quite as big as a brisket, but take just as long to smoke properly. Coated generously with coarse black pepper (which Wayne calls a "fifth food group"), the reward is silky tender beef richer than most any other cut.

NICK PENCIS

STANLEY'S FAMOUS PIT BAR-B-Q: TYLER

Being a barbecue rock star isn't much of a stretch for Nick. He spent plenty of years on the road touring with his many bands. This seasoned drummer has since traded long hours on the road for long hours working the pits in his East Texas barbecue joint. Stanley's has a long history in Tyler and Nick is just the latest in a line of owners, but he keeps looking for ways to up his game and refine the smoked-meat palate of an entire region averse to well-smoked brisket fat. That brisket is plenty good, but Stanley's is famous for ribs.

• • • DOUBLE-RUBBED BABY BACK RIBS • • • • • • • • • • •

MEAT: 2¼- to 2½-pound slab of IBP pork loin back rib

RUB: White sugar, brown sugar, paprika, chili powder, black pepper, garlic, cumin, salt, basil. Apply the rub and let them sit overnight. Apply a new coat just before they go into the smoker.

WOOD: Texas-grown pecan—down, split, and seasoned 6 months or more

PIT: ⅜-inch thick steel barrel pit with offset firebox—straight-shot style with two 12-inch stacks

FIRE: 275 to 300 degrees

TIME: Approximately 4 hours

IT'S DONE WHEN: Place tongs under the slab, with tong tips extending no further than the halfway point of the slab. If the slab bends and starts to break under its own weight, pull it off and wrap it up.

REST THE MEAT: 30 minutes prior to cutting

PRO TIP: Removing the membrane is tedious and not entirely necessary. Leave the membrane on and just score it with the tip of your knife.

That's a whole lot of ingredients for a Texas rib rub, but who can argue with the results? For the first two years of the *Texas Monthly* Barbecue Festival, these ribs took home Best in Texas. That's an impressive feat given any competition, but only the best in Texas are invited to the event. These days even the humble Nick Pencis will gladly tell you that his are the best ribs in Texas.

ROY PEREZ

KREUZ MARKET: LOCKHART

Roy is a naturally quiet man who shied away from the spotlight when he first started cutting meat at Kreuz Market, but it didn't take long before he was hamming it up with the customers. These days it's one of his favorite parts of the job—Roy told me that he's disappointed when someone stops by without saying hello. As manager of the pit area, it's part of his job to chew the fat with customers and take photos with those who want to capture his greasy white jacket and well-groomed mutton chops. That's especially true when former Texas Ranger pitcher Nolan Ryan stops in for sausage or some of Kreuz's famous shoulder clod.

··· BEEF SHOULDER CLOD ······················

MEAT: Beef shoulder. No special meats as long as you know what you're doing because even poor-quality meat can turn out awesome

RUB: Food-grade salt, coarse ground black pepper, cayenne pepper, in that order

WOOD: Good ole post oak, aged at least one year

PIT: ¼-inch steel pit with offset firebox

FIRE: 600 to 800 degrees

TIME: 4 to 6 hours

IT'S DONE WHEN: The pin goes in with almost no resistance (Roy carries a stainless steel rod about the size of a pencil that is sharpened to a point at one end).

PRO TIP: I don't know if I qualify as a pro but I'd say, "Love what you're doing and everything will fall into place."

· ·

You'll hear plenty about the "low and slow" mantra of Central Texas. Here at Kreuz they smoke a lot hotter. A shoulder clod of around fifteen pounds cooks up in less than six hours. The result is a firmer slice of beef that must be consumed immediately lest the juice evaporate. If you come away from the pit with butcher paper piled high with meat (like everyone else does), save the sausage, ribs, and pork chop for last, and eat the clod first while it's still hot and juicy.

EMILIO SOLIZ

TWO BROS. BBQ MARKET: SAN ANTONIO

Emilio Soliz wanted to be a chef in his early career. He seemed to be on the right path to that dream after hitching his wagon to one of San Antonio's most successful chefs—Jason Dady. Then came Dady's newest venture—Two Bros. BBQ Market. As his Twitter handle—@PitmasterEmo— reveals, Emilio now feels more at home holding the title "pitmaster." In just a few years at Two Bros., Emilio has gone from a "long-haired hippie" (his words) to a man who takes his top position at the pits seriously. His attitude shows in the seriously smoked meat coming from his well-worn pits—serious enough to grace the cover of this book..

• • • CHERRY-GLAZED BABY BACK RIBS • • • • • • • • •

MEAT: Whole 1½- to 2½-pound rack of pork baby back ribs

RUB: Proprietary rub used. You can substitute a 1:1:1 blend of kosher salt, mesh ground pepper, and smoked Spanish paprika. The glaze is natural cane sugar cherry syrup.

WOOD: Texas-grown post oak, split and no more than 4 pounds per log

PIT: Custom-built three-door ¼-inch-thick steel box pit with offset firebox

FIRE: 180 to 250 degrees

TIME: 3 to 4 hours

IT'S DONE WHEN: The ribs pull apart easily by hand, but are not falling off bone

REST THE MEAT: Not more than 30 minutes

PRO TIP: Smoke ribs for 1½ hours with no glaze. Then use the syrup to baste ribs throughout the cooking process until finished. This will apply a nice glossy glaze that isn't too sticky but creates a beautiful smoked, sweet finish.

• •

The purist in me wants to like the more traditional St. Louis ribs better than these fancied-up baby backs, but the sweetness is more subtle than you'd expect, and the smoke isn't hidden. Don't let your butcher paper go without them.

TOOTSIE TOMANETZ

SNOW'S BBQ: LEXINGTON

When Snow's BBQ in Lexington was named best barbecue in Texas by *Texas Monthly* magazine in June 2008, Tootsie Tomanetz became an instant star in the barbecue world. It's odd that her significant skill as a pitmaster was "discovered" only after more than thirty years of tending pits. As one of the rare female pitmasters in Texas, she says some folks insist on calling her a chef because they don't feel comfortable applying the pitmaster moniker to a woman, but Tootsie is no doubt a master of the many pit types out behind Snow's. Even several years removed from the initial stardom, she still gets asked every Saturday morning to pose for photos. Always humble, this reluctant star says she is just a "plain old country girl" who has lived her entire life in either Lexington or Giddings, just seventeen miles away, and would just as soon keep a low profile. That's going to be tough if she keeps showing up at 2 A.M. every Saturday to cook some of Texas's best pork, and she has no plans to stop, even at age seventy-seven.

• • • PORK STEAK •

MEAT: Boston butt sliced into steaks 2 to 3 inches thick

RUB: Equal parts coarsely ground pepper and table salt. Apply rub at least a day before smoking.

WOOD: Texas post oak cooked down to coals

PIT: Rectangular steel pit with a hinged steel lid

FIRE: Apply a thin even layer of hot coals onto bottom of cooker. Place meat on the grate after the lid gets warm.

TIME: Cook the steaks over direct heat for about 6 hours. To hold the meat just let the fire die down after the 6-hour cooking time.

IT'S DONE WHEN: A fork slides in easily

REST THE MEAT: No need

PRO TIP: Mop the meat a couple of times on either side with a mix of water, butter, onion, Worcestershire sauce, and dry mustard

• •

It's a pork shoulder, but in Tootsie's words, "There's no need to ruin it by pulling it to pieces." She suggests slicing it as you would a brisket, noting that it can be just as attractive as a sliced brisket if done with care.

MANDO VERA

VERA'S BACKYARD BAR·B·QUE : BROWNSVILLE

During two visits to Vera's in my travels, Mando was affable and quite willing to discuss his cooking process. We even shared our first cow eye together, but attempts to reach him have failed since then, so this recipe is cobbled together from my notes along with some help from Lolis Eric Elie's detailed description of Mando's cooking process in *Smokestack Lightning*.

• • • BARBACOA DE CABEZA • • • • • • • • • • • • • • • • • • •

MEAT: A skinned and thoroughly cleaned cow head with tongue attached. Brains are no longer left intact.

RUB: Do not season the meat. Wrap it tightly and completely with aluminum foil.

WOOD: Burn mesquite wood down to coals. Do not allow burning wood or wood that has not been incinerated into the pit. The coals should be hot on your open palm.

PIT: A hole in the ground. This one is roughly six feet, by four feet, by four feet deep and lined with bricks.

FIRE: This is inexact, but once the flames have subsided and there is nothing but coals,

spread them evenly along the bottom of the pit and load the wrapped heads over the top of the coals. Wet burlap is laid over the heads before a metal lid is placed over the pit and dirt is shoveled onto the lid until the lid is covered.

TIME: At least eight hours after the pit has been covered.

IT'S DONE WHEN: Well, once you pull off the lid it's not going to cook any longer.

REST: No need. Pull the meat from the head and serve immediately with a sprinkling of table salt.

PRO TIP: If the coals don't feel quite as hot as they should, then let the meat cook longer.

• •

The legend of Vera's is that the subterranean pit as it exists would not meet current permitting requirements, but it has been "grandfathered" and can be used so long as the business continues to operate. Alfred Valdez with the Brownsville Public Health Department confirmed the grandfather clause at Vera's. The joints between the bricks do not form a solid barrier from the earth on the other side. I asked hypothetically if the Health Department would allow a similar subterranean pit of solid concrete since it formed a continuous barrier, and he confirmed that such a pit would be permit-able. This form of cooking may be endangered, but it's not the Health Department that will make it extinct. All we need is a little concrete.

GARY VINCEK

VINCEK'S SMOKEHOUSE: EAST BERNARD

Gary is a third-generation Czech. His great-grandfather came over from Europe and quickly started making sausage. This is the recipe they use at the store today, which is why Gary wouldn't budge when I asked for it. He's been running Vincek's since he bought the place in 1985. Before that he worked at Dozier's in Fulshear. The pits he uses today are either the ones he inherited when he bought the place or ones built just like them.

· · · SMOKED BRISKET · · · · · · · · · · · · · · · ·

MEAT: IBP briskets from 12 to 14 pounds

RUB: In descending order, paprika, salt, black pepper, chili powder, granulated garlic, cayenne pepper. Apply rub just before smoking.

WOOD: Pecan in the smoker, B&B lump oak charcoal in the concrete cooker

PIT: Start in a custom-built stainless-steel-lined concrete block smoker (fat side up), and finish on a cooker with 10-inch thick concrete walls and modified conveyor belts for grating (fat side down).

FIRE: The heat stays below 240 degrees in the smoker. There's no thermometer on the cooker, but the meat stays about 18 inches above the fire.

TIME: The beef smokes for 12 to 14 hours then is transferred to the direct-heat cooker for 3 more.

IT'S DONE WHEN: You can stick a fork into the meat and turn it easily.

REST THE MEAT: The meat is held on the cool side of the cooker until it goes to the serving line.

PRO TIP: Mop the meat with a mixture of oil, vinegar, and Worcestershire sauce, but only when you're already checking the meat.

· ·

This two-step method for brisket is a unique combination of the Central Texas norm of indirect smoking and the Hill Country tradition of direct-heat cooking over coals. Here Gary uses charcoal to finish the briskets, which is a rare fuel to find in any Texas barbecue joint. When asked about wrapping the meat to help it cook, he said flatly, "I'm not cooking a roast."

ACKNOWLEDGMENTS

Nick and I need to first thank our wives. This was an admittedly selfish endeavor that took many weeks on the road, far from home with few breaks in between. Nick left a pregnant Erin McWhirter at home with a toddler, and I left my wife, Jennifer, at home with two young children and a broken elbow. Did I mention they are selfless angels? We also need to thank our employer, Good Fulton & Farrell Architects who gave us the time off and kept our jobs waiting for us when we returned. Their support was immense.

While on the road there were many people that offered incredible hospitality, including Jerry and Lee Anne Cadell, Ron and Catharine Brehm, Jessica and Ryan Soliz, Jennifer and Dave Singer, Josephine and James Wise, Ronnie and Sandra Imhoof, and Tammy Chambless who all gave us a place to sleep, and Randy Rouse who provided more beer than I can remember.

Dallas food writer Scott Craig and the writers at *Texas Monthly* sparked my interest in the beauty of Texas barbecue, so I guess I owe them the most. Nancy Nichols gave me a shot to write my first bona fide article about Texas barbecue and turned it into a cover story.

I've had plenty of companions along the way on this barbecue road, but the most stalwart (besides Nick) were my good friends Sam Watkins and Clark Key. I would know much less about the foodways of Southeast Texas if it hadn't been for the guidance of Chris Reid and Michael Fulmer. The importance of dance hall preservation in Central Texas wouldn't have been brought to light without the efforts of Steve Dean.

He'll search for all the holes in this book now that I'm his competition, but Robb Walsh has been a helpful barbecue mentor and a tireless advocate for the hardworking pitmaster. Author Lolis Eric Elie provided one of the best barbecue road trip books to date in *Smokestack Lightning* which provided more than a little inspiration for this book.

I am forever in debt to the many readers, advocates, and ambassadors of my blog, Full Custom Gospel BBQ, which I started with my friend Sam Watkins in 2008. Back in its infancy another friend, Alli Dryer, saw the blog's potential and pushed me to make it bigger and better. Without permission, she started the @BBQsnob Twitter account and thrusted me into the world of social media which has done much to further the mission of discovering great barbecue.

No one made my name more visible to Anthony Bourdain than Leslie Brenner, so I need to thank her for being my partner in the BBQ-Gate tango. My incredible agent, David Hale Smith, may have helped a bit with that visibility, too.

With the only payment being my eternal gratitude, Kat Benner went over every line of this book to make it somewhat readable before it ever made it to my ever-patient and thoughtful editor, Libby Edelson. The book wouldn't have the same photographic depth without the precedent set by Wyatt McSpadden, and it definitely wouldn't look the same without the talented design of Suet Chong.

Lastly, and most important, we all need to thank the pitmasters. They are the true prophets of smoked meat, and without them we'd just be eating roast beef.

THE BEST

In the words of Texas barbecue expert Robb Walsh, "There is no best barbecue, any more than there is a best symphony or a best painting." While I agree in principle, I think there are only a few joints out there that create a *true* masterpiece out of smoke and meat. Roy Perez at Kreuz Market in Lockhart smokes the finest pork chop in the state; the most memorable joint I've ever visited is Prause Meat Market in LaGrange; the best bite of brisket I've had was at Black's Barbecue in Lockhart; and the best breakfast in Texas is brisket at Snow's BBQ in Lexington. All of these joints put out phenomenal barbecue, but few do it consistently. The joints that do so aren't all legendary, but they all have something in common—a dedicated and talented purveyor of smoked meat worthy of the title "pitmaster." Much respect is owed to *all* of those who toil in soot-covered and smoke-filled pit rooms every day, but with all of the respect due to them, and to Robb Walsh, these are the best barbecue joints in Texas.

FARGO'S PIT BBQ—BRYAN, TEXAS
PITMASTER—ALAN CALDWELL

As a pitmaster, Alan Caldwell is an enigma—welcoming and hospitable, but so deeply guarded about how he smokes meat that I don't even know what kind of smoker or wood he uses. There isn't an item on his menu that isn't spectacular, but what he does with pork spareribs is art. He turned this poultry skeptic into a smoked chicken believer and his brisket fat will make you never order lean beef again.

LOUIE MUELLER BARBECUE—TAYLOR, TEXAS
PITMASTER—WAYNE MUELLER

Taking over from a legend isn't easy, but Wayne has done more than just steady the ship at Louie Mueller since the untimely death of his father. Beef ribs that were already great are now some of the best in the state. People order house-made sausages by the cooler full, and the peppery brisket is aggressive, unapologetic, and sumptuous. I know there's a proud papa looking down into the pit room.

PECAN LODGE—DALLAS, TEXAS
PITMASTER—JUSTIN FOURTON

In the few years that Pecan Lodge has been open, it has put out some of the best brisket in the state,

and has done so consistently. Home-made pork links are a welcome change from the commercial sausages prevalent in the region, and the pulled pork will leave you wondering why all Texas pitmasters haven't embraced the pig shoulder. They recently added beef short ribs to their menu, and there are none better in Texas.

VERA'S BACKYARD BAR-B-QUE—BROWNSVILLE, TEXAS
PITMASTER—MANDO VERA

In a region where barbacoa is worshipped, a trip to Vera's can double as Sunday mass. Vera's is the only joint in the state still cooking beef heads with wood smoke, so it isn't much of a surprise that it's the best barbacoa I've eaten. What is a surprise is how much I still long for it now that I'm eight hours away from it.

FRANKLIN BARBECUE—AUSTIN, TEXAS
PITMASTER—AARON FRANKLIN

There are very few things in life for which it's worth waiting in a two hour line. I can tell you from experience and without hesitation that the brisket at Franklin Barbecue is one of those things. The bonus is, when you line up for the brisket, you also get to try incredible pork spareribs and luscious pulled pork. In short: get in line.

BIBLIOGRAPHY

Burka, Paul. "Texas Primer: The Farm-to-Market Road," *Texas Monthly*, April, 1983.

Burnett, John. "When the Sky Ran Dry," *Texas Monthly*, July, 2012.

Carriker, Robert. *Boudin: A Guide to Louisiana's Extraordinary Link*. Lafayette: University of Louisiana at Lafayette Press, 2012.

"Century-Old Obelisks Mark U.S.-Mexico Boundary Line," August 30, 2010. http://www.cbp.gov/xp/cgov/about/history/did_you_know/obelisk/obelisk.xml

Cowen, Tyler. *An Economist Gets Lunch: New Rules for Everyday Foodies*. New York: Penguin Group (USA) Inc., 2012.

Cox, Mike, "Hoo Doo," August 3, 2003. http://www.texasescapes.com/MikeCoxTexasTales/145MasonCountyHooDooWar.htm

Cox, Paul. *Texas Trees: A Friendly Guide*. San Antonio: Corona Publishing Company, 1988.

Demers, John. *Follow the Smoke: 14,783 Miles of Great Texas Barbecue*. Houston: Big Sky Press, 2008.

Durham, T.R. "Salt, Smoke & History," Gastronomica, winter, 2001.

Edge, John T. "BBQ Nation," *Saveur*, June/July, 2011.

Edge, John T. "Pitmaster: An Homage and Rumination," lecture at the University of North Carolina, 04/06/11.

Elie, Lolis Eric, ed. *Cornbread Nation 2: The United States of Barbecue*. Oxford: Southern Foodways Alliance, Center for the Study of Southern Culture, University of Mississippi, 2004.

Elie, Lolis Eric. *Smokestack Lightning: Adventures in the Heart of Barbecue Country*. Berkeley: Ten Speed Press, 2005.

Engelhardt, Elizabeth S. D. *Republic of Barbecue: Stories Beyond the Brisket*. Austin: The University of Texas Press, 2009.

"Farm/Ranch to Market Facts," February 6, 2013. http://www.dot.state.tx.us/tpp/hwy/fmfacts.htm

Fehrenbach, T. R. *Lone Star: A History of Texas and the Texans*. Cambridge: Da Capo Press, 2000.

Fussell, Betty. *Raising Steaks: The Life and Times of American Beef*. New York: Houghton Mifflin Harcourt Publishing Company, 2008.

Henry, Terrence and Mose Buchele, "Raise the Steaks! Beef Prices Soar," May 9, 2012. http://stateimpact.npr.org/texas/2012/05/09/why-cattle-prices-are-so-high/

Kelso, John. *Texas Curiosities, 3rd: Quirky Characters, Roadside Oddities & Other Offbeat Stuff*. Guilford: Globe Pequot Press, 2007.

Lange, Marty. "Eye of the World," *Texas Monthly*, July, 1992.

Lipscomb, Jessica, "Patillo's Barbecue Reopens Landmark Restaurant on Washington Blvd.," December 5, 2011. http://www.beaumontenterprise.com/news/article/Patillo-s-Barbecue-reopens-landmark-restaurant-on-2340570.php#ixzz2K9KLZNJr

Lopez, John. *Texas Barbecue 101*. Fort Worth: Great Texas Line Press, 2008.

Mackay, Jordan. "Cooking by Feel," *The Art of Eating*, autumn, 2011.

Maurer, Ed, "What Happens to Meat in the Smoker...a Look at the Art and Science of Barbeque," http://steeltownbbq.com/3.html (February 6, 2013).

"Maximizing Spice Flavors," *Cook's Illustrated*, July/August, 2003.

McLagan, Jennifer. *Fat: An Appreciation of a*

Misunderstood Ingredient, with Recipes. New York: Ten Speed Press, 2008.

McSpadden, Wyatt. *Texas BBQ*. Austin: University of Texas Press, 2009.

Morthland, John. "Meat Feat," *Texas Monthly*, November, 1997.

Morthland, John. "The Other Cabeza de Vaca," *Texas Monthly*, May, 1997.

Moss, Robert F. *Barbecue: The History of an American Institution*. Tuscaloosa: The University of Alabama Press, 2010.

Myhrvold, Nathan, Chris Young, and Maxime Bilet. *Modernist Cuisine: The Art and Science of Cooking*. Bellevue: The Cooking Lab, 2011.

Patoski, Joe Nick. "Pit Stops," *Texas Monthly*, May, 2003.

Patoski, Joe Nick. "Smokin!" *Texas Monthly*, May, 1997.

Plushnick-Masti, Ramit, "Water Trucked to Nearly Bone-dry Texas Town," January, 30 2012. http://www.foxnews.com/us/2012/01/30/water-trucked-to-texas-town-where-wells-ran-dry/

Shahin, Jim, "It's the Pits," June 14, 1996. http://www.austinchronicle.com/issues/vol15/issue41/food.bbq/future.html

Sharpe, Patricia. "BBQ 08," *Texas Monthly*, June 2008.

Sharpe, Patricia. "Texas Primer: The Chilipiquin," *Texas Monthly*, November, 1987.

Smith Jr., Griffin. "The World's Best Barbecue is in Taylor, Texas. Or is it Lockhart?" *Texas Monthly*, April, 1973.

Staten, Vince, and G. S. Johnson. *Real Barbecue*. New York: Harper & Row, Publishers, Inc., 1988.

Underly, Kari. *The Art of Beef Cutting: A Meat Professionals Guide to Butchering and Merchandising*. Hoboken: John Wiley & Sons, Inc., 2011.

Vine, Katy. "Of Men and Meat," *Texas Monthly*, February, 2012.

Walsh, Robb, "Burrito Wrap-Up," April 8, 2004. http://www.houstonpress.com/2004-04-08/restaurants/burrito-wrap-up/

Walsh, Robb. *Legends of Texas Barbecue: Recipes and Recollections from the Pit Bosses*. San Francisco: Chronicle Books LLC, 2002.

Walsh, Robb, "Texas BBQ Pork: The Brown Pig," September 7, 2011. http://robbwalsh.com/2011/09/texas-bbq-pork-the-brown-pig/

Walsh, Robb. "Zen and the Art of BBQ," *Saveur*, June/July, 2011.

Warnes, Andrew. *Savage Barbecue: Race, Culture, and the Invention of America's First Food*. Athens: University of Georgia Press, 2008.

Witzel, Michael Karl. *Barbecue Road Trip: Recipes, Restaurants & Pitmasters*. Minneapolis: Voyager Press, 2008.

Witzel, Michael, "The Texas Pig Stands Drive-In," November 8, 2008. http://michaelwitzel.com/wordpress/the-texas-pig-stands-drive-in/

The pitmaster oral histories from the Southern Foodways Alliance are a great resource and can be found at http://www.southernbbqtrail.com/texas/index.shtml.

The Handbook of Texas Online was used heavily as a resource for multiple items regarding Texas history: http://www.tshaonline.org/handbook.

PHOTOGRAPH INDEX

INDEX

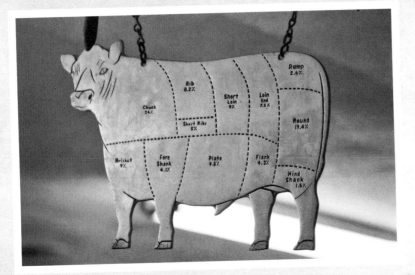